THE WORLD'S
WICKEDEST MEN

THE WORLD'S WICKEDEST MEN

AUTHENTIC ACCOUNTS OF LIVES
TERRIBLE IN THEIR POWER FOR EVIL

by ANDREW EWART

TAPLINGER PUBLISHING COMPANY
New York

First published in the United States, 1965

TAPLINGER PUBLISHING CO., INC.
119 W. 57th Street
New York, New York 10019

Library of Congress Catalogue Card Number:
66-10331

Printed in Great Britain

CONTENTS

PREFACE

WICKEDNESS, it can be argued, is a relative term. Often, like beauty, it is in the eye of the beholder. It is as varied as the relative outlooks of the "Wee Free" churchman in the north of Scotland, who believes that it is wicked to hang out washing on Sundays; the Roman Catholic, who regards divorce as sinful; and the orthodox Jew, who regards eating pork as abhorrent; one man's pleasure certainly can be another man's damnation.

But, religious views apart, there are actions and courses of conduct which followers of all religions and of none unite in condemning. Some are beyond argument—murder is such a case. But what of mass murder—war? Does that qualify, by definition? Or does it depend on what one is fighting for, or against? Then there are border-line cases: euthanasia, the speeding of painless death to end needless suffering. Is that a wickedness, or a kindness? Or does it depend on whether one is a doctor, or a lawyer?

Such considerations are outside the scope of this book, but they serve to show how important it is for anyone embarking on studies of human wickedness to set out clearly his terms of reference.

The problem of good and evil has exercised the great thinkers of all ages. Early philosophers sought to rationalize the existence of God through his antithesis, the Devil. If there is no embodiment of evil, they argued, there can be no embodiment of good. Therefore, if God exists, so, too, must the Devil.

In this twentieth century powerful minds tend to deride such conceptions as simplifications. Good and Evil, say our latter-day ideologists, are comparative terms, not absolutes.

Certainly few today would claim to be either saints or devils. We like to think of ourselves, no doubt, as rather decent people with, perhaps, a dash of mischief for seasoning. We are, however,

7

still prepared to offer our admiration to those rare beings who have sufficient strength of character to dedicate themselves exclusively to the service of others, without thought of praise or reward. But isn't that admiration tinged with incredulity—aren't we inclined to defend our own, more self-centred behaviour with the consoling belief that such altruism "isn't quite human"? And how do we react to those opposites—also, fortunately, rare— who seem to devote their lives with the same singleness of purpose to evil-doing? Aren't we tempted to think that they are "too bad to be true"?

In such a climate of opinion, any attempt to pick out for special attention "the best" or "the worst" of mankind may lay itself open to the charge of special pleading. Some gentle, kindly soul is sure to point out that there is so much good in the worst of us and so much bad in the best of us.

What standards, then, can be used in assessing human wickedness so remarkable as to be worthy of inclusion in a rogues' gallery of recorded history? Well, it can be observed that the four great faiths which have withstood the erosion of time (Christianity, Judaism, Mohammedanism, Buddhism) have in common one abiding principle:

DO UNTO OTHERS AS YOU WOULD HAVE OTHERS DO UNTO YOU.

If, therefore, one man's influence on others significantly improves the human condition, then that man, by my definition, can be said to be Good. Conversely, those whose influence brings wretchedness or ruin to others can be called Bad.

This book is a study of human wickedness defined in such terms. All the men described in its pages are chosen because they have defiled those to whom they owed responsibilities as husbands, lovers, parents, children, friends, leaders, or rulers.

The first criterion in the selection of the infamous is that every character must have made some impact on the history of mankind. Many of them will, no doubt, have their apologists, but each and every one of them, in my opinion, has left the world worse than he found it. More, his brief appearance on the stage of time has degraded not only the *milieu* in which his reputation was built, but human society as a whole. Yet it is true that some had outstanding qualities; others were instruments of their age.

PREFACE

To Genghis Khan goes the dreadful distinction of being
responsible for a heavier toll of human life than any other man
whose deeds are known to us. If, therefore, the mass butchery of
our species be the ultimate in wickedness, then "The Scourge
of God" must assuredly be the wickedest who ever lived. Yet,
compared with Adolf Hitler, Genghis Khan was a decent human
being—fair-minded, generous and, occasionally, even merciful
within the lights of his own civilization. He, at least, did not have
the advantage of centuries of enlightenment, culture and
philosophy to draw upon—he was a simple savage, following
the tradition of his nomadic kind : to destroy utterly anyone and
anything which might threaten the existence of his people in the
slightest degree. Although he exterminated well over a score of
millions of human beings, he also drew up a code of law, known
as the *Yassa*, which is almost incredible as the work of an
illiterate Asiatic nomad.

What can be said of Hitler other than that he gave his own
people a new purpose and re-kindled national pride only to
destroy them for the second time in fifty years—without a shred
of remorse? Behind him he left desolation, despair, hatred.

Yet, if Hitler richly deserves his place among the Wicked
Ones, so too does the most Godly of the characters to figure in
these pages—a man who sought nothing for himself and lived
only to increase the power and the glory of his Mother Church.
Torquemada is, perhaps, the classic case of bigotry: the "unco-
guid" individual who is responsible for wretchedness and suffering on a vast scale because of his unshakeable conviction that
he is saving souls. The ghoulish tortures and lingering agonies
inflicted on "sinners" in the name of God by this uncompro-
misingly holy man surpass in horror the exterminating ovens of
the Hitler regime. And both Torquemada and Hitler, for utterly
different reasons, sought the obliteration of the Jews.

* * *

Sometimes it happens that a single crime can leave a more
lasting mark on history than the annihilation of an entire race.
There is a stupefying enormity about genocide which overwhelms
the senses, whereas the murder of two little children in the
Tower of London, because they might have threatened a

scheming tyrant's boundless ambition, can outrage the public
conscience more sharply. Thus Richard the Third of England
is blackened forever in history as the assassin of the little
princes, whereas the actual instruments of this most shameful
act are forgotten. Richard's reign was, indeed, a tragedy fit for
a Shakespeare to recount, although, if one puts his excesses
alongside those of, say, Ivan the Terrible, he seems a tame-
enough villain. One has, however, to remember the sanctity of
human life and the dignity of the individual in England and to
contrast this with the indifference to the rights of man in Russia.

Many Englishmen can be moved by the fate of the little princes
in the Tower and yet remain indifferent to Ivan's bestial
savageries.

*   *   *

It is when one approaches the sphere of sexual behaviour that
the ground shifts under one. Compare, for instance, the moral
attitudes of Victorian England with the Cinquecento in Italy,
that age of unbridled lust in which a popular harlot was given a
Pope-scale funeral. Cesare Borgia was a product of the fifteenth
century, yet the abnormalities of his notorious family disgusted
even that dissolute period. Despite that, it would be harsh to
judge the Borgia Pope, Alexander VI, by the Vatican standards
of today.

Casanova and the Marquis de Sade were two eighteenth-
century libertines who have added their names to the languages
of the West—but were they the worst of their times? They are
known to us intimately through their writings, and what a contrast
in behaviour do they present! Most of us would, I suppose,
regard Casanova as a gallant and an entertaining character and
the Marquis de Sade as a moral leper. Yet, if his boastings are to
be believed, the Venetian's conquests ran into thousands whereas
the French libertine sought, through practical experience and
experiment, to catalogue sex perversions and fantasies. There is
no doubt about the judgment of succeeding generations on their
written works: Casanova's *Memoirs* are regarded as literature
of a high order whereas de Sade's far more pretentious volumes
are rejected with disgust and horror.

It is doubtful, however, if de Sade's debaucheries could

approach in lasciviousness those of the Roman Emperors of the Julian-Claudian house and, in particular, Caligula and Nero.

It is difficult to believe that a cultured people like the Romans, with such a high regard for honour and dignity, could have submitted to the rule of a succession of monsters who made matricide and fratricide instruments of State. Nero qualifies for inclusion in this book because, during the fourteen years of his rule, he committed almost every major crime known to man and left such a legacy that, even today, his name is a by-word for infamy.

*   *   *

There is a figure of our own century who was sincerely believed by many to be the Devil Incarnate. This was Rasputin, surely one of the most astonishing men of all time. That a peasant should have become, to all intents and purposes, the real ruler of Imperial Russia is, in itself, incredible, but that this weird creature, with unkempt beard and filthy black fingernails, should have succeeded in seducing hundreds of women, from the highest to the lowest in the land, defies imagination. Even the story of his death lends credence to the Satanic legend. He gulped down a plateful of cakes containing enough cyanide to kill a dozen men—and showed no ill effects: then he drank goblets of poisoned wine— with apparent relish. Bullets were pumped into him, he was stabbed in a dozen places, bound and thrown into an icy river. When he was found, one arm had been freed and his lungs were full of water—he had, in fact, met his death by drowning.

*   *   *

The choice of Stalin for this catalogue of villainy has recently been endorsed by one of his closest collaborators and eventual successor, Nikita Khrushchev. For three decades, the Communist world hailed Joseph Vissarionovich Djugashvili as the greatest man of all time—now the same sources are describing him as the greatest criminal known to history. This dramatic switch-over of superlatives is based on statistics, only now becoming available, of the reign of terror which "Uncle Joe" clamped on the 160,000,000 people of all the Russias.

It seems certain that, when the counting of fallen heads is

complete, Stalin will have been responsible for a higher grand total of victims than Hitler. According to Sovietologists, 1,000,000 were slaughtered in Russia from 1928 to 1939, and a further 16,000,000 perished during the same period—half from famine and half from administrative murder—in the ghastly forced labour camps of the Arctic and Siberia. According to the official figures, 25,000,000 human beings went "missing" from the Soviet census returns during the period of Stalin's rule and the dictator himself, even on his own specially prepared figures, could not account for 14,000,000 of that total. For political massacres committed against his own people, Stalin unquestionably far outdid Hitler—in fact, it is impossible to find any tyrant with a comparable record of political murder in all recorded history.

* * *

Why should Don Salvatore Lucania figure among such world-shaking merchants of evil? Was he not just a cheap gangster, strutting his brief hour through the non-stop melodrama that is crime in America? Are such hoodlums not a dime a dozen in the United States even today? Far, far from it. The evil influence of "Lucky" Luciano is seriously underestimated even now, nearly two years after his peaceful death in Naples. For Luciano was the boss man of an international organization with ramifications as widespread in crime as the Comintern's in international politics. He was the controlling genius of Dope International, the most fantastic conspiracy in the history of world-scale crime. Luciano directed the illicit trade in habit-forming drugs from the Middle East, through Italy and France, to the eastern seaboard of America. He amassed profits on a scale unrealizeable by any other business or trade and in the process he was responsible for the unbelievable wretchedness and suffering of hundreds of thousands of drug addicts from the Levant to New York's East Side. And his wickedness lives after him.

* * *

Perhaps the most controversial selection for inclusion in this book is a man who put no one to death or the torture, who did not peddle drugs, who was far from a by-word for lasciviousness but who, in the author's view, was one of the most intellectually damaging men of our times.

Senator Joseph Raymond McCarthy was a loud-mouthed, vulgar braggart, with no regard for learning or truth. Yet he fathered an evil which swept like a prairie fire across the United States of America, producing among sensitive minds everywhere, astonishment growing into embarrassment and eventually into disgust, that a nation which regarded itself as a beacon of liberty for the world should have been degraded by such a mindless mountebank as Joe McCarthy. Yet for five years this ignoramus, who admitted that he "discovered" Communism only two months before he organized what was to become the most disgraceful witch-hunt in American history, paralysed the will of two U.S. Presidents and interfered with the course of his country's foreign policy.

To a generation which had already experienced the phenomenal rise of another loud-mouthed braggart from penniless tramp to conqueror of most of Europe, it was not beyond the bounds of possibility that Joe McCarthy might have won supreme power in the United States. If this seems an absurdity to Americans, it seemed equally absurd to their allies that such a figure of fun could have caused such panic in the U.S. Government, or purged the liberal elements of the nation of many of their most distinguished thinkers. He achieved all this without a political party, programme, or organization behind him. He was manifestly a cynical liar, a buffoon and a blatant opportunist— yet he rocked the United States to its foundations, and he was responsible for yet another "ism" which can still make all decent men shudder—McCarthyism.

* * *

These, then, are the men who, if the verdict of human society counts for anything, have, by reason of the lives they led, richly deserved the opprobrious superlative—"the wickedest in the world".

Chapter 1

NERO . . . AND HIS FAMILY

FEW men in the history of the human race have equalled Lucius Domitius Ahenobarbus—known to history as the Roman Emperor Nero—for all-round unadulterated evil. He was a monster; and in the fourteen years during which he misruled the Roman Empire he committed almost every major crime known to man.

So evil was Nero that his wickedness has become a legend. Every schoolboy has heard how Nero fiddled—in fact he sang— as Rome burned. He has gained equal historical notoriety as the man who dipped early Christians into boiling pitch and used them as living torches to light his chariot races.

Yet Nero was far from exceptional, either for his age, or, still more, for the Imperial House of which he was the last Emperor. Monster as he was, Nero was but the worst of a bad lot—the Julian-Claudian royal house which was almost certainly the wickedest royal family in history.

It was founded by Julius Caesar, whose life of debauchery— with lovers of both sexes—and death at the hands of his "friends" set the pattern for his successors up to the time of Nero. His successor, the equally famous Caesar Augustus, by the standards of the time was perhaps the best of the line. But the brilliant and amoral woman who was first his mistress and then his second wife, the Empress Livia, developed the art of political family murder into a supreme instrument of State. In the niceties of removal by poison she made her nearest rival in that art, Lucrezia Borgia, appear nothing more than a bungling amateur.

It was to ensure the succession to the imperial throne of her own son and Augustus's stepson, Tiberius, that Livia developed that technique of the physical elimination of all other heirs which became the principal characteristic of the Julian-Claudian succession during the following century.

Tiberius himself, when he came to the throne eventually at the age of sixty, after a cautious start showed himself an apt pupil of his mother. No one was safe from the blood lust of his capricious and tyrannical temper, not even his own nephew and officially adopted heir, Germanicus, who died mysteriously at his headquarters on the Rhine—poisoned by Tiberius at long range. In fact, under Tiberius murder and terror ranged far beyond the immediate domestic circle in which Livia had concentrated her crimes.

Under the rule of Tiberius's favourite, Sejanus, who unearthed a series of conspiracies, real or fictionary, the reign of terror spread. No one in Rome was safe.

By this time Tiberius had left the day-to-day administration of the Roman Empire to Sejanus and retired to the Island of Capri with, according to legend, the pornographic literature of the world to date and twelve well-developed boys. There he remained, satisfying his lusts, for the remainder of his life. Like most of the Julian-Claudian royal house, however, he went in permanent terror of his possible heirs. Not satisfied with the murder of Germanicus he deported and then murdered Germanicus's wife and her two elder sons. The youngest son, known to the Roman garrison on the Rhine as "Caligula" from the tiny jackboots which he wore, survived, along with his three younger sisters. All lived to play key roles in the eventual history of the Emperor Nero.

The only important grown-up member of the imperial house to escape was the sole surviving nephew of Tiberius. A stuttering weakling, known generally as "poor Uncle Claudius", he had been an invalid from birth and was generally assumed to be weak in the head. That was far from the truth. Tiberius, however, let poor Claudius live because he believed that his invalid nephew could be a danger to no one.

At last Sejanus fell. He was replaced by the commander of the Praetorian Guard, which, from that point, was to play a key role in the history of the imperial house. And when the elderly Tiberius caught a cold during a brief sortie from Capri he was murdered by being choked with a pillow.

Some years earlier Caligula, then in his teens, had been adopted along with the Emperor's young grandson as co-heir to the

15

throne. At that time Tiberius had been forced to take Caligula under his personal control as the virile teenager had been discovered committing incest with all three of his sisters, Julia, Drusilla and Agrippina, a classic beauty in her mid-teens. She was destined to be the mother of the Emperor Nero.

Whether Caligula was a party to the murder of Tiberius is uncertain. Probably he was, for he was immediately proclaimed emperor. Little was heard of his co-heir until, in the best family tradition, Caligula arranged for the young grandson of Tiberius to be murdered.

As soon as he ascended the imperial throne Caligula resumed his incestuous relationship with his three sisters. His favourite was Drusilla. To keep the official record straight the Emperor married her off to his friend Lepidus, who, in return for failing to demand his marital rights, was nominated as Caligula's successor.

Sometime afterwards Drusilla died. Caligula was distraught at the death of his mistress-sister. At court there was soon intense competition for the vacant place in the Emperor's bed; his two surviving sisters were among the leading contenders.

Both sisters, after the discovery of their earlier relationship with their brother, had scarcely been in a position to make good matches. As a consequence Agrippina had been married off to a well-bred thug twenty-five years her senior named Domitius Ahenobarbus. One of his mildest criminal activities was swindling. Among his more violent crimes were the murder of one of his slaves, an attack on a senator in the open forum during which the senator lost an eye, and the death of a child whom he ran over with a chariot. Like his Emperor he was in the habit of sleeping with his own sisters. He became the father of the Emperor Nero. For in December of A.D. 37 a son was born—feet first as though to emphasize his incipient abnormality—to Agrippina and her ruffianly husband.

The fact that she was both a wife and a mother did nothing to deter Agrippina in her efforts to become Caligula's mistress. She failed, however, to hold his permanent affections. But she had an overweening ambition, unequalled by any other member of the royal house, to rule Rome one day. She was in no way particular what means were needed to that end.

Discarded by her emperor-brother she formed an alliance with his former favourite Lepidus—who had also been dropped from favour when his usefulness came to an end. She became the mistress of Lepidus and persuaded him that if they could murder Caligula she would put him on the imperial throne—with herself as Empress. She persuaded her youngest sister Julia to join the conspiracy. Caligula's secret police were, however, informed. An obscure spy named Tigellinus, of whom more will be heard, warned Caligula of the sisters' plot. Caligula summoned his two sisters to France where he was inspecting troops. They could not deny the allegation of conspiracy. Lepidus was executed forthwith. Both sisters were banned to a small island.

Agrippina was forced by Caligula to travel all the way from Lyons to Rome with the ashes of her lover Lepidus in an urn hanging round her neck.

By this time Caligula, as a result of a disease believed to be congenital, was rapidly going mad. The mild regime which had characterized the first few months of his reign had given place to a reign of blood and terror even more vicious than in the days of Tiberius. Moreover Caligula was able to satisfy all his lusts by supervising personally executions and orgies, which were mixed up indiscriminately.

The Emperor's madness progressed rapidly. No one knows how many, high and low, were put to death. He declared himself a god and had a temple erected for his own worship. He appointed his favourite charger consul and a member of the Roman Senate. Within four years of becoming Emperor he had squandered the vast fortune carefully amassed by his skinflint predecessor.

Fears and self-interest combined to produce numerous conspiracies to murder the mad tyrant. Many were discovered and grisly reprisals followed. But at last, in January of A.D. 41, Caligula was murdered in his palace by two leaders of his own Praetorian Guard.

Almost the sole survivor of the main Claudian-Julian royal line was "poor Uncle Claudius". To the intense surprise of that stuttering old gentleman, who privately had become a historian of some distinction, he was declared Emperor by the Praetorian Guard—after he had agreed to pay a substantial sum to all the officers and men.

At once Claudius pardoned his nieces Agrippina and Julia and restored their forfeited estates. The elder woman hastened back to Rome to pursue her thwarted ambition in a palace where intrigue and murder might achieve anything.

Agrippina's four-year-old son Lucius Domitius had seen little of his beautiful mother up to that time. For the first two years of his life, while she had been one of the leaders of Caligulan society, the child was left to the care of two Greek nursemaids. Soon after Agrippina's banishment his elderly father had died. The little boy was then left to the care of his father's youngest sister (and mistress) Domitia Lepida junior.

The boy's aunt, whose moral attributes were certainly no higher than those of his mother, had little interest in her nephew. His upbringing was entrusted to two household slaves—one of them a dancer and the other a barber, with each of whom his aunt is believed to have slept from time to time. But by the time of Agrippina's return her son's aunt had become one of the most powerful women in Rome. She was the Emperor's mother-in-law, and Claudius had always been under the thumb of the women around him, and of the freed Levantine slaves on whom he relied for everything.

From the first of her three marriages Domitia Lepida had a daughter named Messalina who, on the threshold of her teens, had demonstrated that she had inherited her mother's proclivity towards amorous adventure. At the age of fifteen the strikingly beautiful slip of a girl had married "Poor Uncle Claudius", who was then separated from his second wife and had long been living with a professional prostitute. Messalina was probably attracted by the considerable family fortune which Claudius administered as head of the family.

Messalina was still a teenager when by the whimsy of fortune her husband Claudius became Roman Emperor, and she Empress. Three weeks later she presented Claudius with a son —the question of whose paternity provided the basis for much speculation.

Both Agrippina and her younger sister Julia had their eyes on the same target . . . the Emperor's bed. As his nieces they both had personal access to Claudius, who was notoriously susceptible to young women. Julia at once attempted to make the running.

Messalina, as was to be expected, reacted sharply. Claudius was still infatuated with his young wife and Julia was charged with intriguing against the imperial marriage. She was banished along with her lover, the noted Spanish-born philosopher Seneca, who, despite his Stoic principles, was devoted in practice to the pleasures of the flesh.

Agrippina was more astute. She formed the opinion that Messalina's extra-marital adventures (which by this time were becoming notorious) would ensnare the Empress sooner rather than later. Agrippina was content to wait. She also believed that her trump card in the fight for power lay in her young son Lucius Domitius, whom, up to that point, she had largely ignored. Along with the infant son of Messalina, who had been named Britannicus, Agrippina's child was one of the two possible heirs who could be expected to succeed the elderly Claudius. Agrippina, therefore, took the boy under her personal supervision.

At the same time she set about refurbishing her somewhat tarnished social reputation by marrying a leading Roman intellectual. The "salon" which she established in his house was soon the haunt of Rome's leading writers and philosophers.

Agrippina had a political acumen rare in her sex. She realized that before any active bid for power she needed a "fifth column" inside the imperial court.

The Roman Empire now was being ruled by a handful of former Levantine slaves whom Claudius had freed many years earlier to administer the family estate. When he became Emperor they had merely taken it over as the Imperial Estate. They were all men of great ability and devoted to Claudius. Agrippina decided that Pallas, the Imperial Treasurer, offered her the best opportunity. Obviously, with the whole of Imperial Rome's finances in his grasp he was a man who could not be bought— with money. Agrippina, of course, had never been reluctant to sacrifice herself if the stakes were high enough. As a Roman princess she offered herself to the one-time Levantine slave. He took the bait. She became his mistress—and he her spy in the government.

In the course of the year A.D. 46 Claudius, inspired by Pallas, decided to celebrate one of the main Roman anniversaries by a sort of schoolboy military tattoo. One of the companies would be led by his six-year-old son Britannicus, the other by the nine-and-a-half year old Lucius.

The future Nero was a sturdy boy, big for his age. He was well coached. The way he handled his horse and his company drew ovations from all sides. Britannicus was scared. He lost control of both his mount and his company. Claudius, who adored the boy, was upset. Agrippina was radiant—and Messalina livid. Soon afterwards someone tried to murder Lucius by placing a snake on his pillow when he was having an afternoon nap. Messalina had decided to extend her homocidal activities.

By this time the Empress had become the scandal of Rome. She had persuaded Claudius to give her a separate wing of the royal palace. There on the pretext of recovering from "severe headaches" she staged a series of orgies. Lovers followed in rapid succession, her choice was catholic—actors, slaves, the young bloods of Rome, even the Parthian Ambassador. Ruthlessly she covered all traces of her debaucheries—by murder.

Claudius permitted her much freedom and she continually interfered in the government. Time after time she came to him with a secret report that one of the ex-lovers who had become embarrassing or dangerous to her was plotting treachery. Claudius, the only one in Rome who did not know the facts, always ordered immediate execution.

Carefully Agrippina watched the situation develop. It could not go on indefinitely. After Claudius had departed to campaign in south-eastern England the orgies of Messalina became even more flagrant. She challenged the leading harlots of Rome (and some of the more enthusiastic amateurs among her friends) to an amatory contest. The aim was to prove who could sleep with most gallants in one night. At dawn, after the twenty-fifth lover, the leading harlot confessed herself beaten. Messalina herself continued till high noon.

Eventually the nymphomaniac Empress became infatuated with the best-looking young man in Rome, Silius, on whom she showered presents, including furniture from the royal palace and other imperial property.

She persuaded Silius that they should murder Claudius and marry, after which she would make Silius Emperor. When

Claudius returned to Rome Messalina approached him with a made-up story about an astrologer predicting that "her husband would die within a month". By this she persuaded Claudius to give her a "temporary divorce" that would get round the prophecy. Afterwards they would remarry!

Claudius left Rome on an official visit to the Italian coast. In his absence Messalina hurriedly married Silius. The ceremony became a sexual orgy in which the bridegroom carried the near-naked bride through the streets followed by guests clad only in leopard skins.

Pallas, and the Emperor's most trusted freedman Narcissus, had long been carefully watching Messalina. This time she had played into their hands. Narcissus rode at speed to meet Claudius to tell him what had happened. Outside Rome Claudius was greeted by a panicking Messalina who told him "it was all a joke". The old man's vanity had, however, been wounded. Under the influence of drugs provided by Narcissus and Pallas he ordered his wife's death. He also ordered the execution of her lover and of the wedding guests. So at last the way was open for Agrippina to achieve her lust for power.

It was common knowledge that Claudius could not live without a woman in his bed. At once Agrippina appeared in the palace to comfort him. But there were other contenders favoured by various parties at court, including his second wife by whom he had a daughter.

Claudius, strongly influenced by Pallas, made up his mind to marry his niece. But she was already married.

That mattered little to Claudius, who regarded the temple recently erected in his honour in Essex as but just recognition of his own divinity. As though by divinely-inspired coincidence Agrippina's husband died leaving her a large fortune. All Rome knew that death had been by poison. Under Roman law an uncle could not marry his niece, but Claudius, regarding himself as a god, brushed aside such man-made rules. He married Agrippina as his fourth wife. At last she was Empress.

Claudius was infatuated by the full-blown beauty of his new wife who by this time was thirty-two. He could deny her nothing. When she swept all Messalina's creatures first from the court and then from administration he raised not even one little finger.

Agrippina had begun to plan for the future. She began to take steps to ensure that she remained ruler of Rome after the death of Claudius—which clearly could occur at any time. The key to all her plans was her son, Lucius Domitius.

First move was to suggest that Lucius should become betrothed to Claudius's child by Messalina, a daughter named Octavia. The girl was already betrothed to one of the younger members of the Senate. That meant nothing to Agrippina. She accused the senator of incestuous relations with his sister! When the accusation was made before the Senate the young man was removed from the list of senators. After being involved in such a scandal, clearly he could not marry the Emperor's daughter. A few weeks later the unfortunate man committed suicide. Thereafter Claudius was easily persuaded to agree to his daughter's betrothal to his stepson.

With her son designated the Emperor's future-son-in-law Agrippina began to impress on Claudius the danger to the Claudian succession should he die suddenly leaving his son Britannicus a minor under a regency. She suggested that his daughter's future husband should be made co-heir. Although Claudius may have had private doubts about the true paternity of the boy, he loved Britannicus dearly. Agrippina kept repeating her suggestion. Pallas, who no doubt received his reward, supported it. The precedent of Augustus, who had nominated his son-in-law Tiberius as successor, was much quoted. In the end Claudius capitulated.

By an Imperial Edict of Adoption dated 25 February, A.D. 50, the Emperor Claudius formally adopted his stepson Lucius Domitius with the Imperial title of Tiberius Claudius *Nero* Drusus Germanicus. By signing that edict Claudius put his name to his own death warrant. His life was in Agrippina's hands. She determined to end it as soon as circumstances permitted, though she realized that the necessary preparations would take some time.

The official adoption meant that Nero would be committing *legal* incest by marrying Claudius's youngest daughter. Agrippina removed that obstacle by having the girl adopted by another family.

Nero, at the time of his adoption, was a well-built, friendly

22

and robust lad of twelve. He neither knew nor cared about his mother's dark designs for him. His interests were artistic—poetry, music, sculpture and painting. Otherwise he was ill-educated. But like most Roman boys of his age he was a passionate devotee of chariot racing. For hours he could expatiate on the technique of the charioteers, on the merits of the horse teams and on the other gossip of the circus arena.

Agrippina decided Nero must be suitably trained for his chosen destiny. She summoned to court the philosopher Seneca, who had returned from banishment in Corsica only a few months earlier. It was a shrewd choice. Young Nero was provided not only with one of the most eminent intellects of the age as a tutor; he was also given a guide, philosopher and "ghost" who could be depended on to write and teach Nero to recite the proclamations, speeches and other public pronouncements which Agrippina was certain that her son—when Emperor—would shortly be called upon to make.

In the meantime Britannicus, who, according to some reports, suffered from epilepsy, was pushed more and more into the background. On one occasion when he addressed Nero by his former name of Lucius, immediate offence was taken. Agrippina reported to his father. The tutor of Britannicus was accused of imparting subversive ideas to the boy. The tutor committed suicide. He was replaced by one of Agrippina's creatures, who kept Britannicus in something approaching comfortable captivity.

Agrippina knew that the real key to the succession of Nero on the death of Claudius, of course, lay in the Praetorian Guard. She began reorganizing the high command. Two commandants who had opposed her when she first became Empress were removed. She trumped up against them charges of failing to maintain discipline. Claudius removed them. At Agrippina's request he appointed to command of the Guard a veteran soldier named Afrianus Burrus, a one-time protégé of the Emperor Livia who for long had been administrator of the Imperial estates. Agrippina had reason to know that she could depend on Burrus.

In preparation for the seizure of power on Claudius's death Agrippina used every possible device to ingratiate young Nero with the Senate and other influential Roman citizens. Claudius himself was persuaded formally to introduce the young man to the Senate. A few months later Nero was much praised for his first speech to that august body—a speech written by Seneca in which he persuaded the Senate to agree to the restoration of freedom to the island of Rhodes.

Nero, exercising his Imperial privileges, also appeared in court as a judge. His judgments were praised. They had previously been prepared by Seneca.

When Nero became fifteen he was married to thirteen-year-old Octavia, daughter of the Emperor by Messalina. By Roman law each was too young to marry, but Agrippina secured special consent from Claudius.

Gradually Nero came to be accepted by the mass of the Roman people as the inevitable successor to Claudius. However, Agrippina and her schemes had one implacable enemy in Narcissus, the Emperor's chief secretary. Carefully he watched her, seeking for any false move that would give him an opportunity to take action against her. After Messalina's death Narcissus had hoped to find a collaborator in the Empress. Since his fellow minister Pallas occupied a special place in her affections, he was rebuffed. That was why he became her opponent in everything—and used his influence to further the claims of Britannicus against those of Nero.

Narcissus at long last got the sort of evidence he had been seeking. He is thought to have warned Claudius of Agrippina's affair with Pallas. In the midst of a drunken stupor which was a nightly occurrence the Emperor muttered: "It is just my unfortunate fate to have to put up with the dissolute lives of all my wives—and then to deal with them."

When a spy conveyed warning, Agrippina realized that time was short. If she were not to fare as Messalina had done, she had to act before Narcissus could rouse Claudius to condemn her. Against Narcissus she could do nothing as long as Claudius lived.

On previous occasions Agrippina had had dealings with Locusta, a woman of Gaul who was known as a specialist in herbs—and poisons. Now she sought her help again. She had decided to enlist to her aid the Emperor's particular love for mushrooms.

The most probable of several differing accounts of what

NERO . . . AND HIS FAMILY

followed reports that on the evening of 12 October in the year
A.D. 53 Agrippina had prepared a special dish of mushrooms
for her husband. On the largest and most appetizing she sprinkled
poison. The plate was carried from an ante room to the Imperial
dinner table. To allay suspicion, Agrippina first chose some
mushrooms for herself—being careful to leave the best ones for
the Emperor. Claudius suspected nothing. He gobbled up the
most succulent of the mushrooms and in a moment or two was
violently ill. Quickly he lost consciousness and was carried out
apparently "drunk as usual".

The constitution of the elderly invalid was, however, tougher
than anyone had suspected. With the help of nature he was able
to get rid of the poisoned mushrooms: although still ill, he
showed every sign of recovery.

Frightened and furious Agrippina decided that it was a case
of now or never. The Emperor's Greek physician knew of the
plot. He was accustomed on such occasions to tickle the
Emperor's throat with a feather to cause him to vomit. This
time Agrippina induced him to paint the feather with poison.
It worked. Claudius slumped dead. In one of the anterooms
Agrippina with Pallas, Seneca and Burrus, who were all in the
plot, feverishly made arrangements for the succession. The death
of the Emperor was kept secret. But the leaders of both the
Praetorian Guard and of the Senate were privately advised of
what had happened. Most of the morning was spent in three-
way haggling between the conspirators, the Guards officers and
the Senate. There was tough bargaining. Eventually Agrippina
agreed to pay a substantial "accession grant" to all the Guards
officers and men. The Senate was pacified in other ways. Rumours
of the Emperor's death had spread, so a bulletin was issued saying
he had had a good night and actors were summoned to the palace
to entertain the sick man.

Soon after midday the gates of the palace opened. Nero
appeared with Burrus at his side and Pallas, Seneca and others
behind him. At a signal from Burrus the Praetorian Guard
shouted "Long live the Emperor Nero". Shy and bewildered by
the rapid course of events, the seventeen-year-old who had so
suddenly become Emperor mounted a platform. He spoke a few
sentences written by Seneca. His key point was that the Praetorian

Guard would be paid his "accession gift" at once. The Guard cheered again.

That same evening Nero was received with acclamation by the Roman Senate. They proposed to bestow on him the title of "Father of the Fatherland". Seneca was at his elbow to help him to stutter out a few words declining this honour on account of his youth. Nero was still amazed and confused by the turn of events. Only twenty-four hours before he had seen the Emperor collapse at the dinner table. He went in fear of his formidable mother, and not for a moment had he doubted her story that Claudius was suffering from a sudden stomach complaint. Then in the middle of the night he had been dragged from his bed by his mother to be told he was now Emperor. Nero scarcely knew what to think. But he had no doubt who had gained him the Imperial throne. That night when asked by a Praetorian Guard to give the password for the night he gave "Optima Mater" (Best of all Mothers).

That admiration for and obedience to Agrippina was of short duration. The death of Claudius was the signal for a new wave of terror. All who had opposed Agrippina as Empress fell victims. The first was Narcissus who, as Claudius's chief secretary, had in the previous few weeks written letters seriously compromising her. As soon as he returned from his cure he was thrown into prison and forced to commit suicide. One senator was condemned for *lèse-majesté* merely on hearsay evidence repeated by his slaves. Among other equally notable victims were some of Messalina's former lovers.

Seneca, although quite prepared to achieve high office by doubtful means, was at heart a mild and peaceful man. He had hoped that the regime of his charge Nero would be marked by justice and mildness—as he had made Nero promise in the first major speech which the new Emperor made to the Senate. The reign of terror instituted by Agrippina appalled him. Burrus, to whom also she owed much, shared Seneca's opinion. That Seneca would dare to convey his horror to Nero never occurred to Agrippina; yet that is exactly what he did.

The revelations of his mother's crimes filled the new Emperor with shock and terror. He was appalled to discover that his adopted father had been murdered. Nero could not bring back the dead. But under Seneca's guidance he freed and restored to office those victims of his mother's terror who were still alive. Naturally tension rose steadily between Seneca, who by this time was virtually chief minister, and Agrippina, who saw her power slipping. Within a fortnight of becoming Emperor, Nero, acting on Seneca's suggestion, publicly rebuffed Agrippina during a reception of Armenian ambassadors.

A week or two later the Emperor Nero met a young girl of exceptional beauty in one of the corridors of the imperial palace. He was much impressed and asked who she was. He discovered her name was Akte and that she was a freed slave of Greek-Syrian descent in the household of his wife Octavia—with whom he did not cohabit and whom in fact he detested. Up to that point Nero had known little if anything of love. He fell head over heels in love with Akte. She was equally attracted to the good-looking, well-built young Emperor and she had no objection to becoming his mistress. Nero showered gifts on the girl and came to obey her slightest word. He was so much in love that he decided to divorce Octavia and marry Akte as his legal wife.

When Agrippina knew that her son proposed to make a serving maid her daughter-in-law her fury was terrible. There was a violent scene in which Nero threatened to abdicate and retire in peace to Rhodes with his mistress. Up to this point Nero had been intimidated by his mother. Now, when the clash of interests threatened to rob him of his desire, for the first time in his life he openly defied Agrippina.

Within a month of Claudius's death, Agrippina knew that the power for which she had so long sinned, plotted and murdered had begun to slip through her fingers. To emphasize that he was now the master, Nero sacked Pallas, Agrippina's lover, from the post of Imperial Treasurer. That astute operator took his farewell after laying down only one condition—that he should never be asked to account for any of the funds which had passed through his hands.

Agrippina, without a scruple, decided to dispose of Nero just as she had so many others. The rightful heir Britannicus was still at court. So she plunged into a new conspiracy to install Britannicus on the throne in place of her own son. However, Britannicus was injudicious enough to let his resentment at the recent course of events become obvious. He was watched: soon Nero and Seneca had word of the plot. Nero was his mother's son. He did not hesitate for one moment. Britannicus must die.

Nero summoned from prison the poison expert Locusta and told her to prepare a poison for Britannicus. It gave him only diarrhoea. Locusta was threatened with death unless she produced something really effective. But Britannicus was now on the alert; everything he ate and drank was tasted for him. Nero, however, knew that he had to succeed and he did indeed possess the flair of the true poisoner. He invited Britannicus to dinner along with Agrippina, Seneca, Burrus and his wife Octavia, as well as some of his usual boon companions. It was arranged that a slave should serve Britannicus with a hot drink—so hot that he could not drink it. A suitably-treated jug of cold water was conveniently nearby. The water was added to Britannicus's drink; moments later he slumped forward dead.

His first murder successfully accomplished, Nero blandly informed his guests as the corpse was carried out, "There is no reason for excitement. . . . Britannicus has just had one of these epileptic fits from which he has suffered in the past."

All the guests were appalled. But it was Agrippina who was the most shaken. White and shivering she sat and watched Britannicus's body disappear. Just three months after she had murdered her husband she realized that she had met her match —in her own son. The cold bloodedness with which he had carried out the murder appalled even the most accomplished murderess in Rome.

The body of the dead Britannicus was at once removed to the Field of Mars and, on Nero's orders, was burned to prevent any investigation into the cause of death. Next day Seneca was deputed to inform the Senate that Britannicus had died as a result of an epileptic fit.

From the moment she saw Britannicus slump forward, Agrippina knew that it was open war between herself and Nero. Her only hope was to remove him. Her current plot was foiled by the death of Britannicus, but at once she began to search for another suitable "pretender". At the same time, in preparation for a coup d'état or a court revolution, she began to suborn senior officers of the Praetorian Guard. Nero reacted by removing

28

all guards from Agrippina and sending her to live in an old palace where from time to time he visited her ceremoniously.

All Rome knew of the conflict between Nero and his mother. Soon a rumour spread that she had found a suitable "pretender". This was a descendant of Caesar Augustus in the female line who was the same distance in descent from the great emperor as was Nero himself. Agrippina was said to be ready to marry this man and to make him Emperor in place of her son. How far the plot went is uncertain.

Nero certainly received warning of what was afoot from an actor who was taking part in a theatrical performance which—as a result of the new Emperor's artistic inclinations—were becoming a regular feature of palace life. Nero was very drunk when he learned of his mother's new bid to overthrow him. He went literally mad with drunken rage.

"First she threatens to make the army march against me and use Britannicus to drive me from the throne," he shrieked. "But Britannicus is gone. Now she has found another one. . . . There must be an end to it." Then he screamed to Seneca and Burrus, who had rushed to him, "Kill her".

Seneca had watched the Emperor's outburst with growing trepidation. Whatever Agrippina's crimes might be, he was too astute to let Agrippina be executed out of hand. Gradually he persuaded Nero to take a more rational course. In the end the Emperor agreed to the despatch of a commission headed by Seneca and Burrus which was to try—and execute—her.

The commission set out at daybreak for Agrippina's residence. When they challenged her she answered with a powerful speech. She was a clever woman and a brilliant actress. She appeared to break down. She spoke of her "mother's heart". Soon the commission was on the verge of tears. She pleaded that she must be allowed to see Nero for the last time. The commission returned to an impatiently-waiting Nero. He agreed to see his mother.

Agrippina assured Nero that what he had been told was a vile libel. She was completely innocent. She had only his interests at heart. Her histrionics prevailed—for the time being.

The young Emperor had other interests in these first few months of his reign apart from combating his mother's bids to oust him from the throne. He had decided he was an artist. With the aid and encouragement of Seneca he started to write light verse. But his absorbing interest lay in music. He summoned the leading singers and performers on the zither to the palace and insisted that they perform hour after hour, until they were exhausted. Then he decided he too would be a singer. Alas, his voice was thin, reedy and uncertain in pitch. He decided he must study singing. Thereafter a great part of the day was spent in vocal exercises—sometimes as he lay on his back—to the despair of Seneca and others who had to put up with his out-of-tune bawling. His throat became Nero's main preoccupation; he went in constant fear of catching cold.

Nero sought other diversions. Wearying of the wise words and the constant admonitions of Seneca, he gathered round him a group of the Roman "teddy boys" of the age. Their chief was his greatest friend Marcus Salvius Otho, whose scandalous exploits had led to innumerable thrashings with a whip by his father. Otho, elegant, well-spoken and well-mannered, fascinated the young Emperor and, if the great Roman historian Tacitus is to be believed, initiated Nero into the satisfaction of homosexual lusts. It was Otho who induced Nero to join in nightly adventures which rapidly became the scandal of the capital.

Clad in clothes borrowed from their slaves, Nero, Otho and a group of other spivs toured the brothels and cabarets, smashing dishes, assaulting the customers and generally plundering wherever they went. The streets of Rome at that time were unlit, so as they were making their way home completely drunk the group of ne'er-do-wells found new entertainment in beating up innocent passers-by returning late to their homes. Some of the victims retaliated in kind and more than once Nero returned to the palace with evidence of the shrewdness of their blows. His doctor provided him with medicaments which concealed the visible signs if not the pain of the blows.

On one such nocturnal encounter Nero encountered the senator Julius Montanus with his wife. Nero fell on the lady and tried to "insult" her. Her husband rushed to the defence of his wife and struck back at the rowdy. The Senator obviously knew how to use his fists for he forced Nero to release his wife. Nero went home nursing two black eyes and various other weals and bruises which not even the skill of his physicians could conceal. In consequence he was forced to remain out of sight for several days.

From acquaintances at court the Senator discovered that it had been the Emperor whom he had struck. He was misguided enough to write Nero a letter of apology. But Nero was no sportsman. When he received the letter he was furious and screamed, "This man knows he struck Nero—and he still lives." This was reported to the Senator. He recognized in the one phrase his own death sentence. A few hours later he committed suicide before worse befell him and his family.

After this Nero was more circumspect in his nocturnal rioting. He took with him an escort of Praetorians and gladiators who followed at a discreet distance.

Nero also was still fascinated by chariot racing in the arena. Just because his mother had forbidden him to have anything to do with the sport he appeared at the circus and exercised his team of horses amid the plaudits of the crowd. But he was not particularly skilful; at one corner his chariot overturned and Nero literally bit the dust of the arena. Thereafter he confined his chariot practice to a quiet hollow—a site on which today stands the Vatican.

Little was heard from Agrippina for nearly two years after her narrow escape from execution at the orders of Nero. Without real friends and with no supporters she led a humdrum life in an old house where, like other ladies in similar circumstances since, she spent her time writing her "memoirs". She still thirsted after power, however. But she had learned a lesson. She now abjured conspiracy, preferring instead to make a new effort to win back the regard of her son—and so her own power.

Although she was over forty, Agrippina was still a strikingly beautiful woman. So she decided to be not Nero's mother—*but his mistress*. Three years after his succession Nero had a mistress only nominally; for all practical purposes, though not in name, Akte had become his true and loving wife. She was, however, a simple girl who knew nothing of amatory finesse. In this direction Agrippina had nothing to learn.

Though Agrippina was virtually barred from the Imperial palace, in accordance with Roman custom Nero still visited her for certain intimate family festivals. At one of these, when the young Emperor was sated with good food and wine, Agrippina

31

started to exercise her wiles. By lascivious kisses and other tendernesses she aroused Nero—and persuaded him to forget that she was his mother. Nero succumbed. His relationship with Agrippina was to become much more than a temporary sexual deviation. In some ways to have her as his mistress satisfied some deep-seated morbid complex by demeaning a woman whom previously he had feared.

As soon as Seneca discovered what had happened he was appalled. Applying the maxim of "a woman to fight a woman" he summoned Akte to his aid. She poured reproaches on Nero, who, in consequence, felt his whole world slipping beneath him. Yet he could not forget his experience with Agrippina, nor the morbid satisfaction it had given him. He saw in himself a new Oedipus. His mother had become for him the cause of agonizing suffering and of a terrible inner conflict.

"Whatever she did had become a burden to him," states Tacitus, "and so he decided to put her to death."

Nero poured out his problems, and his decision, to his boon companion Otho. Clearly it was unthinkable to bring Agrippina before a Roman court. Poison was the obvious means for handling such a problem, but Agrippina was reported to possess a formidable pharmacopoeia designed to prevent any such fate. Moreover the analogy with the death of Britannicus might prove too close.

Nero was still pondering on the problem when he went to Baiae on the coast for the festivities marking the beginning of spring. There his one-time teacher Anecitus, whom he had appointed commander of the local fleet, produced a special attraction, a ship which opened in the middle, throwing its cargo of wild animals into the sea. Either Nero or Otho had a brilliant thought; here was the perfect method of disposing of Agrippina.

Agrippina was invited to join Nero by the sea. He met her on the landing stage and accompanied her to a country house which had been prepared for her on the other side of the bay. That evening he invited her to a banquet to be given by Otho in his honour. Agrippina was delighted and gladly accepted.

That evening a ship was sent to bring her across the bay, here about a mile broad. During the banquet Nero showed his mother the greatest respect. Towards midnight the banquet

ended. As Nero escorted Agrippina to the quay he told her: "My
dear mother look after your health. Remember that it is only
you that I love—and that through you alone I rule." He kissed
her hand, her cheek and her bosom and watched her go on board
the galley that was to take her across the bay.

When the ship was a good distance from the shore the captain
pulled the lever which opened the centre portion of the hull.
Agrippina and her lady-in-waiting were dropped into the water
and partly trapped under a heavy lead canopy which had been
placed over them to ensure that they would drown. When the
lady-in-waiting, trapped in the water, shouted "Save the
Empress", she was beaten to death with boathooks by the crew.

Agrippina herself knew that this was an attempt at murder.
She therefore made no cry for help but started to swim for the
shore. During her period of banishment she had spent much
time diving for sponges and was an adept and powerful swimmer.
She covered the half mile to the shore in safety. Then by a
devious route she made her way to the house where she was
living.

Nero returned to his seaside villa to wait impatiently news
of his mother's death. When at last the ship's captain arrived he
reported that Agrippina had met her death in an accident at sea.
Nero was still pondering the implications of his action when a
slave arrived to tell him of Agrippina's remarkable good fortune
in her escape.

Nero was seized with panic. He was not fooled by the tone
of his mother's message. He expected at any moment to see her
march in at the head of her slaves to murder him with her own
hands. He ordered that the guards round the villa be strengthened
and summoned Seneca and Burrus. They were singularly un-
helpful. The Emperor knew his mother must die. With that sly
ingenuity for which he was already famed he knew that he must
now find a pretext for her "legal execution". Though his advisers
were unable—or unwilling—to help, Nero himself was never for
long at a loss in devising devilment. Very soon he devised a
means to secure his end.

He summoned the slave sent by Agrippina to tell of her
"fortunate escape". As the slave repeated the message Nero
adroitly let a dagger clatter on to the floor.

"Seize him," he shouted. "My mother has sent this man to murder me. Look at the dagger on the floor."

Burrus, head of the Praetorian Guard, still declined to act, but the Imperial navy was more helpful. On Nero's order the captain of the murder ship and two other naval officers took horse for Agrippina's residence. The three men entered the house and burst open the door of Agrippina's room.

"If you come to inquire after my health," she said, "I am well. If you come to commit a crime I decline to believe that my son has given an order for the murder of his mother."

None of the three assassins said a word. One lashed at her head with a cudgel. She fell back on the bed, yet so great was her strength that it required repeated stabs from the assassins' daggers before she lay dead.

The captain went into the garden and told the terrified slaves to build a pyre. Agrippina's corpse was carried out on a sofa and thrown on to the fire so that no one would be able to prove the manner of her death. The actor Minester, who had long been one of her lovers, was found. He too was murdered and his body thrown on top of that of his mistress. The three murderers then returned to Nero—and informed him that his mother had been executed for attempting his murder.

* * *

Nero is believed to have had another reason for the murder of his mother. According to some authorities she is believed to have tried to prevent his marriage to one of the reigning beauties of Rome, the famous Poppaea Sabina, with whom the Emperor was now infatuated. Poppaea in her extreme youth had been married to one of the Praetorian Guard commanders under Claudius; this man had been replaced at Agrippina's instigation by Burrus. Since her husband's enforced retirement Poppaea had led a very quiet life in which her main interests had been in preserving her beauty and in buying elegant clothes.

When Nero first met Poppaea is uncertain. Whatever the exact circumstances, after divorcing her elderly husband she married Otho, the Emperor's favourite. Whether this was at Nero's instigation is uncertain. Nero soon became infatuated and, after a slight show of resistance, Poppaea became the Emperor's mistress, replacing the faithful Akte. The disgruntled Otho, after for some time sharing Poppaea's bed with his friend the Emperor, was despatched as governor-general to the distant province that now is Portugal.

Poppaea was determined to be Empress, and Nero sought the means to satisfy her ambition. He already had a wife—Octavia, the younger daughter of the Emperor Claudius, with whom almost certainly he had never lived. The disposal of Octavia presented a complicated political problem. His betrothal to her had been the reason for his adoption by Claudius and clearly involved his succession to the Imperial throne. He could easily divorce Octavia, but if she married again, as the daughter of Claudius she might well be held to have a good claim to the throne, in which case her next husband could become a serious rival.

Nero at first intended to divorce Octavia on the grounds of infertility, but there was evidence to suggest that he had never consummated the union, so he abandoned that course.

Burrus, now in his mid sixties, died suddenly; according to one rumour, from poison given at the instigation of Nero. His place as chief security officer was taken by the one-time spy Tigellinus, the man who had warned Caligula of Agrippina's treachery. Within a short time Tigellinus had established himself as the classic secret police chief of a dictatorship. According to one historian, from the moment he felt secure in his position, "Terror became the order of the day". Like his modern successors, he was a man of ingenuity. To solve the problem of Octavia he introduced a good-looking Greek slave, a flute player, into the Empress's boudoir. The neglected woman was inevitably found in his arms. Adultery was sufficient grounds for divorce. So Nero ended his marriage and twelve days later married Poppaea.

Nero, however, still treated Octavia with great circumspection and as a parting gift presented her with a house. By this time there was in Rome growing opposition to Nero and his terror. The divorce of Octavia, last of the direct Julian-Claudian line, aroused widespread unrest. Protest meetings were held outside her house. To stop these disorders, Nero ordered Octavia to retire to the country. News of her banishment was the signal for a riot which was suppressed only after the Praetorian Guards had charged the rioters with drawn swords and beaten them back with whips.

Poppaea, against whom most of the discontent was directed, was furious. In the streets the crowds shouted and booed at her. At last she went to Nero and on bended knee claimed that her life was in danger from the followers of Octavia. To Nero this called for only one solution: Octavia must be removed from the scene. He summoned Anecitus, one of the naval officers who had taken a leading part in the murder of Agrippina, and outlined the latest imperial murder operation.

For the benefit of the Senate and the Roman people, explained Nero, it would be announced that Octavia had been organizing a revolt to take over power. To win over the Imperial navy to her side she had seduced Admiral Anecitus. She would be arrested for treason and deported to a small island. Her death could be expected to follow.

Nero assured Anecitus that if he played the role allotted to him he would be highly rewarded. Otherwise he would die. Anecitus accepted. Octavia's arrest and deportation to a small island followed; but the lady had something of her father's character. She declined to commit suicide. She was therefore beaten over the head by her guards, her wrists were slashed and she was left to bleed to death in a Turkish bath. The pusillanimous Senate passed a resolution thanking the gods for delivering the Emperor from this new danger.

Seneca by this time was at loggerheads with the Emperor. For some time Nero had been impatient of the elderly philosopher's tutelage. In addition Seneca had become involved in various financial scandals. It was alleged by his enemies that his usury had precipitated a revolt among the British tribes in South-east England some time previously. A split became inevitable. Emperor and philosopher parted with exaggerated expressions of high regard, but Seneca retired with resentment smouldering against the man for whom he had done so much.

For a long time Nero dallied in Naples, where the still-surviving Greek influence was to his taste, singing, writing poetry, playing the zither, and appearing as an actor in his private theatre with Tigellinus acting as prompter in place of Burrus and Seneca.

Yet Nero was a shrewd judge of the Roman character and knew that his reign of terror could continue unabated only so long as he gave the mob circuses to entertain them. He therefore announced a great summer festival.

The carnival was held at midsummer of the year A.D. 64 at a lake on the outskirts of Rome. On the water was built a large raft to accommodate the Emperor and his guests while all round the shores were booths where the Roman citizens were invited to eat and drink as much as they liked—at the Emperor's expense. Among the trees were other small buildings in which were some of the most beautiful and attractive women in Rome. There were beautiful Greek slaves, prostitutes, virgins from aristocratic families, middle-class wives, and some of the most prominent beauties of Roman society. Most of them were either half-clothed or naked. They had been officially "requisitioned for service" on the Emperor's orders. It would be a mistake to presume, however, that the majority of them were opposed to obeying Nero's command.

As twilight fell the satiated Romans made their way towards the "houses of joy" hidden in the woods. At once fights broke out as fierce competition developed for the best-looking girls. Thereafter developed one of the most unbelievable orgies of all time. Half of Rome was involved. Gladiators could be seen in the embraces of daughters of senators, slaves with their mistresses, and distinguished figures of Roman official life with glamorous young slaves. Pandemonium reigned throughout the night. There were innumerable disturbances in some of which men were killed. And women in considerable numbers were throttled or beaten to death by their drunken lovers-for-the-night.

While the Bacchanalia raged around him Nero lay on his raft by the side of Poppaea enjoying the cooling breezes of the mid-summer night. This midsummer orgy, however, was but the prelude to even more sensational events.

After that wanton night by the lake Nero withdrew to his country home at Antium for a rest. It was there early on the morning of 19 July that he was awakened by a messenger.

"Rome is on fire," the Emperor was told. The famous Circus Maximus was already a mass of flame and the imperial palace was threatened.

Nero mounted a charger and headed for Rome, three hours' fast riding distant. When he reached his capital and saw the flames consuming Rome, Nero was entranced. He could scarcely contain his excitement. It was an occasion to be celebrated by a great artist such as himself. Donning Greek robes he quickly made his way to an eminence from where, in safety, he could observe a spectacle which must have been something like that around St. Paul's Cathedral in London after the bombing in September, 1940.

Nero celebrated the burning of Rome in his weak tuneless voice and accompanied his song on a zither. He sang of the destruction of another great city—Homer's story of the fall of Troy.

For more than a week the city blazed furiously. When the flames at last died down much of the city was destroyed. The origin of this great fire, like others including the Great Fire of London in 1666, has been the subject of bitter controversy among historians. Contemporary witnesses who watched the fire in Rome are, however, agreed—it was started by Nero. There are widely-differing accounts of what happened. Some reports claim that the fire was actually started by Nero's minions darting through the narrow streets of the old city with flaming torches.

Nero's true reason for putting Rome to the flames is still a matter of historical argument. Some authorities suggest that he wished to revenge himself on the Romans for their support of his murdered Empress Octavia. Apologists claim that he wished only to clear away the ancient slums and replace them with splendid new buildings. It is perhaps more probable that Nero (gross and bloated although still only twenty-six) was by this time a little mad and the thought of the spectacle of the city in flames had excited his "artist's soul".

Whatever the facts the citizens of Rome, not unnaturally, took a strong view about the burning of their homes. Their anger was concentrated on the man whom they were sure was responsible.

Nero, with that flair for evil which never deserted him, knew how to exploit such a situation. By the middle of the sixth decade since the birth of Jesus Christ the sect known as the Christians was becoming something of a nuisance to the Roman authorities. Members of it had spread from the Middle East all over the

Empire. According to the historian Tacitus, in the capital itself they had attracted "all the disgraceful and evil elements until they had a considerable body of adherents".

The Roman authorities had decided to act against the Christians. Nero decided to kill two birds with the one stone. He therefore publicly blamed the Christians for setting Rome on fire. In fact he took action which at one and the same time would appease the angry citizens of Rome and get rid of many of the troublesome Christian sect.

Thus began Nero's first great persecution of the Christians. Tacitus reports that, as an entertainment, the Emperor dealt with the Christians in three ways: 1. He ordered them to be dressed in the skins of wild animals and thrown to dogs which tore them to pieces. 2. He crucified them. 3. He had them dipped into boiling pitch and, after dark, used as human torches. As a refinement of this last method he had his garden specially equipped for the human flares. Then dressed as a charioteer the Emperor, amid the plaudits of a specially-arranged crowd, raced round the arena in his chariot illuminated by the light of the burning Christians. No one knows how many Christians were martyred in the butchery ordered by Nero in A.D. 64. It was a very large number. Although after a time the mass murders waned, persecution continued. Three years later St. Peter and St. Paul became martyrs to the Nero terror.

While the Christians burned, Nero plunged into the task of rebuilding his burned-out capital. But if the ordinary people were kept quiet by his butchery of the Christians, both the military and civilian leaders around him had become weary of his insatiable blood-lust. In the months before the fire there had been a number of abortive conspiracies. The burning of Rome gave new impetus to the plotters. One group of senior officers of the Praetorian Guard proposed to place Seneca on the throne; an intrigue in the Senate centred around a Senator called Calpurnius Piso, who was something of a Grand Seigneur. It was proposed that, after Nero's assassination, he should marry Antonia, the sole surviving child of Claudius by an early marriage, and should become Emperor. By the early months of A.D. 65 the two plots had coalesced.

The assassination attempt was fixed for 19 April, the last day of the festival of Ceres. The conspirators had decided to adopt the tactics used against Julius Caesar, while one conspirator fell on his knees before Nero (and held his legs) another would stab him.

However, the conspirator chosen to stab Nero made somewhat demonstrative preparations in his own home. His freedman secretary suspected the truth. He went home and told his wife. She was a formidable woman who had no intention of her husband becoming involved in any murder plot. After a domestic scene she forced her husband to go during the night to Nero's country house to disclose the plot.

Nero was in a fury. He summoned Tigellinus. Two of the principal conspirators were arrested and taken to Nero's residence. In Nero's presence they were tortured with a series of barbaric instruments until they disclosed the names of their fellow-conspirators. One of the names dragged from them was —Seneca.

That same afternoon, by which time most of the plotters had been rounded up, Nero set up a sort of "field general court martial" consisting of himself, Tigellinus and another officer. One after the other the plotters were dragged into the sunshine before the garden table—and condemned. Seneca was accorded special treatment. An officer was sent to him to inform him that he had been named as a conspirator. He sent back the officer to Nero denying the charge. But relations between the Emperor and his former mentor were tense for Seneca had made complaint about certain aspects of the great fire. The officer was sent back to the famous philosopher with a message that he must kill himself. He did so in a manner worthy of his stoic philosophy.

Altogether seventeen conspirators were sentenced to death, three voluntarily committed suicide, and a number, including one who had betrayed his fellows under torture, were freed.

The conspiracy was merely an open manifestation of the growing discontent with Nero which was shared by all sections of the Roman people. The Emperor was warned of the discontent by Tigellinus, and prescribed his invariable remedy in such circumstances, a bigger and better orgy. He proposed to repeat the carnival by the lake of the previous year. But the Senate for once opposed him, "to avoid further scandal".

Nero, therefore, announced that he would personally honour with his presence a Festival of Song to be staged in the Pompeius Theatre. He had no sooner taken his seat in the royal box than there was a growing chorus of shouts "Come and sing yourself" . . . whether it was spontaneous is open to doubt.

At first, pretending bashfulness, Nero declined. As the cries for the appearance of the "great artist" increased he bowed to public demand. A few minutes later clad in the costume of a zither player (which he had thoughtfully brought with him) the bloated figure of the Emperor appeared on the stage. In his croaking, tuneless voice he sang, and sang, and sang. The royal performance went on from four in the afternoon until the fall of the summer dusk. By the time he approached the end Nero, hoarse but still indomitable, rose on his toes and strained his neck in a desperate effort to reach the high notes which he had set for himself.

It was one of the greatest comic turns of history, yet the audience applauded wildly, for scattered among them were large numbers of the plain clothes police of Tigellinus. While the lower orders who failed to applaud were encouraged by a rap on the head, senators and others who either yawned or openly laughed had their names taken down for future punishment.

This comedy had scarcely ended when the news of the sudden death of Poppaea broke. The reason for her death remained a mystery. She was pregnant at the time and Nero was wildly excited about the prospect of the birth of an heir. One account claims that she had a miscarriage, but that is probably a half truth. More probable is the rumour which swept Rome at the time. Nero, returning home in the middle of the night from one of his usual orgies, was involved in a stormy scene with his wife. In a drunken temper he kicked the pregnant woman in the stomach and she died from her injuries. Whatever the facts Nero certainly was heart broken. He gave her a grandiose funeral, but her death marked a turning point in his life.

He could never forget Poppaea and constantly craved for her in his bouts of erotic delirium. The mistress of one of his boon companions was installed as Mistress of the Wardrobe with the task of acting as "Madame" of the Royal brothel. It was her function to find girls and boys who bore some resemblance to the dead Poppaea to share the Emperor's bed. Night after night, clad in his dead wife's garments, these prostitutes of both sexes were taken to him.

At last a youth named Sporus, clad in one of Poppaea's most elegant gowns, satisfied Nero. He seemed to believe that his wife had returned. The youth was castrated and given the name of Sabina, one of the family names of the dead Poppaea. Thereafter he became the Emperor's "mistress".

But the gratification of Nero's erotic peculiarities also required the re-enactment of mythological sexual orgies. For that purpose the Mistress of the Wardrobe kept a list of the various prostitutes of both sexes supplied to her master with notes of their individual erotic qualifications.

His lusts were not sexual only. Steadily the total of the victims of his sadistic and bloodthirsty demands rose, until the whole of Roman society went in living terror. One historian has described the last years of Nero's reign as "Murder on an endless belt".

As always with Nero there was method in his madness. By this time the fortune he had inherited from Claudius was dissipated and he was desperately short of cash to maintain the expensive orgies which had become part of his life. He ordered Tigellinus to concentrate the Neronian terror on the richest men in Rome and throughout the Empire. He became the head of a sort of Murder Incorporated with an acumen which would have aroused the envy of the late Mr. Albert Anastasia, his twentieth-century successor. One by one the millionaire Senators and others with equal fortunes received the imperial command: "Kill yourself". And the secret police messenger made it clear in each case to the doomed millionaire that he had better leave a substantial portion of his estate to the Emperor less a worse fate befall his unfortunate dependants.

The death roll was huge and the profits commensurate. Nero, however, was as weary of Rome as Rome was of Nero. In the year A.D. 66 he determined to satisfy the ambition of a lifetime and make an extended visit to Greece, where he would stay to take part in the Olympic games of the following year. He left the government in the hands of one of his freedmen, Helius, and on 10 August left Rome accompanied by a varied suite, the most notable members of which were his "mistress" Sporus-Sabina and the inevitable secret police chief Tigellinus. They stopped at the modern Benevento, where another abortive attempt was made to assassinate him, before sailing from Brindisa in the latter half of the month. En route the party called at Corfu, where, in the famous temple of Jupiter, Nero sang an ode to the god. From the autumn of A.D. 66 until the spring of 67 Nero remained in Corinth, for the most part living the life of a carefree tourist, but occasionally joining Tigellinus in efforts to clear up the aftermath of the Benevento assassination attempt.

On this occasion Nero decided that the Olympic Games must be extended to include both drama and music. The town of Olympia, however, had no theatre. So Nero ordered the construction of a playhouse in time for the games. There the Emperor won the laurels both as the "greatest tragic actor" of the time and as a singer. He was determined also to exhibit his prowess as a charioteer. Although during the race he lost control of his team and fell out of his chariot, the judges tactfully decided that he was the winner.

Nero, like many other travellers, was enchanted by Greece and lingered on into the spring of the following year. During these last months of his "holiday" he decided to "regularize" his relationship with Sporus-Sabina who was his constant companion. With Tigellinus playing the role of "father of the bride" the ceremony was duly carried out according to the rites of the Roman religion. The Greeks, who were not particularly shocked by this type of union, drank the health of the "newly-wedded couple" coupled with the hope that they would have many children.

By this time the Roman Empire was seething with revolt. Almost all the commanding generals were involved in a plot to remove Nero and replace him as Emperor with the veteran Commander-in-Chief in Spain the seventy-three-year-old Galba. When Nero at last reached Italy in March of A.D. 68 open revolt had broken out in Gaul. The revolting general had issued a proclamation accusing Nero of being "Murderer . . . Matricide . . . Poisoner . . . but worst of all a dreadful singer who did not even know the rules of the art". That insult alone brought any reaction from the by now completely besotted Emperor. The revolt in Gaul was suppressed; but the generals still plotted. Nero seemed indifferent.

Then less than three months after his return from Greece he suddenly decided to pay a visit to Alexandria in Egypt. Despite his apparent indifference Nero knew the end of his reign was near. His main interest probably was to save his life. He may have intended to flee Rome for good and to take refuge in Egypt, for he gave orders for a company of German mercenaries to be sent on ahead of him to await him in Alexandria and to act as a guard.

His departure was fixed for 8 or 9 June. On the afternoon of the 8th he slipped quietly out of Rome and made for his country home in the Servilian gardens fifteen miles from Ostia. There he informed his personal bodyguard of Praetorians that he was leaving for Egypt. Two years earlier these men had accompanied him to Greece gladly. This time the officers told him bluntly that they did not intend to go. He was faced for the first time with open mutiny, and one officer significantly quoted to him a couplet of Virgil:

> *"Is it then so great a misfortune*
> *to give up life"?*

That was the beginning of the end. Nero realized that he was finished as Roman Emperor. He pondered for hours on the problem: should he flee to the most distant province of the Empire or appear in the Forum and in a great speech declaimed in the classic manner ask for the forgiveness of the Roman citizens for all that had gone before? He was still pondering that problem when he went to bed. At midnight he woke up. There was a deadly silence. He went into the garden—the Praetorian Guard had disappeared! Nero panicked. He shrieked for help. Two of his freedmen appeared. He pleaded with them to find him a place of refuge. For the next few hours he made a tour of the nearby country houses of his friends. No one would take him in. When he returned he found all his servants had vanished—along with a gold vase of poison which he had had prepared the previous day.

He was still undecided what to do when the verse of Virgil quoted by the officer came back to him. He decided to take his life. He would drown himself in the Tiber. But when he reached the bank he drew back in terror and ran home.

Slowly he recovered his nerve. He put aside all thoughts of suicide. One of his freedmen Phaon had a small house hidden in the countryside four miles from Rome. He suggested to Nero that this house would be a safe refuge. Desperately Nero seized upon the idea. He would go there at once. Armed with two daggers but still in his nightshirt and with bare feet he jumped on a horse. As he galloped off he shouted to Sporus-Sabina, who had been wakened, to follow him.

The direct route to Phaon's house was across the breadth of Rome. Nero declined to face a passage through the city. He insisted on riding in the midst of a severe storm of thunder and lightning round the periphery of the city. By this time the city itself was in turmoil. An all-night sitting of the Senate was taking place. The Praetorian Guard were bribed to back Galba by a promise of double the gift they had received on Nero's accession. They shouted, "Long live the Emperor Galba; away with Nero."

Nero and his small party was only a few hundred yards away. Nero heard the shout. He panicked again. He abandoned his horse and followed by his companions set off across the stony ground in his bare feet. He made slow progress, but eventually the little group reached Phaon's house. It was locked. Nero was forced in his nightshirt to climb a wall and then to crawl through a hole into the courtyard.

Inside he sank on to a bed. In a corner crouched Sporus-Sabina shivering with terror. Phaon broke the silence; he told Nero there were two choices now open to him ... to kill himself or to face public execution. Nero was astounded. After his flight he had believed he was safe, at least for the time being. It took time to convince him but at last however he agreed. He asked that a grave be dug for him. As he watched tears welled from his eyes and he murmured: "What an artist will disappear with me".

He seemed to have no idea how to kill himself. Phaon urged him to use his daggers. Naïvely he urged his companions to kill themselves first so that he would see how to do it. They declined. At last he plunged a dagger into his breast. For some minutes he remained conscious. But when one of those present attempted to stem the wound with a towel he murmured, "Too late". As he died his eyes fixed in a stare that filled all the onlookers with terror. It mirrored the soul of the man.

As soon as news of his death reached Rome there was a wave of rejoicing. Freedom had been regained "by the sacrifice of the monster". He was only thirty at the time of his death; yet most of the thirteen years and eight months during which he ruled had been a reign of terror.

Only one remained faithful to the dead Emperor—Akte the Greek serving girl who had been perhaps his only true wife. By this time she was a woman of great wealth. It was she who paid for the funeral when his ashes were placed in the mausoleum of the Domitius family on the Pincio.

Many more tyrants were to rule Rome in the centuries that followed, but none of them equalled Nero in sheer evil.

Chapter 2

GENGHIS KHAN

THE people of medieval Europe lived in constant fear that the Mongol hordes—of whom they knew nothing but fearsome rumour—would drive westwards to the shores of the Atlantic like the Four Horsemen of the Apocalypse. To them Genghis Khan was "The Scourge of God".

Thirteenth-century Christian and Muslim sages alike were certain that the terrible conqueror, who had emerged with his armies out of the wastes of farthest Asia to plunder, ravage and murder, was a visitation of divine wrath upon a sinful world. And Roger Bacon, the greatest English thinker of the age, believed that the Mongol emperor was the anti-Christ himself "come to reap the last dreadful harvest".

The fear of the Western world for the man whom Asia knew as "The Emperor of All Men" had all too real a basis in fact, for Genghis Khan, with his superb fast-moving legions of cavalry, exterminated more human beings than any other man in history. He slaughtered even more than Adolf Hitler, who is generally credited with murdering around twenty million human beings between 1933 and 1945. If the total of slaughtered human souls be the ultimate test of wickedness Genghis Khan assuredly was the wickedest man who ever lived.

It would, however, be a mistake to assume that this fabulous conqueror—his character and conquests are known from little more than legend—was basically evil.

The Mongol host which swept across Asia and half of Europe sacked cities, devastated whole countries and slaughtered their peoples on an almost cosmic scale without any real malice. The Mongol nomads valued human life less than the soil which nourished their beasts. To secure better grazing they slaughtered human beings *without hatred*—simply to make an end of them.

Unlike the Nazi Führer, Genghis Khan never killed for ideological reasons—he knew nothing of ideology and little of religion. He was a simple warrior chief of a nomad people born to wage a perpetual struggle for existence, and ruthlessly eliminating any and all who might threaten that existence in any way.

He was a cruel and, in later life, a brutally sadistic man, but he was not fundamentally evil. Contemporary records suggest that, according to his own savage lights, he was often fair, generous and sometimes even exceedingly merciful. He left behind him a code of laws, the *Yassa*, almost incredible as the work of an illiterate northern Asiatic nomad, and certainly he was more broad minded than his contemporaries in Europe. He had a fiery and savage temper and, as was customary, he liked to get drunk. During his life he had five hundred wives and concubines, yet he remained devoted to his first wife who became his Empress.

He died as he lived, unspoiled by his conquests, yet he left a mark on history which survived until modern times.

One legend claims that the Mongols were descended from the Biblical Japhet. Another asserts that the founder of the clan was succoured by a wolf—an Asiatic counterpart of the Roman legend of Romulus and Remus. Whatever their origins, the Mongols remained unknown to the world until the seventh century when they were mentioned in the writings of Chinese scribes. Little more was heard of them for half a millenium. But by the twelfth century their ruler Kabul Khan, the great-grandfather of Genghis Khan, had established the overlordship of the Yakka or Great Mongols over the other wandering tribes north of the Gobi. Yesukai the father of Genghis Khan was known as a Siberian Princeling "the master of forty thousand tents".

By that time the Yakka Mongols had seized the best of the grazing lands which stretched from Lake Baikal in Siberia to the Khingan Mountains which today border modern Manchuria. It was in a Mongol encampment-village in that region in 1164 that Yesukai's first-born came into the world in the big felted tent which was the chief's home. The father was absent on a raid at the time of the birth. He killed his enemy and on his return gave the newly-born the name of his foe—Temujin, which meant "Finest Steel". The fable that Genghis Khan—as the boy was to be known in history—was originally a smith probably comes from

the Turkish form of the word Temurji. The Chinese version
T'ie mou jen however contained a curious prophecy—Supreme
Earth Man.

Temujin was a hardy boy, as were all Mongol children who
survived infancy. As he grew up he became noted for great
physical strength. Spare in build, he became even as a boy one
of the best wrestlers in the tribe; also he was a fine shot with bow
and arrow. Ruthlessly he employed his talents to impose his will
on his fellows.

Feuds were a commonplace of Mongol life, especially in a
polygamous household like that of Yesukai. The younger children
were particularly jealous of the first-born son of the senior wife,
who was Temujin's beautiful mother Houlun. One of his younger
half-brothers, with whom Temujin was on bad terms, stole a
fish which Temujin had caught. Mercy was not in the vocabulary
of a teenage Mongol. The younger boy was slain where he stood.

As he entered his teens Temujin was a tall youth with high
shoulders and a lightly tanned skin. Long reddish hair hung round
his shoulders, but his grey-green eyes were curiously unMon-
goloid; they had not the slightest trace of a slant.

Temujin was in his mother's tent when one day a Mongol
horseman galloped up. The rider came to say that Yesukai had
been poisoned by enemies and lay dying; he wanted to see
Temujin. The thirteen-year-old youth rode as fast as he could.
But he was too late. His father was dead; he, himself, was now
Chief. At once he was faced with open revolt. The great majority
of his father's lieutenants decided that they would not pay
tribute to a thirteen-year-old boy. His mother Houlun took
immediate action. With the nine yak-tails which was the standard
of the Mongol chieftains she rode after the deserting notables
and persuaded them to turn back. But only part of the clan took
the oath of fealty. Soon Temujin was threatened by both revolting
members of the clan and those who were in feud with his family
and had long waited just such an opportunity to overthrow the
power of the Yakka Mongols.

The story of the next four years is the record of the teenage
Temujin's struggle to regain his heritage. Much of the time he
was in hiding. He was tortured by his enemies when he was
caught and on more than one occasion he escaped death by a

hairsbreadth. But he was indomitable. Cunning kept him alive and his growing wisdom kept the remnants of the clan about him.

In these years of struggle qualities which set him apart from the rest of the Mongols began to develop. Temujin began to demonstrate an exceptional skill in organizing and deploying his forces, however small they might be. Gradually he began to dominate the turbulent sections of the tribe. Soon the Mongols began to mutter that Temujin and his brothers, who had loyally stood by him, were getting strong! He was brutal. He was hard. But so were his enemies. Gradually the tribe came to appreciate that they were dealing with a leader of exceptional ability.

By the time he was seventeen Temujin was again master of the Mongols. He decided to marry. He set out for a neighbouring clan where, while his father was still alive, he had become betrothed to a small grey-eyed beauty, then aged nine. Her name was Bourtai. She was his first, and perhaps his only true love. Despite the hundreds of other wives and concubines which, according to Mongol custom, he took in the years that followed, Bourtai was to remain principal wife as long as he lived. She was to be Empress of one of the greatest empires the world has ever known.

When Temujin had restored his authority over his own Mongols the rest of the nomad clans of Mongolia were far from accepting him as overlord. Bitter inter-tribal warfare flared up among the clans in the Gobi region. No quarter was given: none was expected. During this period of strife, the Merkits, a tribe from the north from which Temujin's mother, Houlun, had been stolen eighteen years before, took the opportunity to raid in revenge. The Mongols were caught by surprise. Temujin himself was able to leap from his bed and on to horseback, then at the head of his private guard he cut his way to safety. Bourtai however was captured by the invaders. In accord with the rules of tribal justice she was awarded to the kinsman of the man from whom Houlun had been stolen.

Temujin secured reinforcements from an allied clan and set out in pursuit of the raiders. He caught up with the Merkits at their first encampment and made a surprise attack. Riding furiously among the wrecked and overturned tents Temujin kept shouting his wife's name. Hearing his voice she ran out from hiding and caught his rein. In a moment she was in the saddle in front of him. Some months later she gave birth to a boy. Some expressed doubt about the paternity of Bourtai's first-born, who grew up moody and difficult, but Temujin never faltered in his devotion to his wife.

There was no truce in the non-stop struggle for supremacy in the Gobi. The Mongols were still the weakest of the tribes. Temujin had to lead his men repeatedly into battle. With success his forces gradually grew until he was in command of a formidable army of fifteen thousand men.

The Mongols became devoted to their young chief. When, in one action he was wounded in the throat by an arrow, he fell as if dead. As soon as his absence was noted, two of his lieutenants returned to find him. After sucking the blood from his throat they washed the wound with melted snow. Because he sorely needed food, one of his lieutenants led a raid on a nearby enemy camp to get it. Then, after Temujin had eaten, they set out for the Mongol camp. They were overtaken by a blizzard and forced to halt. While Temujin slept his lieutenants stood for most of the night holding a leather cape to give him shelter from the snow.

The success of Temujin and his Mongol cavalry in these repeated skirmishes began to attract attention. At last his chief rival, who led some thirty thousand men, decided he would have to end the Mongol power for good.

The Mongols were en route from summer to winter pastures when they were attacked. Their long tented carts or *kibitkas* were spread out along a valley. Quickly Temujin rallied his forces. He used the wagons to form a hollow square covering one flank. Then he made preparations for what Field-Marshal Montgomery would call a "set piece battle". He had thirteen thousand men and was encumbered by women, children and animals. His enemies numbered thirty thousand, divided into light and heavy cavalry. Hour after hour the struggle raged. But Temujin was already a general of marked ability. By superb handling of his forces in this, his first pitched battle, he repulsed the attack. Six thousand of the enemy were killed. The wounded were pitilessly put to the sword. Seventy enemy chiefs were led captive before him. As a warning to other possible aggressors,

Temujin, according to legend, had those seventy chiefs boiled alive in cauldrons.

Nothing succeeds like success. From all over what is now Mongolia men flocked to the standard of the nine yak-tails—the emblem of the man who had the knack of victory. His other virtues also were much discussed. According to an old Mongol legend it was said that "he permits the hunter to keep his kill, the soldier to keep his spoils, and will take his coat from his back and give it as a gift".

Temujin had become the most talked-of man among all the illiterate wandering clans of north-eastern Asia. Gradually, from among the leaders who swore him fealty and from the daring youths he marked out as having the qualities of command, he chose the men who were to gain fame as his generals. The eleven Orkhons were to become known as the Kiyat—the Raging Torrents. As they swept across Asia and Europe in the years that followed, that description was not belied. Of these commanders Bayan and Muhuli were two tried and crafty leaders of great experience. Another was Chepe Noyan who had once been the Khan's prisoner and had been won over by generosity; he was impetuous and a dashing commander of cavalry. Subotai Bahadur, a sagacious princeling from the north, was another to be set down in military history as one of the great cavalry commanders of all time.

Despite the increase in numbers under his command, complete victory yet eluded Temujin, indeed in one big battle his principal enemies the Karaits won a great victory. Some wavering clans went over to them; so by the beginning of the thirteenth century the Gobi region was divided virtually into two rival camps.

One of these groups, however, was commanded by a supreme military genius. In the fighting thousands died. Leaders of the principal families were put to death summarily. The best of the fighting men who were captured were given the choice between death or joining the legions of Temujin. The women were shared out: the most desirable became wives of Mongols, the rest became slaves.

At last in a great battle Temujin broke the remaining power of his enemies. Until that point his life had been shaped by the actions of his enemies. Now he had the appetite to conquer, and that applied to everything and everyone in his path. His troops were despatched in various directions. To the east they reconnoitred right up to the Great Wall of China itself. To the west they advanced along the historic caravan routes into Central Asia and to the borders of the Muslim world.

The next twenty-one years were to see an almost unparalleled era of conquest. If Temujin had developed his military skill he had become also something of a statesman. He knew that to conquer he must have a sure base and that depended on the peoples of the Gobi region. Therefore, in the year 1206, he summoned a great council of khans—a *Kurultai* as it was known in their language. He told them they must choose one man to rule all the peoples of Asia—in a word a Mongol Emperor. The choice was inevitable. By unanimous acclamation of the assembled chiefs Temujin was elected *Genghis Kha Khan*, the supreme ruler, Emperor of All Men.

The way had been opened for the Mongol conquest, which in the next century would spread across half the world—and exterminate a sizeable proportion of the population of the known world. First, however, Genghis Khan had to make preparations. In the months which followed his elevation as Genghis Kha Khan he evolved the great Mongol battle plan. It would meet with unvarying success until more than fifty years later it encountered its first check at the hands of the Mamelukes in Egypt. The strategy and tactics devised by this illiterate Asiatic nomad would have done credit to the most sophisticated general staff of the twentieth century. This was how Genghis Khan operated:

1. There was a meeting of the Mongol general staff presided over by the Khan himself and attended by all senior officers who would take part in the operation. A plan was worked out; the best routes of advance agreed, and specific tasks allocated to the various units.
2. Spies were sent out and patrol actions undertaken to secure prisoners for questioning.
3. As soon as the signal was given by the Khan the doomed country was entered from several points at once; each division of the army moved independently towards its objective. The various commanders had an independence and discretion that their present-day successors, constricted by

directives sent by radio, would envy. All, however, were
ordered to keep in touch with the Kha Khan or with his
Orkhon commanding the front by a system of couriers unparalleled at that time or indeed for centuries thereafter.
4. Some divisions invested the large defended cities while other
bodies ravaged the countryside and massacred the inhabitants. Supplies were gathered in from the land which had
been overrun and a base for the next stage of operations was
established.

Genghis Khan, like all the great captains of history, knew that
the secret of success lay in two things—surprise and speed. The
first was an inbred attribute of all Mongol tactics developed
through the centuries. The second was provided by the stupendous
mobility of the Khan's *tumans* (cavalry divisions). These horsemen of the Khan could traverse hundreds of miles at a speed and
with a battle efficiency which a modern armoured division would
find difficult to better.

When Genghis Khan turned his eyes eastward the ancient
civilization of China was in a state of advanced decadence. The
Khan knew much about Cathay . . . or Khitai as he called it and
as it is still called in some central Asiatic tongues. Technically
he was a vassal of the Golden Emperor, who ruled from his
fabulous palace not far from present-day Peking. For his help in
subduing an earlier border revolt along the Great Wall he had
been awarded the ceremonial title of "Commander Against the
Rebels."

In the course of the long-drawn struggle against the ancient
Chinese ruling house of Sung—which still controlled much of
southern China—the Golden Emperor had asked for Mongol
reinforcements. Genghis Khan sent several *tumans*, led by the
redoubtable Chepe Noyan, who had the nomad's instinct for
memorizing the lay of land. When he passed through the Great
Wall on his way home Chepe Noyan had stored in his mind a
detailed picture of northern China. This was reported to Genghis
Khan as soon as the *tumans* reached home.

In the year 1210 the Golden Emperor who had honoured
Genghis Khan died. He was succeeded by his son, an incompetent
named Wai Wang. Genghis Khan decided that the moment had
come for his first great foreign adventure. So when the new

Emperor sent an envoy to the Mongols to collect tribute, Genghis Khan met him with open defiance.

"I had thought," he said, "that the Son of Heaven must be an extraordinary man. But an imbecile like Wai Wang is unworthy of a throne. Why should I humiliate myself before him? Our dominion is now so well ordered that we can visit Cathay. Is the dominion of the Emperor so well ordered that he can receive us? We will go with an army that is like a rushing ocean."

Genghis Khan had thrown down the gauntlet to the greatest civilization in Asia. It was winter time and snow covered the Gobi. Yet he sent out ambassadors and spies. With the princes of Liao in northern Cathay he made a pact—that they would strike from the north as he struck from the west. Spies who penetrated the Wall watched the defensive preparations of the Chinese. Other agents stirred up unrest among the border tribes.

As the spring melted the snow Genghis Khan advanced for the first time against a major military power. Much historical controversy has taken place over the actual strength of the Mongol Horde. On occasions it reached a strength of a quarter of a million, but during this first great invasion of China probably was much smaller.

The main body consisted of 100,000 battle-scarred warriors commanded by the Khan himself. He and his Imperial Guard were all mounted on black horses and clad in leather armour.

Galloping across the barren plateau in a vast cloud of dust the Golden Horde reached the Great Wall of China—that vast rampart hundreds of miles long—in so short a time that virtually no defence of the Wall was organized. After all, secret agents had been tampering with the border tribes for months past. The Mongols passed through without loss or delay. As soon as the Horde was through the Wall the Mongols spread out across the face of Shansi and the neighbouring provinces of western China. Each unit's commander knew what to do. They depended on no base for supplies. Their transport was an integral part of the forces and they lived on what they could find.

Chepe Noyan was in the van. Soon his scouts reported that the first main Chinese army was ahead. Actually the Chinese general had lost his way in the gorges of a range of hills. Before he could re-organize the Mongol Orkhon swung through hill passes, known to Chepe Noyan from his previous visit to Cathay, around the flank of the Chinese force until an attack could be launched upon its rear. The Chinese were annihilated. Those who surrendered were massacred. The few who escaped flew to the east; fear and panic spread as they passed.

Panic is infectious. As was so often to happen in the future, defensive armies became paralysed by the mere thought of the Mongols. A second army barring the Mongol advance wavered and fled without striking a blow. So Genghis Khan with his main forces reached the first of the defended cities.

Leaving *tumans* to screen the cities the Mongols pressed on towards the capital Yen-King. But the devastation and horror wrought by the Horde had aroused the Chinese people. New armies began to appear on all sides. When he reached the outer gardens of Yen-King itself, Genghis Khan was a great enough commander to know that the opposition was too formidable. Without a moment's hesitation he gave the order for withdrawal. He would live to fight again another day.

After a winter's rest, and recruitment, the re-grouped forces of the Khan again advanced beyond the Great Wall in the early spring. Once more they scored sensational victories. Again the Horde massacred hundreds of thousands of Chinese. This campaign brought Genghis Khan to realize that, while the Mongol cavalry could always out-manoeuvre and defeat the slow-moving Cathayan armies in the open, his forces were not yet equipped for or strong enough to capture strongly-fortified cities. After being himself wounded, Genghis Khan again withdrew to the Gobi.

During the third season of his campaigning against China he made only a few raids just to prevent the Chinese becoming complacent. A normal nomad chieftain would no doubt have left well alone and rested content with the vast booty he had captured. But Genghis Khan was not ordinary. He had seen the wealth, the luxury and the civilization of Cathay. He was obsessed by lust to conquer—and destroy.

In the spring of 1214 he again passed through the Wall. This time he had three vast armies each operating under independent command. While the flank armies moved out to right and left, Genghis Khan himself cut across northern China like a scythe.

In an incredibly short time the army of the centre under his command reached the Pacific coast near modern Tientsin. Spread out across a vast area of northern China the Mongols systematically settled down to besiege the strongest cities. Time after time they gathered thousands of peasants from the land, herded them like cattle and drove them ahead as a human shield to enable them to reach and breach walls and fortifications. Often the city dwellers were so petrified by terror of the Mongols that they opened their gates. Genghis Khan, in these early days, was still comparatively merciful. He spared those who surrendered their cities—but the people of the countryside were massacred and the houses and crops burned or trampled underfoot. Cattle were either killed or driven away.

It was total war—and war to the death—war such as was not to be seen again until the twentieth century. Certainly no such conflict had ever been envisaged by the highly-civilized but decadent Chinese. However, the armies of Cathay were not the only opposition the Mongols had to face. Soon famine and pestilence spread across the land. These took toll of Mongols and Chinese alike. The Mongol Horde became seriously weakened. Many men were sick and horses were feeble from lack of corn.

Genghis Khan was encamped aroung Yen-King, the capital, which already had held out for several weeks. Now it was clear that either the Mongols must take the town quickly or retreat once more. The officers of the Horde pleaded with the Khan to let them make an all-out attack. He refused. Instead he sent a strange message to the Son of Heaven in his marble palace.

"What do you think now of the war between us? All the provinces north of the Yellow River (most of northern China) are in my power. But I am going back to my homeland. Could you permit my officers to leave without sending gifts to appease them?"

It was an astounding message, yet Genghis Khan was being perfectly logical. He knew he could not take Yen-King. He needed the wherewithal to pay his officers; if the Golden Emperor sent gifts his prestige would diminish.

Some of the stouter spirits among the Mandarins around the Son of Heaven wanted to refuse the request, some even advocated a sortie against the Mongols in their weakened state. But the fear of the Horde which had gripped so many in China had affected the Emperor also. He submitted to the Khan's suggestion and sent gifts of five hundred beautiful slave girls, an equal number of youths, fine herds of stallions and vast quantities of gold and Chinese silk. He agreed to a truce and gave a princess of the Imperial House to Genghis Khan as a wife.

Then Genghis Khan marched back towards the Gobi. On the edge of the desert he halted; as was Mongol custom, all the captives were slaughtered. There was no place for slaves in the encampments of the Gobi.

Now came sensational news. Demoralization of the Chinese had gone further than Genghis Khan had realized. The Emperor himself, the Son of Heaven, had fled towards the south, despite the fact that his ministers had prophesied revolt and chaos if he did so.

Mongol spies were despatched back into China. Their reports showed that the Chinese ministers had been right; their dire predictions were coming true. Chaos in China was increasing.

In the light of that intelligence Genghis Khan despatched his most serviceable division south at speed towards the Yellow River to try to cut off the escape of the craven Son of Heaven. However, his lead was too great for even the swift Mongol horsemen to catch up. The Emperor escaped over the river into the dominions of his enemies—the Sungs. The Mongol division went on a private campaign of conquest and massacre in the course of which it was almost trapped. But it fought its way out and returned to the Khan.

The brilliant Subotai, greatest among the Orkhan generals, was sent into north China with freedom to act as he wanted. He achieved the conquest of Korea.

In the Gobi some of the Mongols were becoming restive at the absence of the Khan, so the trusty Chepe Noyan was sent to restore calm.

Genghis Khan now was short of troops for a campaign, but he shrewdly judged that there would be little resistance in the Chinese capital. He despatched the Orkhan Muthuli with only five thousand Mongols and an indiscriminate assortment of tribal mercenaries and Chinese deserters to attack the town. Yen-King could easily have been defended. But the Chinese were demoralized and disorganized. As soon as the Mongols appeared the troops inside the city mutinied.

Looting broke out. Eunuchs from the Imperial Palace were seen fleeing with precious gold and silver ornaments. A number of ladies left to their fate in the palace were ravished by the soldiery. Fire broke out. In despair the Chinese general took poison. In scenes of indescribable horror the capital city of Cathay fell to Muthuli's men, who, with unbridled licence, slew wherever they went.

Genghis Kha Khan was now fifty years of age and had conquered the greatest empire in Asia and probably in the world of that time—the domains of the Royal House of China. The conquest of the whole of China would yet take many years, and was not achieved in Genghis Khan's lifetime.

Several million Chinese had been massacred during the campaign of conquest—no one has ever been able to estimate the total. But China presented the same problem to Genghis Khan as it had presented to every other conqueror. There remained still more hundreds of millions of its people.

The Kha Khan realized that, contrary to his usual practice, he could never reduce the whole vast extent of northern China into depopulated grazing land. He, therefore, appointed Muthuli military governor with orders to prosecute the conquest of the southern empire of Sung. As a token that Muthuli was indeed viceroy the Khan bestowed on him an embroidered banner emblazoned with nine yak-tails.

Genghis Khan had no use for palaces or cities, so he retired to the Gobi that he loved. Yet it was to be in the capital of Cathay that his grandson, the great Kublai Khan, would receive a strange visitor from Western Europe called Marco Polo.

During his campaigns Genghis Khan had closely observed the Chinese administration. He had come to admire the Mandarins who had carried on the fight after their desertion by the Emperor. Some were men whose knowledge deeply impressed the illiterate Kha Khan. These he took back with him to his home at Karakorum. One was a tall, distinguished mandarin having a beard that reached to his waist and a deep sonorous voice. His name was Ye Liu Chutsai. He lived to be chief minister for

most of the remainder of Genghis Khan's life and during the
reign of his son.

Ye Lieu Chutsai was a man of great culture and wisdom.
Though he admired his master's undoubted military genius, he
strove constantly to combat the sadism and blood lust into
which the primitive instincts of the old conqueror had gradually
been transformed.

In his silk-lined pavilion at Karakorum Genghis Khan
admitted: "To crush my enemies, to see them fall at my feet, to
take their horses and goods and hear the lamentation of their
women . . . that is the greatest happiness of all."

During Genghis Khan's absence on campaign local rulers in
Tibet and Turkestan made incursions into the Gobi region and
caused some disorder in the Mongol homeland. When the Khan
started to redress this situation, operations took him ever farther
westward along the caravan routes of central Asia. Inevitably he
clashed with Muslim military might, then at the height of its
power. The great Muslim potentate of the time was Muhammed,
Shah of Karesim. His empire stretched from India to the Arabian
desert, from what is now Soviet Central Asia to the shores of
the Persian Gulf. At first Genghis Khan and the Shah were
cautious and carried on intermittent trading. The showdown
came when the Shah slew one of Genghis Khan's envoys. Of all
men the Mongol leader was the last to tolerate that. In the
spring of 1219, at the age of fifty-five, Genghis Khan left his
capital on a new journey of conquest.

The Mongol campaigns which followed were among the
greatest in the annals of military strategy. At their conclusion
Genghis Khan was master of an empire stretching across fifty
degree of latitude—an empire unequalled until that of Britain
seven hundred years later. He changed the course of human
history, spreading terror and destruction as far as Eastern Europe.
In the process he exterminated something approaching ten per
cent of the population of the world known at that time.

Wherever the Mongol Horde went its progress was marked by
piles of corpses and the blackened husks of ruined cities. The
Mongols carried out Genghis Khan's precept of "stone dead
hath no fellow" by atrocious treachery and cynical disregard
of promises.

The first great massacre was in the city of Bokhara, one of the most famous cities of Islam in Central Asia. It was defended by a wall that would have taken months to breach.

Genghis Khan expected a hard fight, but the Shah fled—quickly followed by the Turkish troops he had left to defend the city. The Mongols allowed the Turkish force to get out of the city, then trapped it against the banks of the River Syr and slaughtered every single man.

Abandoned by their defenders the elders and imams of the city decided to surrender Bokhara—*in return for a solemn promise that all citizens would be spared*. The gates were opened and the Mongols poured in. In their midst was the Kha Khan himself, a fantastic figure in a white felt hat with eagle feathers and red cloth streamers hanging down from the ears (they were designed to hold the headgear in the fury of Gobi desert blizzards). His long coat was of black sable with a girdle of gold plates. Uninhibited by any religious sentiment he drove his charger up the steps and into the interior of the principal mosque to the terror of the worshipping Muslims.

"Who is this man?" cried one terrified bystander.

"Hush," replied an elder, "he is the wrath of Allah which has descended upon us."

Genghis Khan actively encouraged such superstition. Like all the great captains of history he knew that one of the secrets of war is to paralyse the *mind* of his enemy.

"The sins of your emperor are many," he told the crowd in the mosque. "I am the wrath and flail of heaven come to destroy him. Give him neither protection nor aid."

Then the Mongols systematically plundered the city. When the last gold ornament had been recovered from the cellars and wells he ordered that all inhabitants, to whom safety had been promised, be driven out on to the plain around the city.

"It was a fearful day," said a Muslim chronicler who later reported the carnage. "One heard only the weeping of men, women and children who were to be separated for ever. The women were ravished by the barbarians under the eyes of those who had no resource but sorrow. Some of the men rather than witness the shame of their families rushed upon the Mongols and died fighting."

Massacre of the rest followed. The city was put to the fire and a vast pall of smoke arose from the funeral pyre which had been Bokhara.

That set the pattern for the campaigns which followed. Samarkand, Merv, Balkh, Tashkent, Nasipor were all captured, ruthlessly looted and their populations exterminated. At Herat more than a million and a half corpses marked the course of Genghis Khan's vengeance.

In one city some people saved themselves by lying down in the midst of knots of corpses. The Mongols heard of this. Genghis Khan thereafter ordered that the heads of all inhabitants of captured cities be cut off. From that day the progress of the Horde from Central Asia to Central Europe was marked by huge pyramids of bleaching skulls.

In the ruins of another city a few Persians survived. Spies warned Genghis Khan that there had been survivors. A regiment of cavalry was sent back. They hunted the survivors like animals through the ruins until none remained. In fact, the Mongol advance was like a giant hunt. Every possible device was used to root out and destroy each and every human being. In one city a mullah was forced at the point of the sword to ascend the minaret and to summon the faithful to prayer. As the survivors appeared from their hiding places they were butchered by the Mongols.

When the Golden Horde abandoned a city they trampled and burned anything that had been left standing. At Urgench, where they had suffered severely because of a long and stout defence, they took a particularly savage revenge. They built a dam to cause the river to overflow and submerge the ruins. For centuries thereafter the river's sudden change of course was a puzzle to some geographers.

While Genghis Khan subjugated Asia down to the Indus, Subotai with an army of twenty-thousand horsemen swept south-westward in pursuit of the Shah, who died a fugitive. The Mongol cavalry swept round the southern end of the Caspian, through the passes of the Caucasus into Europe and crossed what is today the Ukraine. On the Dnieper they annihilated the army of the Duke of Kiev before driving on towards that old Byzantine city itself which, because of its gilded domes, the Mongols christened the Court of the Golden Heads. Kiev was destroyed and its inhabitants massacred just as it was again in 1942 and 1943 by Hitler's invading army.

The carnage at Kiev has seldom been equalled in human history. Old people were tortured, women ravaged and children hunted like animals. Only utter desolation remained—a desolation made even more ghastly by the pestilence and famine which followed. The effluvia of decaying bodies was so great that even the Mongols avoided Kiev.

Just before that massacre on the Dnieper, Genghis Khan had ended his all-conquering campaign in Central Asia. The last stand of the Kharesim Empire was broken on the banks of the Indus. But the hot steamy climate of India was inimical to the warriors from the north and Genghis Khan withdrew round the Roof of the World back to his homeland.

As the Horde left the smoking ruins along India's north-western borders the Khan gave his customary order—kill the captives. Once again hundreds of thousands who had been captured and kept as slaves during the campaign were massacred. Only the women of the Muslim rulers were spared—to be taken to the Gobi.

Genghis Khan had, however, begun to ponder on the enormous carnage, for his chief adviser Ye Liu Chutsai had told him: "It is time to make an end of killing." Of Muslim savants, with whom the Khan frequently discussed the ethics of their faith, he asked whether they thought that the blood he had shed would be remembered against him by mankind. He had tried, he said, to understand both the wisdom of Cathay and of Islam, which he had studied from his captives.

"I have pondered the wisdom of the sages and I can see that I have slain without knowledge of what to do rightly." But his savage nature was not easily to be denied. He ended, contemptuously, "But what do I care for such men—or their views?"

The veteran conqueror was beginning to feel the effects of his various wounds. He seemed to understand that his time on earth was limited. To a great council on the banks of the Syr—at the point where two years earlier he had first invaded the Kharesim Empire—he summoned all the Mongol potentates.

From all the vast territories which the Mongols had overrun

the viceroys and the commanding generals hurried to meet
Genghis Khan. They came from the fringes of the Arctic Circle
and from the Caspian, from the shores of the Sea of Japan and
from the Caucasus. Two in particular filled the heart of the old
man with joy—Subotai, who had ridden at breakneck speed half
across the world from the borders of Poland, and his nine-year-
old grandson, Kublai, from the Gobi, who one day as Emperor
in Cathay, would extend the Mongol dominion to the Equator.

To the assembled council Genghis Khan gave instructions:
that the signs of revolt which were apparent in his empire should
be ruthlessly suppressed; that his enlightened legal code, the
Yassa, should be enforced and that his son should succeed him.

As soon as that great council of the Mongols ended, the old
Khan set out for the Gobi, where for nearly a year he rested with
his first wife Bourtai by his side. But he could not for long
remain inactive. News came that remnants of his former foes were
gathering along the borders of Tibet. In mid-winter Genghis Khan
set out to suppress the revolt. Marching through blizzards and
crossing the rivers of Central Asia on the ice, the Mongol Horde
pressed on to find formidable opposition barring its path. For a
time it seemed that disaster faced Genghis Khan. Yet once again
the supreme military genius of the Khan triumphed. His foes
were overcome; another half a million people died. By now his
name alone was enough. Thousands lay down before the Horde
and let themselves be massacred without putting up the slightest
opposition.

The revolt having been utterly crushed, Genghis Khan again
turned for home. But even yet he could not rest. One great
opponent remained—the ancient Empire of Sung in southern
Cathay, which had so far defied all the Mongol efforts to overthrow it.

Ye Liu Chutsai, by this time the Khan's most trusted adviser,
protested at the proposed annihilation of the great Sung
civilization.

"If these people be slain, how will they aid thee or make wealth
for thy sons?" he asked the Khan.

Genghis Khan was reminded of the Chinese sages he had
captured in his earlier campaigns in northern China; these men
too had become his ministers and his advisers. After careful

thought he unexpectedly told Ye Liu Chutsai, "Be thou then master of the subject peoples—serve thou my sons faithfully." But he would not forego the conquest of the Sung. He rode out again for China. Crossing into the northern dominions, which he had conquered years before, he forded the Yellow River in the winter of 1227 and headed south.

As he encountered the warmer climate of sub-tropical China he received news from the other end of the world—his first-born Juchi had died on the Volga steppes. He withdrew to his tent but said little. Relentlessly the Horde drove southwards, but now the Kha Khan had lost interest. Even news of victories on the borders of the Middle East failed to rouse him. He ordered messengers to be sent to his son Tuli, who was not far away. When Tuli arrived he found his father wrapped in sables and stretched out on a rug before a blazing fire. Genghis Khan was dying.

"It is clear to me," said the old Khan, "that I must leave everything and go hence from thee."

He had been sick for a long time. The effects of his old wounds were becoming more marked. As he saw the end approach he summoned all the generals of the Horde in Cathay to come to his side. To them he gave detailed instructions on how to complete the annihilation of the Sungs. Then he announced the succession to the Empire which he had created. Tuli, who was by his side, would take over all the lands of the east. Another son, Chatagai, would do the same in the west right up to Poland. Each would be responsible to his third, and favourite, son Ogotai, who would rule as the supreme Kha Khan in Karakorum.

After that Genghis Khan died uncomplainingly. He had parcelled out his possessions, the greatest empire and most formidable army known up to that time, just as if they had been the tents and herds of his ancestors.

The death of Genghis Khan paralysed the Mongol Horde. Without his hand to guide them the Orkhons abandoned the campaign against the Sungs—and turned for the Gobi. The Khan's body must be shown to the people and handed over to Bourtai for burial. His death spelt danger. To deny his enemies a pretext for rallying and to obviate general revolt among the subject peoples, the death of the Khan was kept secret. The troops escorting the bier cut down every single person they encountered until the funeral procession had reached the safety of the Gobi sands. The number of those who died along the funeral route has never been accurately calculated. But historians have estimated that in all China Genghis Khan exterminated eighteen million human beings.

No one knows where Genghis Khan was buried.

Under his son, Ogotai, the Mongol Empire continued to expand. In the east Mongol power was consolidated in northern China and Korea. Moreover the Mongol legions started to eat into the Sung Empire to the south. After suppressing trouble that flared up in what had been the Kharesim Empire, the Mongols swept on to conquer Armenia and Georgia. Everywhere they went they continued Genghis Khan's policy of mass extermination.

The Mongol speed and fighting power destroyed the Russian and Danubian peoples and in the battle of Liegnitz in 1241 delivered modern Silesia into their hands. Western Europe was saved only because Ogotai drank himself to death.

Under his successors there was a period of family squabbling, but eventually order was restored and the path of conquest resumed. The last of the Abassid Caliphs of Bagdad was tortured to death and nearly a million of his people were slain. What is now Iraq, and which since ancient times had been one of the granaries of the Middle East, was another region to be overrun and devastated.

In 1259 the advent of the so called Golden Age of the Mongols was marked by the accession of Genghis Khan's favourite grandson, Kublai, as head of the Eastern Empire. His capital was near modern Peking. He took no pleasure in bloodshed for its own sake, for he was a man of culture, educated by the Cathayan sages at his grandfather's court. He won large territories from the Sung Empire with comparatively little loss of life. Yet like his grandfather he was a great conqueror.

His armies drove southwards into what is modern Burma and Malaya; he sent fleets against both Japan and Java. But, like other great military powers, the Mongols had no flair for naval operations—both Japan and the East Indies remained unconquered.

Kublai Khan became a Buddhist; his bloodthirsty brother, Hulago, in Central Asia was converted to Islam. In the old age of Kublai Khan the Mongol Empire began to break up. The inadequacies of medieval transport and communications made it virtually impossible for one man to rule from the China Sea to Poland. By the fourteenth century Mongol unity had disappeared and the Empire was destroyed by the Asiatic conqueror, Tamerlane.

But the descendants of Genghis Khan had penetrated into modern India. Six hundred years after the birth of Genghis Khan his last imperial descendants—known as the Moghuls—fell to the British in the plains of Bengal. Thereafter, until about the beginning of the present century, the last scions of the Mongol imperial family lived quietly in Delhi, and drew a pension from the British-controlled Government of India.

Chapter 3

RICHARD III

OF the long catalogue of crimes which have blackened the name of Richard III of England probably the only one readily associated with him in the public mind today is the murder of the little princes in the Tower of London. Yet in the last hundred years a number of eminent historians, after the most diligent research which resulted in the examination of some previously unconsidered documents, have suggested that he was in fact innocent of responsibility for that shameful deed! However, even if his innocence of that crime were proved beyond all reasonable doubt—which it certainly has not been—the rest of Richard's dreadful record earns him a prominent place among the most loathsome characters in all history.

Considering how brief was his spell of power—he was a military commander before he was nineteen, usurped the throne when he was thirty-one, and was killed at the Battle of Bosworth two years later—Richard managed to pack more wickedness into that span than most degenerates do in a long lifetime. And such was the villainous reputation he left behind him that eventually he was suspected of being implicated in almost every major atrocity committed during his reign. Indeed his very birth, on 2 October, 1452, was commonly regarded as monstrous—he had been two years, men said, in his mother's womb and came into the world feet foremost, with his teeth fully formed and his hair down to his shoulders.

No fifteenth-century gambler would have taken even the wildest of odds on Richard's chance of ascending the throne of England. He was the eleventh in a family of twelve, his ten elders having been born within thirteen years. Five of these children died while Richard was a child and he himself was a slender and sickly boy; even in manhood his bodily strength was feeble, though it must be said that this did not prevent him from displaying great skill as a general and great courage in battle.

Richard was born in an England torn by the bloody Civil War between the Houses of York and Lancaster. Richard's father was Duke of York and the Lancastrian Henry VI was on the throne. There can be no doubt that the savage cruelties of that no-quarter struggle left a deep mark on the growing boy. His father lost his life at the Battle of Wakefield and his conquerors celebrated in ghoulish style by cutting off his head and giving it a mock Coronation with a crown of twisted paper. They even presented this grisly relic to Henry's queen, Margaret of Anjou.

When Richard's mother heard of this defeat she sent the boy off with one of his brothers to Utrecht for their safety while her second son, Edward, was hitting back at the Lancastrians. He soundly defeated them at Mortimer's Cross on the borders of Wales, was received with acclamation in London and declared King. Before a month was out Edward had inflicted another crushing defeat on the Lancastrians on the field of Towton in Yorkshire. Henry and Queen Margaret were compelled to seek refuge in Scotland. They there further infuriated the Yorkists by ceding Berwick-on-Tweed to the Scots.

Back from Utrecht came Richard to be made Duke of Gloucester and his elder brother to be made Duke of Clarence. The House of York now had a firm grip on the throne and the new king, Edward IV, heaped honours on his two brothers. For some time the three seemed to live in harmony until Edward made an unpopular marriage with Elizabeth Woodville. Clarence raised rebellion but Richard remained loyal, a decision which was to serve him well.

The rebels managed to force Edward off the throne and to restore Henry VI. Clarence's reward for his treachery was to be named by Parliament next in succession in the event of failure of male issue of King Henry. In the meantime Edward had taken refuge with his brother-in-law Charles, Duke of Burgundy, and with his help returned to the fray. At the Battle of Tewkesbury he gained a victory of far-reaching consequence.

When the shifty Clarence saw which way the wind was blowing, he quickly changed sides again and sought reconciliation with his brother. But Edward had now lost confidence in Clarence and preferred to lean on Richard, who had remained loyally by his side throughout these vicissitudes. Further, Richard's capacity for generalship had much to do with the triumphant come-back. After Tewkesbury he had given proof of his loyalty by butchering in cold blood the Prince of Wales, Henry's son. This lad was eighteen, just one year younger than Richard himself, and most historians agree that he was the victim of a deliberate act of murder committed when the battle was over and the Prince of Wales was in the power of the victors.

Richard no doubt considered that he was rendering his brother a service by lopping off a dangerous branch of the Lancastrian tree. At any rate this constituted his first crime. In the same month he followed it by another equally contemptible murder—the assassination of the boy's father, Henry VI, then a helpless prisoner in the Tower. The ex-king's body was taken to St. Paul's and put on public exhibition.

Now the direct line of the House of Lancaster was obliterated and Edward IV was never again troubled by rebellion from that source. The Yorkist king promptly compelled all the peers in Parliament to swear allegiance to his eldest son and to pledge that they would accept him as king on Edward's death. We shall see presently how Richard got round that obstacle to his progress towards the Crown.

Meanwhile Richard, the loyal Duke of Gloucester, was well rewarded by his grateful brother with large grants of lands and offices. To cap this shameful chapter, Richard took over in wedlock the betrothed of that Lancastrian Prince for whose death he was directly responsible—Anne, younger daughter of the Earl of Warwick (the Kingmaker).

This cynical piece of effrontery earned him the displeasure of his brother, the Duke of Clarence. Not, of course, on moral grounds but because Clarence had taken to wife Warwick's other daughter and had no mind to split the late Kingmaker's vast possessions with Richard. The mercenary quarrel which raged for years between them tore to shreds the thin veil of family loyalty and to settle it the brothers were allowed to succeed to equal shares of Warwick's property "as if their mother-in-law were already dead". Not only did their rapacious greed know no bounds of decency but it was actually indulged by Act of Parliament!

Soon after this settlement Richard withdrew to Yorkshire. His mother-in-law fled to him to escape from Clarence, a trust which Richard rewarded by keeping her a prisoner for life. This can hardly be regarded as a glorious chapter in England's chequered history.

Edward IV was anxious to smooth over the burning jealousy that divided his brothers, Clarence and Richard because he was preparing an invasion of France. To finance the expedition heavy taxes were voted by Parliament and an appeal was made to the wealthy classes to contribute, "out of their benevolence", to this great national enterprise. These contributions came to be known as "benevolences" and they formed an evil precedent for future ages.

In the event Edward crossed the Channel in 1475 at the head of the flower of England's nobility backed by a magnificent army —and not a blow was struck. The astute French king, Louis XI, bought the invaders off with a handsome bribe of seventy-five thousand crowns, a pension of fifty thousand crowns a year for Edward and lesser amounts for his chief advisers (the Lord Chancellor's "cut" was two thousand crowns a year). What price glory!

Despite this bloodless settlement, taxation became even heavier in England—a property tax of 10 per cent was imposed and King Edward got Parliament to pass an Act which allowed him to pay his debts by instalments spread over twenty years—a royal "never-never", in fact. Richard, who to his credit opposed the "phoney peace" with France, was exempted under the Act, but not so Clarence, whose ill-natured behaviour convinced the King that his brother was plotting to supplant him. Under Edward's own indictment Clarence was committed to the Tower.

Clarence was impeached for high treason and condemned to death. Edward postponed the execution for some time, apparently in the hope that someone would appeal to him for clemency. Brother Richard, however, was significantly silent and, as no one else would make intercession, Clarence was put to death—not by public execution but, to spare him that disgrace, he was drowned, so it is believed, in a butt of malmsey wine.

Shakespeare, as all the world knows, lays this crime, too, directly at Richard's door, making it appear that, although

Edward was more than willing to repeal the sentence of death, Richard, who had set the King and his brother at each other's throats, got the order carried out secretly. It is known, however, that Shakespeare took Sir Thomas More's *Life of Richard III* as his source for the tragedy, and More's work was in fact a copy of the chronicle by Bishop Morton, no lover of the House of York. All that can be said with certainty is that Richard did not lift a finger to save Clarence's life.

The death of Edward IV in 1483 left only two obstacles in Richard's path to the Throne—the little sons of the King. Edward had, in fact, set up a council for the management of the Prince of Wales's affairs until he should reach the age of fourteen. Edward had also decreed that after his death the care of his elder son's person and kingdom should be in Richard's hands. The Prince was thirteen when his father died and the Privy Council fixed Sunday, 4 May, for his Coronation.

The Queen and her friends, who did not trust Richard, tried to insist that the new King should have a strong force of followers to escort him to London, but this was vetoed by the Privy Council. In the end a compromise of two thousand horsemen was agreed. The Queen was a trifle too eager to cut off Richard from every position of influence with her son. The result of mutual suspicions was an undignified scramble to London by the two jealous factions, the Queen's and Richard's.

The two thousand horsemen now proved an encumbrance rather than a protection for the Queen's party and Richard, with his ally the Duke of Buckingham, managed to head them off near Northampton. They arrested most of the noblemen attending the young King and virtually kidnapped the boy. They declared that there was no plot intended against the person of the King, they had acted merely to smash a conspiracy against themselves. Both Richard and the Duke of Buckingham also let it be known that they would be in London for the Coronation and would there answer for their actions. This announcement seemed to allay all anxiety in the capital, but it did not fool the Queen, who at once went into sanctuary in Westminster.

The interruption of the King's journey to London made it impossible to hold the Coronation on 4 May as planned. In fact he entered the city on that day, was met by the Lord Mayor, sheriffs and aldermen and escorted by five hundred citizens to St. Paul's. There he took up residence and received the loyal vows of all Lords Spiritual and Temporal then in London. A Council was hastily convened and Richard was formally recognized as Protector of the King and his kingdom.

It was felt that the King should be removed to a more commodious residence and the Duke of Buckingham proposed the Tower. It should be said that the Tower had often been used as a royal residence and its grisly record as a state prison had not in the fifteenth century made its name so fearful and awe-inspiring as it did in later centuries. No one, therefore, felt apprehensive when the young King was lodged in the Tower. Nor did it seem at all sinister when Richard the Protector proposed that the young King's brother, the Duke of York, should be taken away from his mother, who was still in sanctuary in Westminster, and sent to the Tower to keep his brother company. Indeed Richard's proposal was carried unanimously by the Privy Council.

The Queen, realizing that her influence was gone, handed the boy over to the Lord Chancellor and Archbishop, who met Richard outside the door of the Star Chamber. The Protector greeted his nephew affectionately and went with him to the Tower. Neither that boy, the Duke of York, nor his brother, the King, ever set foot outside the Tower again.

Now England was under a reign of terror. The general tension was increased by the beheading of the powerful nobleman and ally of Richard, Lord Hastings, and it mounted higher with the second postponement of the Coronation. Worse still, on the Sunday fixed for the young Edward's crowning, a sensational sermon was preached by a brother of the Lord Mayor of London proclaiming Richard's right to the Crown.

Then, as if a major publicity campaign had been launched, doubts were cast on the validity of Edward IV's marriage. The suggestion was that Edward and his brother Clarence were bastards and therefore their issue should be cut off from the Succession. In short, to advance his own claim to the Throne, Richard did not hesitate to besmirch his mother's good name by means of an odious and obviously trumped-up allegation.

The last shot in the campaign was fired by the Duke of Buckingham, who went to London's Guildhall attended by other peers and knights and told the Lord Mayor and assembled citizens that the nobles and commons of the realm must make humble petition to the Protector to rule as King. Stressing the "inconvenience" of having a minor as sovereign, he urged the city of London to join the petition. This impassioned pleading met with no response. The people remained mute, the Duke of Buckingham was abashed and the Lord Mayor embarrassed. The situation was saved by some of Richard's and the Duke's servants at the back of the hall shouting "King Richard! King Richard!" and flinging their caps in the air.

This demonstration, about as convincing as a modern Communist state's "election" of a list of single party members, was hastily accepted as the voice of the people, and it served as an excuse to summon Parliament, which met on 25 June to approve Richard's title to the Crown.

It was evidently recognized that this was a makeshift proceeding because another Parliament was called to ratify the Act three months later. The technique of the Big Smear and the rigged meeting had paid off—Richard had usurped the Throne.

The formality of an official deputation from Parliament joined by the Lord Mayor, aldermen and chief citizens of London to present humble petition to the Protector was gone through, and Richard played his part in the farce by pretending to be quite unprepared. He made a great show of reluctance and eventually gave way graciously, saying that it was clear the whole realm was in agreement.

When he had got rid of his petitioners he wasted no time in arranging to assume royal dignity. The very next day he proceeded in high state to Westminster, entered the Great Hall and sat on the marble chair known as the "King's Bench"—from which, of course, the Court of Justice derives its name. He took the royal oath, called his judges, then declared to the people at large that he had that day begun to rule over them. But, just in case anything went wrong, the reluctant Richard had arranged for a considerable force of his followers (the numbers have been variously estimated at five thousand and twenty thousand men) to arrive in the capital from the north at that time. These convenient reinforcements were kept in London until Richard's Coronation was over, then they were sent home.

Such were the devious and shabby methods used by the so-called Protector to oust his sacred charge from his constitutional rights. Immediately the usurper made a great show of caring for justice and mercy. He proclaimed a general amnesty for all offences committed against himself. He took his seat in the Court of the King's Bench. And he set out to give the public a dazzling Coronation spectacle; the Duke of Norfolk was appointed to act as Lord High Steward for the occasion. There were pageants and processions of unparalleled magnificence and the Coronation itself surpassed in pomp all its predecessors.

Richard made sure that the religious rite of anointing invested his person with the sanctity he had lacked before. But despite all the dressing-up, the first revolt against his kingship broke out within three months of the crowning—and the standard of rebellion was raised by the very man who did so much to win him the throne, the Duke of Buckingham. His reason—that Richard had deceived him and won his support for his claim to the throne by faked testimony. It is just as likely that he had sampled quite enough of Richard's policy of intrigue, corruption and violence and that now he felt he must purge himself of evil by overthrowing this Satanic impostor. It has even been argued that Buckingham's insurrection was touched off by his discovery that Richard had been guilty of "a most abominable crime"—in short, the murder of the princes in the Tower.

After Richard's Coronation there was growing public anxiety about the royal prisoners and several movements were set afoot to bring about their liberation. Somehow, somewhere rumours started that both princes had been assassinated. These stories spread swiftly throughout the land. The reports were received everywhere with horror and amazement. Of all the appalling atrocities of the civil war from which England had just emerged, nothing so unnatural as this had come to light. Many found the tale impossible to credit, preferring to believe that the princes must have been sent abroad in secret to defeat intrigues by their friends.

Despite all this tremendous public interest, the precise details of their fate have never been satisfactorily established. That is why, many years later, it was possible for the impostor, Perkin Warbeck, to pass himself off as the younger of the princes—but even he, to lend credence to his imposture, expressly stated that his "elder brother" had been most foully murdered.

Here, at any rate, is a summary of Sir Thomas More's version of the mystery that has intrigued England for five centuries: Richard, about to set out on a tour of the midland and northern counties to consolidate the allegiance of the people, sent a confidential messenger named John Green to Sir Robert Brackenbury, Constable of the Tower, commanding him to put the two princes to death. Brackenbury was horrified and refused to obey the command. Green reported this to his master. "Whom shall a man trust?" asked Richard, and the name of James Tyrell was recommended to him.

The King is said then to have called Tyrell before him and given him a commission to execute his dreadful purpose. Tyrell went to London with a warrant for Brackenbury to deliver up the keys of the Tower to him for one night. Helped by his groom, John Dighton, and Miles Forest, one of the four jailers assigned to guard the princes, he suffocated the sleeping princes with pillows. Then the murderers buried the bodies at the foot of a staircase.

"But," writes More, "it was rumoured that the King disapproved of their burial in so vile a corner; whereupon they say that a priest of Sir Robert Brackenbury's took up the bodies again and secretly interred them in such place as, by the occasion of his death, could never come to light." James, his mission accomplished, reported back to Richard who, according to More, "as some say there made him a knight".

Ever since, historians have been busy picking holes in this account. Most critics single out Sir Robert Brackenbury as the weakest link. The Constable suffered in no way from refusing the King's order. Moreover he remained faithful to Richard and indeed fell in battle fighting for Richard's cause. It is on the face of it most unlikely that Richard would not have taken action against a man in possession of such a fearful secret or that Sir Robert could have held the slightest respect for such a King. Even Sir Thomas More, writing thirty years after the murders, admits that "the thing has so far come in question that some remained long in doubt whether they were in Richard's days destroyed or no".

Whatever the difficulties in the way of resolving the riddle, these facts weigh heavily against Richard: The princes were never heard of after his Coronation; their disappearance was most convenient for the man who had usurped their inheritance so shamelessly; his past record as a ruthless exterminator of any who stood in his path shows that even this execrable deed was well within his compass; he behaved throughout his reign as if he had nothing to fear from the princes; and the stories of their assassination which were rife during his reign were never contradicted by Richard himself.

During the reign of Charles II a most telling discovery was made. While alterations were being made to the staircase leading to the chapel in the White Tower, the skeletons of two boys, whose apparent ages agreed with those of the vanished princes, were found buried under a heap of stones. Antiquaries of the day were in no doubt and Charles had their remains fittingly interred in Henry VII's chapel at Westminster.

It might also be mentioned that, in Henry VII's reign, Tyrell and Dighton were examined about their parts in the crime and both made confessions. Actually few historians place much credence on these, believing that Henry wanted a plausible explanation to end public speculation over this *cause celèbre*. Tyrell was later executed for a totally different offence and Dighton was set free.

Richard had little difficulty in crushing Buckingham's rebellion and he had the Duke beheaded as soon as he was captured. Buckingham appealed for a final interview alone with his former ally but the King curtly refused the request. Perhaps that was as well for Richard as it seems the doomed man planned to plunge a knife into the King's heart. Among the rebel heads to roll was that of Richard's brother-in-law, Sir Thomas St. Leger. All appeals for his life were ignored by the implacable King. Richard indeed saw to it that the last vestiges of Buckingham's futile attempt to unseat him were snuffed out, but he remained aware of a much more dangerous contender for his crown in Buckingham's cousin, Henry Tudor, Earl of Richmond.

When Buckingham was planning his coup, he wrote to Henry, then a refugee in Brittany, telling him that his friends would rise against Richard simultaneously and asking Henry to strike on the coast at the same time. Henry did in fact set out with a small fleet and five thousand mercenaries but, fortunately for him, the ships were dispersed by a storm and the invasion came to nothing.

Richard was not lulled into a false sense of security by this failure; he ordered a constant watch on the coast-line. He knew that the Duke of Brittany was harbouring numbers of important refugees, quite apart from Henry Tudor, whom he had furnished with money and ships for his abortive invasion. After the attempt petered out he continued to give Henry asylum and encouraged him to hope for further aid. Henry found favour also with the new King of France, Charles VIII; so Richard had good reason to expect trouble from the Continent.

In a bid to forestall his rival's plans, which included marriage to Lady Elizabeth, sister of the princes slaughtered by Richard's orders, he even prepared to arrange to marry the girl himself even though his own Queen Anne was still alive. This meant, of course, that he was considering either divorcing or murdering his wife to make an incestuous match with his niece!

He was spared this awkward choice by the death of Queen Anne, a death which seemed to be from natural causes, although suggestions were not wanting that Richard had poisoned her. The rumours of the King's intention to marry his niece now grew stronger, but so great was the revulsion of feeling in the country that Richard was compelled publicly to repudiate any such desire. He made a lavish ceremony of this official denial, calling together the Lord Mayor and chief citizens of London at the great hall of the Knights of St. John and loudly proclaiming that he had never for a moment entertained the idea of marrying his niece. But he made sure that she was well out of Henry's reach by sending her off to a remote castle where she would be well guarded.

Meanwhile both sides made steady preparations for the coming clash. Richard fitted out a naval squadron to repel any invasion from the Continent. He had Henry and his followers proclaimed outlaws and attainted by Act of Parliament as "open murderers, adulterers, and extortioners". He alleged they had shamefully forsaken their own country, putting themselves first in subjection to the Duke of Brittany and afterwards to the King of France in their efforts to overturn the Government of England.

The proclamation went on to describe Henry as of "insatiable ambition and covetousness, pretending title to the crown of England though it was notorious that he had no manner of right to it, for he came of bastard blood, both on his father's side and on the mother's". The fifteenth century had nothing to learn on the use of the smear technique!

Undismayed, Henry pressed on with his plans to invade England and to overthrow the detestable Richard. His propaganda methods were simpler and more effective. He sent letters to all those whom he believed would support his claims in England, couched like this:

> "Right trusty, worshipful and honourable good friends, I greet you well. Being given to understand your good devoir and entreaty to advance me to the furtherance of my rightful claim, due and lineal inheritance of the crown, and for the just depriving of that homicide and unnatural tyrant which now unjustly bears dominion over you, I give you to understand that no Christian heart can be more full of joy and gladness than the heart of me, your poor exiled friend, who will, upon the instant of your sure advertising what power you will make ready and what captains and leaders you get to conduct, be prepared to pass over the sea with such force as my friends here are preparing for me."

On 1 August, 1485, he embarked at Harfleur with all his English followers and a body of French troops in support. He had a favourable wind and landed at Milford Haven on 7 August. Immediately he touched the soil of England, he knelt and kissed the ground, sang a psalm and ordered his followers to advance in the name of God and St. George. He made triumphant progress through Wales and received assurances of massive assistance from all quarters.

Richard's intelligence service seems to have been caught napping, for it was ten days after the landing that the news reached the King, then a few miles north of Nottingham on the edge of Sherwood Forest. At once he summoned his nobles and sent urgent messages to every county threatening death and confiscation to all who did not come at once to aid the King in the field. Despite desertions by many nobles on whom he thought he could rely, he mustered an imposing army and marched in magnificent array to Leicester, where he is supposed to have slept at the Blue Boar Inn, having taken with him his own bed-stead fitted with a false bottom in which the King had hidden about £300. (In those days a very large sum).

Richard marched out of Leicester on Sunday, 21 August, with great pomp, wearing his crown so that all might see he was a true King. He pitched camp about twelve miles west of Leicester near Market Bosworth. Henry's army, about half the strength of Richard's, was also heading for that village. The following morning both armies got ready to join battle. Richard had spent a restless night disturbed by nightmares. He missed breakfast and his chaplains were late for Mass. The day went badly for the King's men. At length Richard heard that his rival was near him, with only a slender guard. He at once spurred his horse forward and engaged Henry in combat. Reinforcements arrived at a critical moment for Henry and the King was urged to flee. "I will die King of England," he is reported to have said. "I will not budge a foot." He laid about him mightily until overwhelmed by weight of numbers and fell crying, "Treason!"

All manner of indignities were heaped on Richard's corpse. Covered in dirt and blood, stripped of every covering and with a halter round the neck, it was slung across a horse's back and carried into Leicester. The body was exhibited to the public for two days, that all men might see that the hated tyrant was dead. Then it was buried at Greyfriars in Leicester with the minimum of ceremony.

Like so many evil beings, Richard, who stopped at nothing to gain his ends, seemed to feel the need for religion—or perhaps to buy back the favour of God—once he had achieved his ambition. He founded two religious colleges and was the benefactor of many Yorkshire churches. Once King, he set out to study the welfare of his country, passed good laws and tried to clean up the corrupt practices of the day. He tried to win the good opinion of the new Pope, Innocent VIII, but that Pontiff received his overtures coldly and exhorted him not to permit in future "what had been done to the offence of God".

Outright hypocrite that he was, Richard no doubt believed that the moral code existed only for lesser men. Thus, he denounced the licentiousness of his enemies although he himself had at least two illegitimate children.

It is clear that he had a remarkable facility for reassuring those who had good reason to fear him and for deceiving those who should have known him through and through. Even his brother's widow, whose two sons were wrested from her protection only to meet early death at Richard's bidding, came to be reconciled to him and in the end even to befriend him. It was noticeable that the more deeply he had wronged a victim on his way to the Throne, the more generously did he seek to make recompense once he was King. Yet it has to be said that, although he was an abnormally evil character, ne was not mean or paltry. He had a taste for the magnificent and opulent in building—he put up a high stone tower at Westminster, built Penrith Castle in Cumberland and constructed important buildings in Nottingham, Warwick, York, and Middleham (now noted for its racing stables) which Richard regarded as his home town.

In dress he was luxurious and he loved to put on the large-scale royal pageant. He ordered his own wardrobe, down to the last minute detail, and himself commissioned merchants for plate and jewellery. So fastidious was he in these respects that one historian says he had the vanity of a coxcomb. We would probably prefer the word "dandy". He was also fascinated by all aspects of heraldry and granted a charter of incorporation to the heralds and officers of arms, giving them Cold Harbour Mansion in the City of London.

His many detractors are fond of describing him as misshapen, or even as a hunchback, but this seems to be wilful exaggeration. Many ancient portraits, which appear to agree with each other in likeness, exist of Richard III, and from them there would seem to be no marked deformity. He appears to have been below average height and to have had one shoulder lower than the other. The face in these portraits shows energy and decisiveness with a hint of malice and deceit emphasized by the long, thin visage and tight lips.

Hall, the English chronicler of that period, says of Richard's appearance that "a man would judge it to savour of malice, fraud and deceit. When he stood musing he would bite and chew busily his nether lip, as who said that his fierce nature in his cruel body always chafed, stirred and was ever unquiet".

How better to end the account of this disreputable chapter in

England's long history than in the words which Shakespeare
puts into Richard's mouth on the eve of the battle of Bosworth:

> *"I am a villain: yet I lie, I am not.*
> *Fool, of thyself speak well: fool, do not flatter.*
> *My conscience hath a thousand several tongues,*
> *And every tongue brings in a several tale,*
> *And every tale condemns me for a villain.*
> *Perjury, perjury, in the high'st degree;*
> *Murder, stern murder, in the dir'st degree;*
> *All several sins, all used in each degree,*
> *Throng to the bar, crying all: 'Guilty! Guilty!'*
> *I shall despair. There is no creature loves me;*
> *And, if I die, no soul will pity me:*
> *Nay, wherefore should they, since that I myself*
> *Find in myself no pity to myself?*
> *Methought the souls of all that I had murdered*
> *Came to my tent, and every one did threat*
> *Tomorrow's vengeance on the head of Richard."*

Chapter 4

CESARE BORGIA

THE age into which Cesare was born—the fifteenth century, or cinquecento, as the historians know it—bore much the same relationship to the previous epoch, the age of chivalry, as our twentieth century does to the nineteenth. It was an age of unbridled licence and immorality, given over to extravagant luxuries and to the cult and worship of external beauty, scorning the old-fashioned virtues and codes of truth and honour. It was a profligate age stained by barbarous cruelties, vile treacheries and dishonoured trusts. Yet the excesses of Cesare Borgia shocked and disgusted even that dissolute period.

It was an age in which erotic literature provided the favourite reading matter for both sexes (*The Decameron, The Facetiae of Poggia*) in which notorious harlots were invested with public acclamation such as is received by today's "sex kittens". When one widely-known Roman courtesan died aged twenty-six she was given a funeral worthy of a Pope and a tomb in the Chapel of Santa Gregoria.

The House of Borgia, from which Cesare sprang, has become a by-word in later history for every form of vice, and indeed the story of that family is studded throughout its long span with ghastly episodes. One writer concludes that "history has made use of the House of Borgia as a canvas upon which to depict the turpitudes of the fifteenth and sixteenth centuries". Yet this House, which traced its origins back to the eleventh century, gave the Church of Rome two Popes and at least one saint. Cesare was a son of the second of these Popes, Alexander VI, who has been described as "the worst Pontiff that ever filled St. Peter's Chair". This man—Roderigo de Lanzoly Borja—was ambitious, worldly, greedy for power, and a prey to all lusts of the flesh. His son, Cesare, developed all these characteristics to the full.

83

THE WORLD'S WICKEDEST MEN

Many contradictory stories surround the birth of Cesare in 1474 or 1476 (the precise date has never been settled) to Giovanna Catanei, an Italian lady who caught the wandering eye of Cardinal Roderigo. Their liaison lasted until 1486 and produced three sons—Cesare, Giovanni Borgia (later Duke of Gandia and murdered by Cesare), Giuffredo Borgia, and a daughter—the notorious Lucrezia Borgia.

Even in these profligate times a bastard was excluded by canon law from wearing the cardinal's hat, yet in time Cesare wore the purple and became a captain-general of Holy Church.

How was the difficulty of his birth overcome? All things could be arranged in those days if you—or your father—could exercise the right sort of influence. So, in 1480, when Cesare was at the most aged six, Pope Sixtus IV (whose own natural sons became his "nephews") granted Cesare dispensation in a Papal Bull from proving his legitimacy. It should be noted in passing that Cesare's father, as Cardinal Roderigo, performed the ceremony of crowning Pope Sixtus.

At the time of his father's elevation to the Throne of St. Peter, Cesare, now eighteen, was attending the University of Pisa. The new Pope did not embarrass himself by inviting his son to the ceremonies in Rome, although he quickly demonstrated that the two chief aims of his pontificate were to re-establish the power of the Church, then the most despised of Italy's temporal States, and to promote the fortune of his children. On the day of his coronation he bestowed on Cesare the Bishopric of Valencia, the revenues of which were worth sixteen thousand ducats a year. That gave the boy a good start in life, you might think.

A letter written by King Ferrante (The Old Wolf) of Naples to his Ambassador at the Court of Spain in 1493 contains the following passage:

"This Pope leads a life that is the abomination of all, without respect for the seat he occupies. He cares for nothing save to aggrandize his children, by fair means or foul and this is his sole desire . . . Rome is more full of soldiers than of priests, and when he goes abroad it is with troops of men-at-arms about him, with helmets on their heads and lances by their sides, all his thoughts being given to war and to our hurt."

Later in that same year of 1493 Pope Alexander created twelve new cardinals to strengthen the Sacred College—and his own hand. One of the twelve was his son, Cesare, now in his nineteenth year. Yet at no time had he taken Holy Orders. For the next three years his adoring father heaped honours and favours upon him.

At twenty-two he was tall, slim and graceful, acknowledged to be the most handsome man of his time. His face was long and pale with a lofty brow and aquiline nose: his auburn hair was worn long and his hazel eyes were large and darting. His health and vigour were remarkable, or he would never have survived his extravagant dissipation. His favourite outdoor sport was hunting the wild boar, which he pursued to the point of extreme fatigue.

In June, 1497, Cesare committed the first of the major crimes which have blackened the history of the Borgias—fratricide. He and his brother Giovanni, Duke of Gandia, were to represent the Pope at the coronation of a new king of Naples. On the eve of their departure their mother gave them a farewell supper. The carousing went on into the small hours. When the brothers left they were attended by only a few servants and a mysterious stranger in a mask.

Once they were in the heart of Rome Giovanni told Cesare that he was going off to amuse himself. He left with one servant, and the man in the mask. Later in the day, when he did not reappear the Pope was alarmed and sent out search parties. A boatman came forward and reported that about 5 a.m. he had seen a man mounted on a handsome white horse, with golden spurs at his heels, riding out of a narrow street to the river's edge. Slung behind him on the horse, so the boatman reported, was the body of a man supported by two men on foot who walked on either side of the rider. When they reached the water they slung the body as far into the river as they could throw. Their victim's cloak floated on the surface and the men threw stones at it until it sank.

The Pope at once ordered a search of the river and the Duke of Gandia's body was dredged up in a fisherman's net. He was fully dressed, with his gloves and his purse containing thirty ducats still at his belt, as was his dagger. The jewels he wore were intact, which made it clear that his murder was not the work of thieves. His hands were tied and there were a dozen wounds on his body. His throat had been cut.

The Pope, outraged and beside himself with grief, ordered the assassins to be traced at all costs. Two months of investigation proved fruitless. Then, dramatically, Alexander ordered that the hunt be called off. The commonly accepted reason for this decision is that the Pope had discovered the identity of the murderers—to his intense embarrassment. The eminent German historian, Gregorovius, states that, if Alexander had not positive knowledge, he had at least moral certainty that Cesare had brought about his brother's death.

Two motives are put forward for the crime. First, Cesare's envy of his brother, whom he wished to supplant as a prince; and second, even more shameful, Cesare's jealousy, springing from incestuous love for their sister Lucrezia, whose favours he is alleged to have disputed with Giovanni. Among the authorities holding this theory is the great Florentine statesman, Macchiavelli. Much is speculation but this is fact, that Cesare stepped into his brother's shoes as Captain-General of the Church.

The following year (1498) Cesare petitioned his brother cardinals to be allowed to put off his habit and ecclesiastical rank, to restore his hat and benefices to the Church, and that he be granted dispensation to return to the world and be free to contract marriage. The cardinals meekly left the decision to the Pope, and Cesare's father found no difficulty in granting all his son's requests. Father and son immediately manipulated the new situation to their mutual advantage—Cesare, the Cardinal of Valencia, which is in Spain, became the Duke of Valence, which is in France.

The price exacted by King Louis XII of France was the dissolution of his marriage by the Pope. This was granted after the formality of a Commission of Enquiry, but Alexander squeezed the last ounce of advantage by proposing the marriage of Cesare to Carlotta of Aragon, daughter of the King of Naples, who was being reared at the Court of France. This would have neatly tied together the Vatican, France and Naples to the danger of Spain. Once that complicated series of wangles, bargains and counterbargains had been agreed, it only remained to put on the Big Show to impress the rest of Europe. Louis XII sent a fleet of three ships and five galleys to conduct the new Duke to France; the Pope, not to be outdone, set up Cesare with a suite of a hundred attendants, including esquires, pages, lackeys and grooms, while twelve chariots and fifty mules were laden with his luggage. The horses of his followers were decked out with bridles and stirrups of solid silver and the richness of the gifts Cesare carried with him staggered even that age of ostentation. In passing it can be noted that Cesare even took with him a pox doctor.

The new Duke himself was a sight to see when he rode out with his princely retinue—he was mounted on a magnificent charger, caparisoned in red silk and gold brocade (the colours of France) and he wore a doublet of white damask laced with gold, with a mantle of black velvet swinging from his shoulders. His cape of sable was adorned with rubies "as large as beans". The Pope watched him go with an escort of four cardinals and sat weeping for joy at the splendour and magnificence of his beloved son.

The pomp of Cesare's arrival at the Court of Louis has also excited the imagination of the fifteenth-century chroniclers. They tell of his superb war-horse shod in solid gold, its head surmounted by a golden artichoke and its tail held in a net of gold studded with pearls. Some say the pack-mules were also shod in gold but most of the shoes were cast by the beasts on the way and left as largesse for bystanders lucky enough to find them.

Louis gave Cesare a cordial welcome, which is more than can be said about his intended bride, Carlotta, who obstinately refused to consider him even for a second. She is believed to have fallen for a young Breton gallant in the service of Queen Anne of Brittany. Baffled by this persistent brush-off, Cesare kept one ace up his capacious sleeve—the Papal dispensation for the annulment of Louis's marriage.

He was on the point of returning to his father still a bachelor —Carlotta remaining obdurate—when he decided to settle for one of two suitable ladies offered to him by Louis as the next best thing. He chose Charlotte, a sister to the King of Navarre. That turned out to be a costly deal for his father as Charlotte's papa insisted on 100,000 livres as a settlement on his daughter and a cardinal's hat for his son.

We are told that seventeen-year-old Charlotte was "the loveliest damsel of France" and that Cesare entered into the marriage very heartily not only for its expediency but for "the beauty of the lady, which was equalled by her virtues and the sweetness of her nature". They spent four months together, then Louis went to war with Milan. Cesare abandoned his bride in favour of the battlefield and never set eyes upon their child born in the following spring. He did not have to do any fighting in the war against Milan—the French avalanche met only token resistance —but he did cut a brilliant figure as he rode into the city by the side of the French king. From that time on he signs himself, "Cesare Borgia of France" and the golden lilies of that country join the red bull of the Borgias on his shield.

The Pope was not slow to cash in on this situation. Seeing his son with all the might of France behind him, he at once gave Cesare the task of bringing back into the Holy See the states of the Romagna, whose princes, outraged by Papal nepotism, had renounced the Pontifical authority, withheld payment of their tributes and, in some cases even had taken up arms against the Church. Pope Alexander could now see the way clear to regain these tributes and at the same time win the Romagna as dominions and dynasties for his children.

Cesare raised in Milan a loan of 45,000 ducats to finance his campaign and he received from Louis three hundred lances and four thousand foot soldiers. These were added to by Papal troops so that he found himself at the head of an army ten thousand strong, well-equipped and supported by artillery. It was the first army in which he had ever marched—and he was at the head of it. In all his twenty-four years of life he had never seen a pitched battle. Yet he overwhelmed two fortress towns— Imola and Forli. These were not in themselves major victories but at Forli he came up against one of the most remarkable women of her day, the redoubtable Countess Caterina Sforza-Riario. This lady had earlier made an ingenious attempt to poison the Pope, for she was determined to oppose the Borgia family by every means in her power, fair or foul. She sent two emissaries to Rome; one carried a hollow cane in which was rolled a secret letter for the attention of Alexander personally. The emissaries were arrested, the letter was found to be impregnated with a deadly poison—an attempt to out-Borgia the Borgias!

This comely termagant of a countess is worth a closer look. Disaster pursued her throughout her life, but she would not be subdued by it. Her husband was murdered, but she ruled Forli in his place and refused to pay annual tribute to the Holy See. Her father, too, was murdered in Milan Cathedral, her brother was poisoned by her ambitious uncle, Lodovico Sforza, in the Castle of Pavia. She had seen her husband butchered and flung naked from a window of the castle which she defended against Cesare and her second husband also was done to death before her eyes by a group of rebels. Instead of pining timidly away, she collected her men-at-arms and rode at their head into the quarter of Forli inhabited by the rebels. There she ordered the massacre of every man, woman and child and stayed to watch the last human being wiped out.

She stubbornly refused to surrender to Cesare even after the town which surrounded her fortress at Forli had capitulated to him. He tried to parley with her, even riding to the edge of the moat, but she promptly tried to capture him by a ruse which was near to being successful. He, therefore, put a price of 20,000 ducats on her capture if alive and 10,000 if dead. It took him a fortnight to reduce the fortress, only to find a smaller citadel within it. That, too, was contested almost to the last man. But eventually he was able to winkle her out of this last stronghold.

Cesare was most impressed by her valour—and her good appearance—treated her with the utmost courtesy and gave her a purse of 200 ducats for her immediate needs. When he left Forli this attractive Amazon rode by his side, dressed all in black and mounted on a white horse. It is said that he made a conquest of more than her territories. He took her to Rome in golden chains and she was given the lovely Belvedere as her "prison". After she had tried to escape she was more safely incarcerated in the Castle of Sant' Angelo. There she stayed for a year until she was freed through the intervention of the King of France. She was allowed to withdraw to Florence to rejoin her children. Then she abandoned her war-like attitudes and devoted herself to good works until she ended her turbulent life in 1509.

Although his successes against Imola and Forli were on only a small scale, Rome gave Cesare a conqueror's welcome on his return. The Pope laid on one of the most stupendous receptions since the early Roman triumphs. Two cardinals rode out of the city to meet Cesare and the entire Papal Court, together with prelates, ambassadors and officials of the city, waited at the gate. The guns of Sant' Angelo thundered in salute. In the Pope's audience-chamber Alexander embraced his son with tears of joy running down his cheeks. Cesare was forthwith made Vicar of Imola and Forli in a Bull of Investiture.

During the lull that followed there was committed in Rome a second crime which has been laid by many eminent historians at Cesare's door—the murder of Lucrezia Borgia's second husband, Alfonso of Aragon. He was a handsome lad of seventeen, one year younger than Lucrezia at the time of their marriage. It was commonly supposed to be a love match, and of it had been born a boy, Roderigo. On 15 July, 1500, Alfonso was set upon by several assailants on the steps of St. Peter's and seriously wounded in the head, right arm and knee. His attackers fled down the steps to where forty horsemen waited to escort them out of the city.

So desperate was Alfonso's condition that he was carried into the Vatican and laid in a chamber of the Borgia Tower where the Last Rites were administered to him. However, he lived until, thirty-three days after the attack, when just as he was thought to be out of danger, he died suddenly, to the great astonishment of Roman society.

"Not," writes Burchard, the Vatican diarist of the day, "from the wounds he had taken, but he was yesterday strangled in his bed at the nineteenth hour."

The Venetian Ambassador to the Holy See reported that, "it is not known who wounded the Duke of Biselli (Alfonso's title), but it is said that it was the same who killed and threw into the Tiber the Duke of Gandia".

The motive? Cesare himself is reported to have declared publicly that he had the duke killed in retaliation for an attempt on his own life. Again, though, there is the suspicion of jealousy, since Lucrezia was prostrate with grief at the news of her husband's death and clearly was devoted to him. She withdrew with her son, Roderigo, to her castle at Nepi where she mourned Alfonso.

It is perhaps significant that when Cesare resumed his campaign against the states of the Romagna in October, 1500, he made his army's first halt at his sister's castle. Once more he was at the head of ten thousand men. France supplied six hundred lances and six hundred Swiss mercenaries joined the force as well as thousands of soldiers of fortune from all parts of Italy. These men were attracted by the glamour of Cesare's name and by the hope of rich booty.

His second campaign in the Romagna opened against an even smaller show of resistance than did the first. Rimini and Pesaro fell without a blow. Just as it was left to a woman to resist him at Forli, so a boy of sixteen at Faenza was the first to provide opposition in this campaign. The boy was Astorre Manfredi and, unlike the people of Rimini and Pesaro, his subjects were ready to stand by their young lord whatever the sacrifices. Further, his grandfather, the ruler of Bologna, sent him a thousand men. This dogged resistance and the foul weather forced Cesare to strike camp and go into winter quarters.

The following April he renewed his assault on Faenza and, despite the most heroic resistance by the beleaguered and heavily outnumbered townspeople—even the women carried heavy stones to be hurled on the invaders—the garrison was battered to submission by a three-day bombardment by cannon.

Cesare met Astorre's peace envoys in a spirit of what appeared to be admiring generosity and agreed that the defeated townspeople should enjoy immunity for themselves and their possessions, a rare concession for a conqueror to make in those days. Cesare also guaranteed Astorre freedom to leave and take his moveable possessions. But this apparent generosity was soon exposed as a stratagem to win the goodwill of the inhabitants for, despite the victor's pledge of a safe conduct, Cesare hauled the gallant youth off to Rome where he was flung into prison. Months later Astorre's body was found in the Tiber with a stone round his neck. So much for the word of a Borgia.

When Cesare returned to Rome in September from his campaigning he learned that his sister Lucrezia had become betrothed to Alfonso d'Este and he joined in the festivities with a will. In fact, according to an anonymous letter, quoted in full by the Vatican diarist, Burchard, he outdid all the other revellers by throwing a supper party in the Vatican for fifty courtesans who indulged in an early form of strip-tease dancing with the servants "and others of higher rank".

Burchard reports that the Pope, Lucrezia and Cesare were present at these goings on and draws a word-picture of the nude women cavorting about on all fours fighting for chestnuts flung to them in a chamber of the Apostolic Palace by the Vicar of Christ—then seventy—and by his son and daughter. Much worse, it seems, was to follow; but perhaps it is enough to record that this was the most shameful orgy ever to desecrate that holy place.

With these, and other equally colourful stories, titillating the gossips of Rome, Cesare decided it was time to check the spread of the tales. He did this in characteristic fashion. He had one of the tale-bearers seized, the man's tongue cut out, his right hand chopped off, and the hand, with the tongue attached to the little finger, was hung from a window of the Church of the Holy Cross.

After the wedding Cesare stayed on at the Vatican until the summer, when he decided to enlarge his conquests in the Romagna and his own power and possessions. His ruthless treachery in the capture of Urbino will serve to show why his name was used as an example to later generations of all that is debased and detestable in human conduct. At that time the town was ruled by a much-loved prince, Guidobaldo da Montefeltre, a cultured and scholarly man, a great patron of the arts, happiest when he was browsing in the magnificent library of the Palace of Urbino.

To him Cesare sent a message that he was marching on the neighbouring State of Camerino, and giving assurance that he had no intention of invading Urbino, begged Guidobaldo to send some provisions and asked him for one thousand men to assist Cesare's enterprise. The latter concluded with protestations of brotherly love—a Judas kiss if ever there was one. This communication not only put Guidobaldo completely off guard but deprived him of a thousand troops. Cesare then sprang on Urbino with the speed of a tiger, attacking from south, east and north. Guidobaldo could do nothing but flee for his life, which he saved by disguising himself as a peasant and making his escape over the hills to Ravenna. Cesare then wrote to his father in Rome, telling him that Urbino was his and excusing the attack by complaining that "the treachery employed against me by Guidobaldo was so enormous that I could not suffer it".

It was unscrupulous behaviour of this sort that caused the great German historian, Gregorovius, to write of "the frightful deeds performed by Cesare on both sides of the Apennines. He assumes the semblance of an exterminating angel, and performs such hellish iniquities that we can only shudder at the contemplation of the evil of which human nature is capable".

Yet Cesare was able to add a refinement to the act of treachery which had lured Guidobaldo to his ruin. On New Year's Eve of the same year (1502) he had arranged a conference with half-a-dozen of his allied princes who had recently signed a treaty with him. Now all these noblemen had for a short time been in revolt against him and the treaty was designed to restore their former allegiance.

Having got them all collected together in the stronghold of Sinigaglia and separated from their bodyguards and their men-at-arms by a cunning ruse, Cesare had them arrested by his strong-arm squads, put on trial at once. In the morning they were executed by strangling. So charming and gracious was he as he lured them to their doom that their suspicions—if, indeed, they had any—were allayed. This stroke of two-faced villainy greatly impressed the Florentine statesman, Macchiavelli, who called it "the beautiful stratagem". Others have described it in less appreciative terms.

If one wonders how, knowing his reputation, so many distinguished people of his day fell for his blandishments only to see the iron hand swiftly shoot from the velvet glove, it must be remembered that behind Cesare was the immense prestige of the Holy Roman Church and it took some time to realize that the Pope and his son were capable of every kind of double-dealing and knavery to enrich themselves and extend their power and possessions.

Once stories of such treacheries began to spread others—more difficult to substantiate—were added to them for good measure, until the Borgias came to be regarded as inhuman monsters capable (and culpable) of every possible act of depravity. One ambassador reported back to his government from Rome in the spring of 1503 that it was the Pope's way to fatten his cardinals before disposing of them—meaning that he enriched them before poisoning them so that he could inherit their possessions.

Mock epitaphs began to be circulated and they spread throughout the country with a speed remarkable in those times of slow communication. One such epitaph was on the Cardinal of Modena, who had amassed enormous wealth in the most questionable manner, and who was one of the many to have been poisoned at the instigation of Alexander VI. The epitaph ended "Terra habuit corpus, Bos bona, Etyx animam"—"The Earth has his body, the Bull (meaning the Borgia) has his wealth, and Hell has his soul."

Of the many lurid stories involving Cesare and the ladies of the Romagna—some, no doubt, invented or embellished by his many noble enemies—one alleging the abduction of the young wife of a captain in the service of Venice is worth mentioning to illustrate Cesare's indifference to scandals of this sort. Stimulated by the indignation of the captain, the Venetian Senate took a hand in the affair and sent an envoy to Cesare to make strong representations for the release of the wife. The envoy assumed a lofty tone and suggested to Cesare that he had done a most unworthy thing and asked that the lady be returned forthwith to her husband. Instead of rebuking the envoy for his insolence, as might have been expected from Cesare's haughty reputation— he sent a mild reply back to Venice begging that the Republic should not believe this charge against him and assuring the envoy that he had not found the ladies of the Romagna so difficult that he should be driven to employ such rude and violent measures!

*   *   *

The Vatican diarist, Burchard, describing the sack of Capua by Cesare's army in July, 1501, remarks with horror on the wholesale violation of the women—"the worst of all war's excesses" —and adds that "the foot soldiers of the Duke of Valentinois (one of Cesare's many titles) acquitted themselves so well that thirty of the most beautiful women went captive to Rome".

A Florentine writer of that period raises the number of captive beauties to forty, reporting that "besides other wickednesses worthy of eternal infamy, many women who had taken refuge in a tower and thus escaped the first fury of the assault, were found by the Duke of Valentinois. . . . He desired to see them all and, after carefully examining them, he retained forty of the most beautiful".

If Cesare enjoyed a rapid rise to power and glory, his fall was even more rapid and, suitably enough, brought about by the most consummate treachery. On the eve of his departure to join the French Army then invading Naples he and his father, Alexander VI, went to sup at the villa of Cardinal Corneto outside Rome, which city was then in the grip of a fever epidemic. The following morning both were fever victims. Within a week the Pope was dead and Cesare was fighting for life.

Although father and son were devoted to each other throughout a lifetime of mutual aid, it is recorded by Burchard that the Pope never asked for his son during that last illness, nor is it anywhere noted that Cesare shed a tear or showed any emotion when the death of his father was reported to him.

Even if the news of Alexander's passing failed to move him it is perhaps as well that he was too ill to know of the scandalous scenes which marred the Pope's funeral. As the clergy were chanting the *Libera Me, Domine* in St. Peter's where the body lay in state on a catafalque, rioting broke out among the soldiers present. The clergy abandoned the catafalque and fled for shelter. The next day the Pope's remains were taken off by six bearers who put the body on show as an amusement for the Roman mobs. Even worse indignities were in store—the carpenters had made the coffin too narrow and too short so they removed the mitre for which there was no room and replaced it with a piece of old carpet. Then they had to force the corpse into the coffin by pounding and squeezing. A disgraceful and dishonourable proceeding even for the remains of the worst Pope in history.

By a strange twist of fate, his son's end was also marred by desecration, and he was to follow his father to the grave within five years. Alexander VI was succeeded in St. Peter's chair by a stop-gap Pope, Pius III, a feeble octogenarian whose reign lasted but twenty-six days. Then Cesare, the arch intriguer and double-crosser, made a major misjudgment. He supported the claims of an implacable enemy of the Borgias, Guiliano della Rovere, in return for his confirmation of Cesare as Captain-General of the Church and the preservation of his dominion in the Romagna. As a result of this support Guiliano became Pope Julius II— and within six weeks of the election Cesare's ruin was complete.

The crafty Julius first allayed Cesare's fears by assuring him of his friendship and support and, indeed, issued briefs to the Church States of the Romagna conquered by Cesare ordering obedience to him. Yet at the same time he notified Venice and Florence, the most powerful of the independent nation-states of Italy that his real aim was to preserve the Romagna, not for Cesare, but for the Church. This was his way of indicating to them that Cesare was out of favour. It is clear that his hidden motive was to strip Cesare forthwith of all power and posses-sions. Venice was not slow to take the hint. Her soldiers quickly captured Faenza and followed up by demanding the surrender of Forli and the other Romagna strongholds still occupied by Cesare's forces.

The Pope at this moment ordered Cesare back to Rome on the specious pretext that Venice was not taking action against the Church but only against Cesare and therefore Julius backed the demand that he surrender all the towns he still held so that there might be a speedy end to the war. Cesare petitioned the Pope to right his burning grievances. The Pope sympathized deeply, then had the Borgia's most famous captain brought to Rome under strong escort. Cesare at last realized that he had been betrayed, bowed to the inevitable and surrendered his Romagna fortresses to the Pope.

That was only the beginning of his misfortunes. Julius con-fiscated Cesare's property wherever possible to satisfy the claims of those who had suffered at the hands of the arrogant conqueror. Then Cesare had a respite—the Spaniards defeated the French in a struggle for the throne of Naples and, as a result, the Spanish cardinals, who were in Cesare's pocket, exerted a new and weighty influence with the Pope.

Cesare, who was now a virtual prisoner at the Vatican, was allowed a safe-conduct to Naples, where he joined up with the

Spanish camp. He was at once given command of an army intended by Spain as the spearhead of an invasion of Tuscany—
with the ultimate object, no doubt, of conquering Florence—
and it looked as though he were to have an opportunity to
re-establish himself and, incidentally, to be avenged on some of
his enemies.

The Pope, however, outsmarted him once again. Julius had
protested direct to Ferdinand and Isabella, the rulers of Spain,
that their support of Cesare would allow him to break his agreement on the Romagna with the Church. So Cesare was arrested,
with the Spanish captain, who had been ordered by his Sovereign
not to interfere, and his admiring friend, Gonzalo de Cordoba,
standing idly by. Thus, in August, 1504, Cesare found himself
on a ship bound for a Spanish dungeon, his hopes in ruins and his
meteoric career in Italy shattered.

He was to make one further sensational bid to recover his lost
glory. He effected a clever escape from his Spanish prison and
managed to reach the kingdom of Navarre where he put himself
under the protection of his brother-in-law, the king, whose
independence at that time was being threatened both by France
and Spain. Cesare put his sword at the service of his brother-
in-law who willingly accepted it. Leading the soldiers of Navarre
against a force of rebels stirring up trouble within the kingdom,
Cesare put them to flight but, outstripping his own men in
pursuit of the fugitives, he was surrounded and forced from his
horse. Still in his resplendent armour, he hacked at his foes in
hand-to-hand combat until a sword-thrust found a gap in his
armour.

He fell dying and was stripped of his armour by the rebels,
greedy for loot, and left, a naked, blood-stained corpse "of no
more account", writes one of his biographers, "than any dog that
died last Saturday".

He was found so by his tardy followers and his body was
carried back to his brother-in-law, who ordered a magnificent
funeral. Cesare Borgia was laid to rest before the High Altar
of Sainte Marie de Viane.

But his remains were not allowed to rest in peace. Two hundred
years later the Bishop of Calahorra, coming upon the slab which
marked Cesare's tomb was so offended by the inscription that he

ordered the remains to be removed from that holy place. The legend that outraged the good bishop ran thus:

"Here in a little earth lies one whom all did fear, one whose hands dispensed both peace and war.

"Oh you that go in search of things deserving praise, if you would praise the worthiest, then let your journey end here, nor trouble to go farther."

Chapter 5

TORQUEMADA

I T is difficult for the twentieth-century Christian, nurtured in democracy and taking freedom of speech, thought, and religious observance for granted, to understand the brutal intolerance and fiendish persecution which marked the spread of Christianity in the fourteenth and fifteenth centuries. Yet no one who studies the period can doubt the sincerity of the churchmen who, in the name of piety, doomed wretched heretics to the most appalling agonies or, indeed, doubt the purity of their motives. Their premise was that the Church of Rome was the true and only Church of Christ; they firmly believed that no salvation was possible for any human being who was not a member of it.

Ignorance of the true faith could not be accepted as an excuse for erring, so the Jew and the Moslem were as irrevocably damned as the savage who had never even heard of Christ. These self-appointed judges of conscience held that the business of the Church was the salvation of souls—for them there was no sin so execrable as heresy. Indeed, heresy was worse than sin—these dignitaries could find it in their hearts to forgive murder, rape, incest—but heresy was a denial of the Church itself.

The tribunal of the Inquisition, the most terrible court in all recorded history, was set up in Castile in the reign of the Catholic sovereigns, Ferdinand and Isabella. For seven hundred years Spain had been under the heel and occupation of the Saracens. Slowly and grimly the forces of Christianity, emerging from their mountain fortresses in the north of the peninsula, had driven the hated Moors south of the River Tagus. But Spain remained a wild and lawless country until the marriage in 1474 of Ferdinand, ruler of Aragon, and Isabella, of Castile, united the divided kingdom. Under their reign the distracted land developed a police system for repression of brigands, a court which curtailed the depredations of the nobles, and a government instilling respect for law and generally quelling all the major elements of unrest. Public credit was restored and the flagrant abuses of the clergy held in check.

Isabella herself would have earned the reputation of one of civilization's greatest queens—had she not been responsible for setting up the Inquisition. But the glories of her reign pale into insignificance compared with this atrocity.

Her decision to establish the court in her realm, Castile, was not lightly reached. Isabella had resisted strong pressure from powerful sources. The man who changed her mind was a compelling advocate in the white habit and black cloak of the Dominican Brotherhood, a tall, gaunt and stooping figure of mild eye and benign countenance—Frey Tomas de Torquemada, Prior of the Dominican Convent of Holy Cross of Segovia. His influence with the Queen was already considerable.

*　　*　　*

Just when the Jews first appeared in Spain is impossible to state with accuracy, but it is known that St. James the Apostle arrived in Iberia, as it was then known, in A.D. 37 to preach the new gospel, so Spain was the first land after Judaea to receive "the Holy law of grace". By the end of the thirteenth century, according to a reasoned estimate by Amador de los Rios, author of the monumental *History of the Jews in Spain*, there were nearly a million Jews in Castile alone. They suffered sporadic persecutions but in the main enjoyed considerable religious liberty until the middle of the thirteenth century. By then many of them had become wealthy and arrogant, flaunting, in too many cases, ostentatious luxury in the faces of the less affluent Christians.

In the thirteenth and fourteenth centuries the persecutions of the Jews set a pattern which was to become all too familiar down the ages—pogroms, confiscations of property, ghettos (then called Juderias or Jewries). By 1412 the Jews had lost all their hard-won privileges—no Jew could be a judge, even in a Hebrew court, or practise medicine, surgery, or chemistry (the professions in which they excelled) and all commerce with Christians was denied to them.

It was, of course, open to them to renounce their faith and receive baptism into Christianity. So severe was the slaughter and the oppression at that period that many chose this way out. These converts were called "New Christians" by the Spaniards and *marranos* ("accursed ones")—by those of their own race. The *marranos* regained all their privileges and found themselves on terms of absolute equality with the Old Christians (pure-blooded Castilians). All the professions were open to them.

It must be made clear that the object of the Inquisition was not the persecution of the Jews. Its concern was with the apostasy of those who, although of the Jewish race, had become Christians by conversion. Any secret return by these New Christians to the religion of their fathers brought them within the jurisdiction of the Inquisition.

Torquemada—the name was not a grim-sounding invention but belonged to an illustrious family of the north—was born in 1420 at Valladolid and, after a distinguished career as a scholar, was elected Prior of the Santa Cruz Convent. So austere was he that he never ate meat or used linen either on his bed or on his person. He observed his Order's rule of poverty so rigorously that his sister had to live as a nun because he could not make proper endowment for her.

Torquemada's influence over Queen Isabella dates from her early years when he was her confessor. He is said to have extracted a promise from her at that time to hunt down all heretics when she became queen.

A Papal Bull of 7 November, 1478, granted Ferdinand and Isabella the power to set up the tribunal of the Inquisition (the Holy Office was the euphemism used) in Castile, to permit the extirpation of heresy "by the way of fire". The tribunal was to consist of three bishops or archbishops "or other God-fearing and upright priests over forty years of age who must be masters or bachelors of divinity and doctors or licentiates of canon law, to make inquisition throughout the kingdom against heretics, apostates and their abettors". Despite the Papal Bull two years elapsed before the sovereigns took action. Then the excuse was a pamphlet published by a New Christian criticizing Ferdinand and Isabella for permitting a fresh outburst of anti-Jewish activity in Spain. The sovereigns delegated their power to appoint inquisitors to the Cardinal of Spain—and so to Torquemada.

*   *   *

Seville was the city chosen for the Inquisition's first ministrations. The gloom of the occasion came as a shock to the gay people of Seville when into their midst marched a funereal procession headed by two white-robed, black-hooded Inquisitors, followed by a Dominican carrying a white cross and behind him a solemn line of barefoot friars. This was the signal for the flight of thousands of New Christians who decided not to risk being hauled before that court. The tribunal chose to assume that this flight was evidence of guilt and demanded of all feudal lords that any such refugees in their territories should at once be returned to Seville for trial. The penalty for ignoring this command was excommunication.

Now many of the most prominent and successful citizens of Seville were New Christians. This savage edict so alarmed them that a group met together and agreed to defend their positions against the Inquisition by force of arms if necessary. The conspiracy was, however, betrayed to the tribunal by the ringleader's lovely daughter. Her motives for this shameful act have not come down through history The immediate result was the arrest of all involved in this mutual-aid pact. They were lodged in prison and brought to trial before the Court of the Holy Office. They were charged with heresy and apostasy.

The three leaders were found guilty as charged and handed over to the secular arm for punishment. They were condemned to be the chief actors in the first *auto da fe* ever held in Seville. The wretched victims were led out barefoot, each wearing a yellow sack of penitence and holding a candle. Surrounded by soldiers they were paraded through the streets of the city in which they had all held distinguished positions. A black-robed Dominican headed the procession holding aloft the green cross of the Inquisition wrapped around in crepe. The procession wended its way to the Cathedral where the doomed men were taken to hear Mass and a sermon. Thence they were led to meadows outside the city where they were tied to stakes and burned to death.

These were only the first of a flood of sufferers, for within a few weeks so many arrests had been made that accommodation for prisoners was strained to the utmost. Then an "Edict of Grace" was promulgated which urged all those guilty of apostasy to come forward, confess and be reconciled to the Church. The effect was staggering—at least twenty thousand converts rushed to avail themselves of the apparent amnesty. But what a diabolical trap they rushed into!

The inquisitors announced a secret condition of the amnesty —that the confessions must be sincere and, as proof of sincerity, the penitents must reveal the names of all heretics known to them. Seldom has such a devilish plot been devised in the name of God. Most of these wretched creatures bought their amnesty at the price of betrayal and the cynical Churchmen hailed their reconciliation as "a glorious thing".

There is little doubt that the malevolent genius behind this shameful double-cross was Brother Torquemada. To him, too, must go the credit for an equally wicked injunction laid on these hapless New Christians shortly after the amnesty. He laid down a black catechism of thirty-seven Articles by which heresy might be recognized and these were so comprehensive that not a single convert in Seville was secure.

Article Four, for example, laid down that, if a man put on a clean shirt on a Saturday and his wife used clean covers on the table on that day, it would be regarded as proof that they were observing the Sabbath in honour of the law of Moses—and so were guilty of heresy. Many of the Articles descended to a level of absurdity but probably the most monstrous was No. 27 which stated that any who held a farewell supper before setting out on a long journey should be deemed to be in heresy—surely that custom has been common among men of all religions and of all times.

Such ordinances made spying a fine art in Seville. One friar formed the habit of spending his Saturday mornings in winter on a convent roof noting the houses of New Christians from which came no chimney-smoke, then having their tenants arrested on suspicion that they would not desecrate their Sabbath by lighting fires!

Burnings of heretics became so frequent that three hundred were consumed by the flames during the first ten months of the

Inquisition in Seville! The court sat in judgment even on some who were already dead, ordered their bones to be dug up and destroyed by fire.

Indeed, so many were the victims of the insatiable Inquisition, that the Governor of Seville had constructed a permanent platform of stone which became known as the Quemadero, or Place of Burning. At each of the four corners of this platform stood a colossal plaster statue of a Prophet which was not merely for ornament; each was hollow so that a doomed heretic might fit inside and there suffer a slow death.

So fanatically ruthless were the inquisitors that the Pope was compelled to intervene. He sent a powerful protest to Ferdinand and Isabella, withdrawing their privilege to appoint inquisitors. The sovereigns found the Papal protest unanswerable; they accepted his rebuke and the loss of their prerogative without demur, but instituted negotiations with the Pope which culminated in the tribunal being given a settled form and Frey Tomas de Torquemada being chosen to head it. First he was appointed Grand Inquisitor for Castile; later his jurisdiction was extended until he found himself at the head of the Holy Office for all Spain, invested with the fullest powers. He could elect or depose subordinate inquisitors at will. As a result the entire character of the Inquisition was transformed.

Torquemada set about reconstituting his Holy Office. He appointed legal experts as assessors, established four permanent tribunals under revised terms of reference—in Seville, Cordova, Jaen, and Toledo—and he set up a chain of roving inquisitors whose duty it was to go where he directed and organize temporary courts. He himself remained at the Court of Ferdinand and Isabella. Now that the Inquisition had become Big Business— all property and wealth confiscated from condemned heretics went to the sovereigns and not to the Church—he had to be in constant touch with the rulers in whose name he acted.

Soon a fifth royal council was added to the four which conducted the affairs of the kingdom and its function was specifically to handle all inquisitorial matters. This was the Supreme Council of the Inquisition established in 1484 (generally known as the "Suprema") and Torquemada was made its president, which enormously increased his power and influence.

This malevolent genius now turned his hand to drawing up a code of jurisprudence for the Holy Office—and this eventually gave the Inquisition an established form which continued with hardly any amendment for three centuries after Torquemada's death. A study of the text of his original Articles reveals the extraordinary spirit that that inspired and governed this terrible instrument of terror, extraordinary in that the wielders of this awesome power are seen to carry out utterly inhuman cruelties out of love for the human species, indeed to save the race from eternal damnation, extraordinary in that they could sincerely believe that the agonizing sufferings they inflicted were acts of mercy and of charity. No more convincing evidence could be provided that there is nothing known to man so devilish as religious fanaticism, for it holds the critical faculties in suspense, destroys all sense of proportion and horribly distorts the intelligence.

If this can be doubted perhaps a description of the tortures employed by these holy men to extract a confession will illustrate the statement. Before the wretched prisoner was "put to the question", as the torture was euphemistically called—these churchmen had a reverence for words, if for nothing less—he was subjected to four stages of mental terror. First came the threat of torture, then he was led to the torture-chamber, shown the implements, the functions of which were carefully explained. After that he was stripped naked and preparations were made for his ordeal; these culminated in the prisoner being laid out on an engine of torture and bound hand and foot. Frequent pauses were made to give him a chance to confess. If the mental terror failed, actual physical pressure was applied.

The available tortures took many forms and the inquisitor was allowed to choose the one most suitable and effective to the case. One scholar of those times listed fourteen varieties, to which must be added many subtle examples of brain-washing and other spiritual torments. Three tortures were commonly employed— the rack, the hoist and the water torture. Ordeal by fire was but rarely employed, when it was used the usual method was to toast the feet of the victim after smearing them with fat. There is one particularly revolting case in 1636 in which ten Jews convicted of having defiled a crucifix were forced to stand with one hand nailed to an arm of a St. Andrew's Cross while sentence of death was read to them.

The hoist was the simplest engine of torture, consisting of a rope running through a pulley attached to the ceiling of the chamber: the prisoner's wrists were pinioned behind him and one end of the rope tied to them. His torturers then slowly pulled on the other end, gradually raising the victim's arms behind him as far as they would go backwards and upwards until he was raised first on tip-toe, then clear of the ground so that his arms took the full weight of his body. At this point he was asked again to confess his heresy. If he refused he was hoisted towards the ceiling, then dropped a few feet until stopped by a jolt that all but jerked his arms from their sockets. Again the question was put to him and, if he remained obdurate, he was given a further drop and so on until he had confessed or was back on the ground. If he stuck that out then weights were attached to his feet, increasing the severity of the torture, until, with shoulders now dislocated, the wretched victim had reached the limit of endurance. There are cases on record in which the victims were left hanging for three hours.

During the torture sessions the inquisitors were always present (by order of Torquemada) with a notary whose job was to make a full record of the proceedings, down to the weights attached, the number of hoists inflicted, the questions asked and the answers given.

The water-torture was more complicated and far more cruel—perhaps for that reason more favoured by the Holy Office. It is worth recording in some detail to show the lengths to which these pious fanatics would go to bring a heretic to repentance.

The prisoner was fixed on a short ladder-shaped engine slanted so that his head was below the level of his feet. His head was held rigid so tightly that the whipcord bit into the flesh. In addition garrotes—lengths of cord tied firmly around a limb with a stick between cord and flesh to form a tourniquet—were attached to thighs, legs and arms. The mouth was now distended and held by an iron prong, the nostrils were plugged and a linen strip placed across the jaws. This would be carried deep into the throat by the weight of the water the torturers poured into the gaping mouth. As the water filtered through the linen the prisoner suffered all the torment of suffocation—he fought desperately to swallow and usually managed to get enough down to keep him conscious. If even then he proved stubborn, the torturers would give a twist or turn of the tourniquet.

The inquisitors must be congratulated on their attention to detail—they made sure that no prisoner was given food for eight hours before the water torture was applied. The notary was particularly instructed to record the number of jars of water needed in each case. Beside this ordeal the rack was almost a kindness.

So much for the sufferings of the flesh.

Infamous, too, was the vindictiveness of the Inquisition in visiting their punishment on the second and the third generation. Consider Torquemada's Article 20 which said:

"If any writings or trials should bring to light the heresy of a person deceased, let proceedings be taken against him—even though forty years shall have elapsed since the offence—let the fiscal accuse him before the tribunal, and if he be found guilty the body must be exhumed. His children or heirs may appear to defend him; but, should they fail to appear or, appearing, fail to establish his innocence, sentence shall be passed upon him *and his property confiscated.*"

The only possible motive for this decree is greed.

There was worse to follow, because men were actually expected to come forward voluntarily and accuse their dead fathers or grandfathers of heretical practices—and disinherit themselves as a result!

Article 9 laid down "lighter penances" for the children (under the age of twenty) of heretics, but of course they could not inherit any of their parents' property—that had already been grabbed by the State—and they were forbidden to hold any office under the Crown. Surely there could be no more wilful flouting of Christ's Commandments than this visiting the so-called sins of the fathers upon the sons unto the third generation!

Another disgusting feature of this medieval brain-washing was the directive issued to the inquisitors for leading an obstinate prisoner into contradictions of evidence which would convict him. Any cunning trick, it seems, was permitted just so long as the letter (but by no means the spirit) of the law was observed. And the slimiest dodge of all was for the inquisitor to promise the prisoner a pardon if he would but confess his heresy.

If the suspect fell for that one, and confessed, then sought the promised pardon, he found himself a dupe of words. He was told that by pardon (*gratia* in Latin, *gracia* in Spanish) was meant remission of part (and usually an insignificant part) of the penalty, or even that all the inquisitor had in mind was the "gracia" or grace of divine favour into which his soul would enter.

Learned theologians filled reams of paper devising specious arguments to justify that monstrous double-cross of a helpless victim. In fact throughout the course of the Inquisition the most sickening hypocrisies were practised to justify the procedures. Here is an example of such scholarly argument:

Question: If the inquisitor enters into a promise, is he not obliged to keep it?

Answer: Such a fraud is for the public good. Anyway, if it is legal to extract truth by torture, it is surely much better to achieve it by *verbis fictis*—dissimulation. However little may be the remission granted, it will always be sufficient to fulfil his promise.

Was no mercy shown to the miserable sinners sentenced to die at the stake? Oh yes. Every condemned man was accompanied on his last journey by two friars who never ceased to exhort him to repent and make confession. If he yielded to their entreaties, he gained the charity of being strangled at the stake before the faggots were lit. But his body was burned after his death.

However self-satisfied were these arrogant bigots who ordained such horrors, the Castilians themselves showed great distrust of this death-dealing instrument in their midst. In part this distrust was due to the secrecy with which its deeds were surrounded. Its trials were not conducted in open court; the examination of witnesses took place in *camera* and behind the veil of anonymity. When a man was arrested he vanished from society until he emerged to play the role of villain in an *auto da fe*. Because of this secrecy the Inquisition wielded a power far greater than that of any civil court. Torquemada's might was in fact more far-reaching than that of his sovereigns, as he held his office directly from the Pope and the Throne could not interfere with him in matters of Faith.

Although Castile felt the first full fury of the activities of the Holy Office, it was in Aragon that the spark of rebellion flared against it. The influential New Christians there, many of whom held high positions at Ferdinand's court, were outraged when the dreaded *auto da fe* was held in their province and decided to meet terror with counter-terror.

Their programme was to massacre the inquisitors. Six assassins were chosen and after several false starts, they murdered one of the inquisitors in church at midnight. But the plot boomeranged —the bloody deed incensed the Old Christians; the mob demanded that the culprits be found and put to the fire.

Far from being intimidated, Torquemada was on his mettle. He arrested scores of suspects and from one extracted a confession and the names of his fellow-plotters on the promise of "grace". When this man claimed the pardon he was piously told that he should receive the grace of not having his hands hacked off, as must the other culprits, before being hanged, drawn and quartered.

One lucky plotter managed to commit suicide in his cell by eating a glass lamp.

Such was the vengeance of the holy Torquemada. For good measure he had fourteen *autos da fe* held in that town in a year, making a tremendous show of ceremonial so that no one would be in ignorance that condign justice was being done there.

Protests against the merciless "justice" of Torquemada were mounting throughout Spain and, on the death of Pope Sixtus IV, a strong bid was made by distinguished Spaniards to have the over-zealous Prior deposed from his office as Grand Inquisitor on the ground that, as he had been appointed by Sixtus, his office ceased on the death of that Pope. Vain hope! The succeeding Pope, Innocent VIII, not only confirmed the appointment, but considerably increased Torquemada's powers and the scope of his jurisdiction. Indeed by a Bull of 3 April, 1487, Innocent commanded all the Catholic princes of Europe to arrest any fugitives wanted by Torquemada and return them to the Inquisition on pain of excommunication. This indicates the far-reaching vengeance of that pitiless man who would not be satisfied until he had hounded the Jews out of any refuge they might have found and bound them to the stake.

Although great wealth was accruing to Torquemada from his share of the confiscations made under the Inquisition, there is positively no evidence that he put any of this to worldly use. He disdained all dignities, refusing the Archbishopric of Seville when that office fell vacant. The only pomp he permitted was said to have been forced on him for his own safety—when he fared abroad he was attended by an escort of fifty mounted staff and two hundred men on foot. He spent his riches on glorifying the religion he served with such fanatical zeal—he had rebuilt the Dominican Convent of Segovia and he endowed the chief church of his native town of Torquemada. He also financed the building of a magnificent church and monastery at Avila. This became his chief residence. His frenzied hatred of the Jews is illustrated by the condition he laid down (with the permission of Pope Alexander VI) that no descendant of Jew or Moor should ever be admitted. However he made ample provision within its walls for the tribunal of the Inquisition and for incarceration of prisoners.

If his personal habits were simple and modest, his public arrogance knew no bounds—he did not hesitate to dictate to his sovereigns in matters of faith and behaved threateningly towards them if they were slow to act at his behest. Anyone below kingly rank found himself in deadly danger if he dared to come into conflict with the Grand Inquisitor.

His greatest triumph was to come after Ferdinand and Isabella, helped by Jewish finance, conquered Granada, the last stronghold of Islam in Spain, on 2 January, 1492, and so ended the Moslem domination of their country, which had lasted nearly eight centuries. Torquemada, the indefatigable, was at their ears insistently whispering that this victory of the Cross would never be complete so long as the Jews remained in the land to pervert the Christians. He brought every weapon to bear, including fantastic atrocity stories and forged letters, to convince his sovereigns that they must banish all Jews who could not be converted to the Holy Roman Catholic Apostolic Faith.

The Jewish leaders, aware of their danger, sent eloquent advocates to the royal court, reminding the sovereigns of their past services to the crown and promising even greater services for the future. And, probably the most persuasive argument of all, they promised to subscribe 30,000 ducats towards the expenses of the war against the Moslems.

It seemed as though the Jews—and the gold—would win until Torquemada himself confronted the sovereigns. In his hands he brandished a crucifix. "Judas," he declaimed to the startled pair, "once sold the Son of God for thirty pieces. Your Highnesses think to sell Him again for thirty thousand. Here you have Him" (crashing the crucifix on the table before the abashed monarchs) "Sell Him then, but acquit me of all share in the transaction." So saying, he stalked out of the audience. His action turned the scales. The ordinance of expulsion was signed at Granada on 31 March, 1492, the very year in which Christopher Columbus brought a new world to their most Catholic majesties, Ferdinand and Isabella.

By this edict all Jews, of any age and either sex, who should refuse to receive baptism had to leave Spain within three months and never return under pain of death and confiscation of their property. It was further decreed that after the three months had expired, no Christian must befriend or assist them, or give them either food or shelter under pain of being accused of abetting heretics.

The Jews who decided to quit their motherland rather than sacrifice what was dearer still—their faith—were allowed to dispose of their property, which, of course, they had to sell at knock-down prices to avaricious Christians, who were all too ready to exploit their helpless position. Often they were forced to sell a splendid home for an ass, or a rich vineyard for a piece of cloth.

Torquemada was not content with thus ruining those he detested. He sent out an army of his Dominicans to go forth into every city, village, hamlet and market-place—even into the synagogues—to persuade these wretched people to receive Christian baptism. Despite the most strenuous efforts by these friar-preachers, they achieved little success as the Rabbis were equally vigorous in encouraging the Jews to stand by their God.

The description of this great exodus from Spain which began in July, 1492, should make every Christian writhe in shame. Forlorn processions of Jews toiling towards the sea in the heat and dust of July, on foot, horseback, by donkey, in carts, the young, the aged, the strong, the weak, some enduring their last days and some their first, took every road that led out of the country that had nurtured their forefathers for centuries.

Every Christian who had in him any spark of human feeling pitied these forsaken people, yet none dared help them because of the decree of their implacable enemy, Torquemada, whose proselytisers were exhorting them to renounce their ancient faith and accept baptism into the Catholic Church. The wandering Jews found that their sufferings were by no means over when they reached foreign shores—they were pillaged and murdered by followers of Christ and Mahomet alike.

France and England received some of the exiles, others settled in the Far East. One luckless colony landed on the coast of Africa and tried to reach Fez across the desert. They were plundered, stripped and left desolate by marauding tribesmen.

Many thousands, despairing of survival, returned to Spain and accepted Torquemada's ruthless terms to become Christians. They were baptised all at once in large groups and the Holy Roman Church thus swelled the numbers of the faithful. The numbers accepting banishment vary in the estimates of Catholic historians from 200,000 to 800,000; Jewish chroniclers put the total at 300,000. The total is some indication of Torquemada's inflexible will and irresistible fanaticism which made him one of the most savage scourges of Jewry in the history of even that tortured race.

What was the result to his country of this great act of zeal? In banishing the Jew and the Moslem—for the Moors were soon to follow when the Inquisition could turn its malevolent attention to the Moriscoes (baptised Moslems)—Spain expelled her merchants and financiers on the one hand and her productive workers in both industry and agriculture on the other. So Torquemada may claim the doubtful distinction of draining the life-blood from his country's veins and reducing the greatest Power in Europe eventually to mediocrity.

By now Torquemada's enemies were multiplying at a rapid rate. Yet, although well conscious of the hatred he stirred up, this intolerant old man ruthlessly pursued his fixed path undismayed. He did, however, increase his precautions against surprise attack. He was never seen out of doors without his large armed escort and he never sat down to dine without a horn of unicorn or the tongue of scorpio on his table as a charm against poison.

His zealous arrogance for once over-reached itself when he began proceedings against two distinguished churchmen of Spain, the Bishops of Segovia and Calahorra, because of their Jewish blood—and this despite a Papal decree forbidding inquisitors from proceeding against prelates unless by special pontifical authority. The Bishop of Segovia was the grandson of a Jew who held an honourable position at the court of Henry IV. So the terrible Torquemada raked up evidence against the long-dead grandfather which, if accepted by the Inquisition, would have the effect of degrading his grandson, the bishop. The Borgia Pope, Alexander VI, to whom the bishop appealed, intervened to give Torquemada his first serious defeat. The Grand Inquisitor was commanded to stick to the letter of the law and leave the bishop alone.

The second bishop, however, did not altogether escape the long arm of the Grand Inquisition. In this instance the bishop was brought to trial but the Pope set up his own judges in the case and they brought in an acquittal. Despite this, Torquemada produced further charges, and this time insisted on his own Inquisition finding the unfortunate bishop guilty. He even forced the Pontifical Court to accept the conviction and to sentence the bishop to loss of all his ecclesiastical dignities. Once the Bishop of Calahorra had been reduced to the lay estate, Torquemada promptly had him imprisoned in Rome, where he died.

This rebuff to the Papal dignity decided Pope Alexander to take measures against the too-zealous Torquemada. He dared not depose him or he would have brought himself into conflict with the Spanish sovereigns with whom he wished the friendliest relations. So he chose a typically Borgian solution. In 1494 he sent Torquemada a brief in which he assured him that he "cherishes him in the very bowels of affection for his great labours in exaltation of the Faith" but, because of his failing health he felt bound to take the heavy duties of his office from his shoulders. To do this, the Pope named a number of assistants whom he armed with powers equal to Torquemada's. In this way he forced the Grand Inquisitor to take a back seat. Further appointments

—and particularly that of a Judge of Appeal in cases of the Faith —confirmed the impression that Torquemada had been superseded, although this most obstinate of men had still one shot left in his locker.

Torquemada published his "Final Instructions" for the Inquisition in 1498, containing sixteen new articles for the administration of justice by the Holy Office. Then in September of the same year, the arch-enemy of the Jews breathed his last in his beautiful monastery at Avila at the advanced age of seventy-eight. His end was peaceful, which is more than can be said of the two thousand wretches he doomed to execution by burning.

He died with an easy conscience for, like most bigots, he could not imagine even the possibility that he might have been in error. Certainly not one of the many who have execrated his name can deny his honesty of purpose, his personal integrity and his utter dedication to his task of ridding his Church of heresy.

Here is the classic case of a man who encompassed evil in the unfaltering conviction that he was doing good. In the judgment of history it is right to vituperate him as a fiend of wicked cruelty yet, depending on one's prejudices, he might well have been venerated as a saint. The human tragedy is that, for three hundred years, Torquemada's spirit of fanatical intolerance and bigotry continued to guide that most merciless instrument of man's inhumanity to man, the Spanish Inquisition.

Chapter 6

IVAN THE TERRIBLE

TWENTIETH-CENTURY Russia is not, by all accounts, a tolerant, tender-hearted country, running with the milk of human kindness. Its links with the outside world are ruthlessly channelled and controlled—but it *does* maintain some links. Sixteenth-century Russia was a vast, closed continent cut off from all outside influence and unable to construct even a rudimentary civilization from its native resources, a land of anarchy and disorder, of dark barbarism. Yet in that secret, shut-off territory where human life was valued at no more than a straw, one man achieved a reputation transcending all others for cruelty. Of this man it has been written that he had "outrun the limits of the sphere within which God permits his creatures to work harm". That man was Ivan The Terrible, the first of Moscow's Czars.

Legend has it that on the day of his birth, 4 September, 1530, all Russia exploded in a thunderstorm of unprecedented violence. His childhood was spent in an atmosphere of savage cruelty— the new head of his family, he himself was later to record, "in my presence stretched out his booted feet on my father's death-bed". Not unnaturally, the boy became nervous and irritable. Seeing men put to the torture, he practised these cruelties on animals so that he would know how to deal with men when his day came. His great delight was to throw dogs from a castle battlement and enjoy their anguished writhings. Worse still, the adults around him encouraged this trait.

Born to rule, Ivan noted the arrogant behaviour of the *boyars* (lords) towards him in private and compared it with their servile and fawning attitude to him at official functions—such as court ceremonials or visits of ambassadors—and he grew to despise them. To test his position, at the age of thirteen he ordered his dog-boys to carry off one of the mightiest of the *boyars* to prison and found they carried out his orders so thoroughly that they strangled the noble on the way! Once assured that his word was law, he set about taking full advantage of his situation. He strutted about the streets of Moscow thrashing whom he pleased, violating any woman who caught his fancy, and always, always applauded by those around him. Yet throughout his life this monster of cruelty was an arrant physical coward, taking to his heels at the least sign of danger.

At the age of sixteen Ivan called his *boyars* together to make two important announcements—one, that he had resolved to marry; the second, that he intended to be crowned Czar. Now the title of Czar, or Emperor, had been brought to contempt by the crowd of Tartar princelets—some of them mere heads of provinces in the pay of Moscow—who had assumed it after the break-up of the Mongol power in Russia. Ivan's ambition was to give it back its real meaning, and its real force. He aspired to make Muscovy a new Roman Empire. His coronation on 16 January, 1547, was made an occasion fitted to herald these hopes. In the presence of a mighty host, all the pomp of Church and throne was mustered. High churchmen prayed that God would grant the new Czar the blessing of truth and justice, while around him his *boyars* scattered gold pieces by the handful as tokens of prosperity to come. Yet the Terrible One, who had dreams of overshadowing the combined glories of Greece and Rome, gave no hint of his vision to the assembled foreign potentates. Just as well perhaps, because few were prepared to acknowledge his Czardom.

His betrothal was organized on the same spectacular scale. All marriageable girls throughout Russia's sprawling land-mass were ordered to take part in what amounted to a beauty competition—the prize being to become the bride of Ivan The Terrible. This sixteenth-century contest to discover Miss Russia did not differ too much from today's Miss World campaign in the United States. It lacked some of the twentieth-century ballyhoo perhaps, but there was a remarkable similarity in the fundamental organization; provincial heats were conducted and the chosen beauties secured a trip to Moscow, with all expenses paid.

In Moscow huge buildings with hundreds of rooms, each containing twelve beds, were got ready to accommodate these medieval Marilyn Monroes. The provincial governors had been briefed to choose only suitably bred girls whose vital statistics approximated to Ivan's requirements and 1,500 of these hand-picked specimens made the trip to Moscow. There further tests narrowed the contestants down to five hundred. When these girls had been suitably installed in the decorated seraglios, Ivan, with one other judge chosen from among his most appreciative courtiers, toured the rooms, presenting each beauty with a kerchief embroidered with gold and gems, which he threw on her palpitating bosom.

The Czar's choice fell on Anastasia, fatherless daughter of an ancient *boyar* family which, despite the many vicissitudes of the princely caste in those days, managed to retain its favour with the throne. Alas, there were suggestions, as indeed there are today, that the whole contest was an elaborate plant and that the final selection was a mere matter of form. At least that is what the unsuccessful rivals are believed to have said when they returned home. As consolation awards, however, they were laden with costly gifts.

Whether or no the selection had been pre-determined, Ivan seems to have been madly in love with his bride. Unfortunately his idyllic honeymoon was shattered after three months by news of the most destructive fire in the annals of the country. It raged unchecked through Moscow on 21 June, 1547, and laid waste a quarter of the capital just when his terrified subjects were beginning to hope that the fair and gentle Anastasia would curb the savage excesses of his turbulent nature. The Great Fire of Moscow seemed to spark off again all Ivan's boyhood cruelties, for when the first delegation arrived a week later to lay complaint against their governor, he had them stripped then poured lighted brandy over them. His fiendish pleasure was interrupted by the news that the great bell of the Kremlin had fallen down. This was taken universally to be an omen of more terrible catastrophes to come. Ivan at once forgot about his screaming victims, called for a horse and galloped off to the scene of the disaster.

The Great Fire left The Terrible without a roof over his head —it even invaded the Kremlin, destroying the Czar's palace, the cupola of the Cathedral of the Assumption, the treasury, the arsenal, monasteries, churches and all the wealth stored within

THE WORLD'S WICKEDEST MEN

them. There was a heavy toll of human life, too—1,700 men, women and children were burned alive. Ivan took refuge on the Mountain of the Sparrows, in the village of Vorobievo, from which Napoleon Bonaparte two centuries later was to glimpse the goal which eluded his conquering army. There Ivan held council to discover the cause of the disaster.

Such was the superstition of the times that Ivan's confessor tried to convince him that the fire was the result of witchcraft. Indeed, the Moscow mobs, incensed by rumours of magicians who tore hearts out of corpses and used them in their sorceries to kindle and spread the blaze, began to howl for blood. A few unscrupulous *boyars* were not slow to take opportunity to pay off old scores by naming scapegoats. Some of these wretched victims perished from this primitive form of lynch law and the murders clamoured for fresh sacrifices.

Ivan chose this crisis to reveal his strength and his ruthlessness. He ordered the execution of the murderers and their followers, using this excuse to crush the most powerful *boyars*. Then he began to plan a reconstitution of the form of government, picking unknown men to fill important posts. From now on he was to make certain that the men around him at the top owed their positions to him. His reforms took some years to get under way —years which were to be marked by disturbances which were to contort and mangle the whole country.

Three years after the disastrous fire he summoned a great assembly of officials in the Red Square in front of the damaged Kremlin to inaugurate his planned reforms, mainly dealing with land tenure. More important for his prestige, Ivan decided to mount a campaign which would destroy the remnants of Mongol power and also remove the considerable obstacles in the way of Russian expansion eastward. So he decided to capture Kazan, the town on the middle course of the River Volga, which was the scene of the first major clash inside Russia between Islam and Christianity, a clash won hands down by the Mohammedans. For Asia Kazan was a commercial and industrial centre and for the Mongol Empire the town was the only solid footing left in Europe.

By October, 1552, the dogged defenders of Kazan cracked and complete victory awaited the besiegers. It needed only Ivan to lead the final assault. But his triumphant *boyars* found him unwilling to assume the role required of him—he shrank from the bloody struggle and preferred to linger at prayer before the altar. "Sire, it is time to lead," cried an excited *boyar* to the kneeling Ivan. "Your men are at close quarters with the Tartars, and your regiment awaits you!" Ivan the Terrible gravely answered this appeal with a text from the Scriptures conveniently advocating the merit of long prayers and he did not budge a yard. It seems that his indignant nobles had to force him to the fight, even going to the extreme length of laying hands on his horse's bridle. The presence of the reluctant hero, however, was enough to win the day. Six thousand Tartars were slaughtered in that final carnage and it did not seem to occur to Ivan to halt the slaughter. When the fighting and killing were over he ordered a Te Deum to be sung and himself planted a great cross to mark this glorious Christian victory.

The consequences of the capture of Kazan were immense— the victory shattered the Islamic wall in Russia; the Muscovites poured through to capture Astrakan and, as colonists followed in the wake of the successful troops to administer the newly-won territories, there began a major expansion of the territories of the Czar. Ivan hardly paused to consolidate these conquests before turning his covetous eyes westwards, to the Baltic and, in particular, to the German colony of Livonia (roughly present-day Latvia).

The hideous behaviour of his army in the invasion of Livonia scandalized even that uncouth age, well accustomed though it was to the barbarities of warfare. Women were abused until they died, unborn babies were torn from their mothers' wombs. Having selected the most comely of the women captives and having spent their lust, the soldiers of the Czar then tied them to trees and practised their marksmanship on living targets. Yet the invasion met only token resistance everywhere. The flower of the Livonian nobility was sent back to Moscow, where the highest-born were treated with gruesome barbarity. The prisoners were led through the streets beaten all the time with iron rods, then subjected to further torture before being put to death slowly.

All this savagery produced a marked feeling of disgust throughout Western Europe. So Ivan set to work to mollify the Pope by

119

asserting that Livonia's misfortunes were due to her people having forsaken the Catholic faith! A boycott of Russia was decreed, however, by the Emperor Ferdinand I. He forbade the sending of Western merchandise, particularly war materials, to Ivan the Terrible. England, under the first Elizabeth, soon found a way round this restriction. Meantime the German Electoral Princes expressed fierce indignation at the Russian excesses.

In practice, however, Livonia was utterly forsaken, so her rulers sought help from the Poles who saw the chance of aquiring a Baltic seaboard and so named a stiff price for their aid. The Scandinavian Powers then started to show interest and soon, wrote a chronicler of that period, "Livonia was like a young lady round whom everybody dances". The result was a struggle for a Baltic empire. It was to last for a century, exhaust two of the principal adversaries, ruin a republic and end in triumph for Russia.

In 1560, while fierce bargaining for alliances and coalitions was going on among the northern powers, Ivan's Czarina, Anastasia, died. His apologists are inclined to suggest that this delightful creature had mitigated Ivan's excesses with her gentle influence, yet the fact seems to be that the day after her death he set about seeking another bride. The action he took added considerable complication to the situation around the Baltic.

What Ivan did was to despatch an ambassador post-haste to Poland to win for him the hand of one of King Sigismund's two unmarried sisters. Sigismund, who preferred to regard Ivan as his natural enemy, was at first extremely ungracious. Eventually, however, he was persuaded to allow the ambassador a sight of the two princesses while they were at church. The younger of them, Catherine, chanced to turn round and her personal charms so captivated the proxy woo-er that he had no doubt she was the one for his master. He must have been a good salesman, too, for he convinced Ivan that this was a match to be negotiated at almost any cost. Apart from the lady's physical attractions, she possessed an even stronger fascination for Ivan. Her brother had no sons and he reigned, by hereditary right, over the important Lithuanian town of Vilna. A marriage with Catherine would allow the Czar of All the Russias to claim in due season his Lithuanian patrimony.

Unfortunately for this dream, Sigismund was by no means in favour of the match—perhaps he, too, could see ahead. Hastily he affianced Catherine to John, Duke of Finland, a brother of the King of Sweden. In 1562 the marriage took place: almost immediately Ivan gave the signal for hostilities between Russia and Poland. The following year The Terrible, in command of a huge army, carried along with him a coffin which he declared soon would receive either Sigismund's corpse or his own. He launched attacks on Smolensk and Polotsk, capturing both these important towns. After that the campaign began to ebb against him, so he attempted to reach an understanding with Sweden. He had not forgotten his designs on Catherine and he tried to include her in his terms with her brother-in-law—he chose to ignore her marriage to the Duke of Finland!

This was such a coarse manoeuvre that he later tried to explain it away by saying that he thought her husband was dead, that he had no thought of taking her for a wife, that he merely wanted her as hostage, etc., etc. Although the royal houses of Europe seemed to be shocked by this flagrant example of wife-trading, the King of Sweden showed few scruples. He promptly captured his unhappy brother and locked him up in the Castle of Gripsholm—and Catherine with him! This set in train a quite disgraceful chain of negotiations between Russia and Sweden during which Ivan insisted on making Catherine the primary condition of any treaty. The wretched King of Sweden could see that this was possible only at the expense of his brother's life—again and again he hesitated on the brink of ordering the execution. Under the strain his mind gave way and he completely lost his reason. He suffered the illusion that he was his own brother and instead of surrendering Catherine to the Czar, offered Ivan the daughter of one of his own concubines.

The Duke of Finland quickly seized his chance—and his brother's throne, consigning the mad king to the dungeon from which he himself had escaped. Catherine alone emerged from these sordid goings-on with her head high. She had resisted the most awful threats and tempting promises, showing all emissaries a ring engraved with the words "Death alone . . ." The story at least had a happy ending for her, and indeed for Sweden, for John, Duke of Finland, although seizing his throne in such

121

astonishing circumstances, proved to be a splendid King. He was to endow the country with a military glory which lasted a hundred years.

Ivan was not allowed lightly to forget the affair of Catherine. The King of Poland succeeded in stirring up plenty of trouble for him at home by persuading the Sultan of Turkey to seek revenge for the capture of Kazan and Astrakan. In 1569 a combined Tartar and Turkish expedition threatened Astrakan. Negotiations for a truce were started, and for a time dragged on. Soon after they were broken off Turks and Tartars appeared at the gates of Moscow. Ivan promptly left his capital to its fate and scurried off to safety in Rostov. Moscow was put to fire and sword—according to some testimony 800,000 people perished and the Tartars, always reluctant to storm the Kremlin, retired taking with them 150,000 prisoners. It was a disaster of the first order and the victorious Khan rubbed salt into Ivan's wound by writing to the Czar as he marched homewards—"I have ravaged your land and burned your capital for Kazan and Astrakan and you, who call yourself the Muscovite sovereign, have not appeared in their defence! If you had possessed either valour or decency you would have shown yourself . . . I want Kazan and Astrakan, and I have seen and known every road in your Empire."

The Czar men called The Terrible swallowed these insults. He humbly begged a truce, offered to yield up Astrakan and even offered to pay annual tribute to the Sultan! Actually he was playing for time and gathering his scattered forces for a return encounter which he achieved—and won, forcing the arrogant Sultan into headlong retreat. But humiliation which the Turks had inflicted left him in a mental turmoil. He laid the catastrophe at the door of the *boyars* and heads fell like apples.

Ivan also turned on Sweden, demanding the whole of Livonia and protesting that all previous negotiations had been vitiated because of Catherine's marriage to John. He repeated his "innocent intentions" in this matter and even asked for a portrait of the daughter of John and Catherine who, he understood, was "fair". Then he tried badgering the new King of Sweden, calling him a tallow-merchant's son and heaping other insults upon him. Their correspondence has been published and it throws a revealing light on this arrogant brute who boasted his his regal lineage and wrote in the manner of a nose-thumbing schoolboy. Take his last letter of the series:

> "You have taken a dog's throat to bark at me. It does not suit me to fight with you in this fashion. If your taste leans to that sort of conflict, take another peasant like yourself for your adversary."

The new King of Sweden was not so easily cowed as his brother. When Ivan, in 1577, decided to settle accounts with Sweden in Esthonia he found John too hard a nut to crack, so, suddenly switching his plan of campaign, he fell upon Polish Livonia. In a few days the whole of that little country, except for Riga, was in his hands. For a second time the wanton brutality exercised by the Russians on the inhabitants and their leaders almost surpasses belief. Ivan, thwarted by the "tallow-merchant's son", was in a towering fury. He had the eyes of an aged Livonian marshal torn out and then had him whipped to death. And the screams of forty virgins, all violated at the same time in a garden, echoed for four hours across the River Dvina.

Even these atrocities, sickening though they are, pale into insignificance beside the terrible punishment inflicted on the free town of Novgorod on suspicion that its inhabitants had been plotting with Poland to remove Ivan from his throne. The year was 1570 and the vengeance visited on the town was totally unexpected, especially as the Czar was fond of visiting the place and his relations with the Archbishop Pimenius of Novgorod were excellent—indeed Pimenius had just returned from a fifteen-week stay in Moscow with a large sum donated by the sovereign to restore a church when Ivan struck.

Suddenly The Terrible announced an expedition to Novgorod by his court escorted by a whole army corps. On the frontier of the province Ivan began systematic destruction of the whole country. Along his entire route to Novgorod he left a desert behind him. His advance guard surrounded the town itself, sacked all the monasteries in the suburbs and took prisoner five hundred monks, then the priests and deacons of every church. These men were herded together in a vast prison and bastinadoed each morning and night. On the eve of Ivan's arrival they were ordered to pay 20 roubles each for their freedom. The few who could do so escaped, but a horrible fate awaited the rest. The

Terrible ordered each one of the prisoners to be flogged to death and their corpses to be taken back to their monasteries and there burned.

The following Sunday the Czar chose to attend Mass. He was met on the main bridge by the archbishop, as was the custom, and, as usual, offered his blessing. Ivan refused the blessing, calling the archbishop a "ravening wolf". Nevertheless he decided to dine with the humiliated Primate. During the meal, when Ivan was making merry, a signal was given, the archbishop was seized, stripped of his insignia and thrown into prison with all his servants. His house was given over to pillage.

Now came the turn of the townsfolk. Implements of torture were set up in the main square of Novgorod and the wretched victims were paraded before Ivan one hundred at a time to be "put to the question" in a parody of the Holy Inquisition. Some were roasted slowly over a fire in such a manner that life just remained in their tormented bodies, then they were put to death by drowning. Covered in blood and gasping for breath, they were bound on sledges, driven rapidly down a steep incline to a spot where, owing to the rapidity of the current, the river never freezes, and there cast into the water. Children were tied to their mothers so that they drowned with them. Soldiers armed with pikes manoeuvred about the river on boats to make sure no victim could escape.

These massacres, according to the official "Chronicle of Novgorod", lasted for five weeks and the number of victims rarely fell below five hundred a day. The total number of important personages done to death at Novgorod is put at 2,770 and no one bothered to count the humbler victims. Although the slaughter was fiendish and abominable Ivan was not entirely satisfied that his vengeance was complete. He had all the shops within the town and all the dwelling-houses in the suburbs razed to the ground; the Czar personally supervised the work of devastation. On 13 January, when there seemed nothing left to destroy, he commanded the few survivors (so many were allowed to live for each street) to assemble before him. He made a most friendly speech to them, advising them to cast off all fear, live peaceful lives and to pray God to preserve the Czar and his Empire from traitors!

Ivan the Exterminator arranged for himself a triumphal return to Moscow to celebrate this "glorious" victory over a helpless community. The joyous entertainment took the form of a masquerade, which was later to be the favourite fun of Peter the Great. Preceded by a jester mounted on an ox, Ivan paraded at the head of his court displaying the insignia of a broom and a dog's head, a symbol which was to become a notorious reminder of his dreadful reign. Even now his lust for blood was not slaked, for he proceeded to root out alleged accomplices in Moscow of the Novgorod plot against him. Ivan selected three hundred culprits and summoned his subjects to the Red Square to watch what was left of them put to agonizing death. A great shock was in store for him.

The great square was garnished with all possible instruments of torture—furnaces, red-hot pincers, iron claws, needles, cords to cut through bodies, great coppers bubbling with boiling water —all this was there but no populace! The people of Moscow had decided to boycott the Big Show. Shaken by the sight of the empty square Ivan sent messengers racing around the city to reassure the sulking citizens—"Roll up, roll up! No need to tremble, nobody will be hurt but the traitors!" At last a few hundred were tempted out of their hiding-places and Ivan treated them to a lengthy harangue. What else could he do with traitors? He would, he said, be merciful and spare 180 lives out of the three hundred condemned to death. He was as good as his word, but he made the unlucky 120 pay dearly for the lives of the rest. An Englishman named Horsey described in ghoulish detail the hideous nature of these executions he claimed to have witnessed. One man, Prince Boris Telepniev, was impaled and lingered on the stake for fifteen hours while his mother was violated before his eyes by one hundred men until she died. Viskovatyi, Ivan's Chancellor, was hung up by his feet and cut to pieces like a butcher's carcass. Founikov, the Treasurer, was sprinkled alternately with ice-cold and boiling water "until his skin came off like an eel's".

Some historians seek to explain such abominable deeds by suggesting that Ivan's mind was disordered. Unfortunately for such a simple excuse, the Czar worked out his Will at this time and it was clearly the product of a balanced, indeed well-ordered mind. He gives sound, reasoned advice to his sons and, in general, the document shows a mastery of the art of government. Further convincing proof of his sanity is afforded by a public debate with an eminent theologian in which Ivan took part the day after the Moscow executions.

The truculent Czar, by now surrounded by foes both outside and inside his country, became conscious of a growing feeling of isolation. He looked to England, where Elizabeth I was on the throne, for a solution to these menacing problems. Intrepid sailors from that little island, who had voyaged to Russia to open up new trade routes and exploit new markets, had made a deep impression on him. He had given them valuable concessions in developing commerce between the two countries. Ivan decided to combine politics and gallantry by seeking Elizabeth's alliance —there is some evidence that he secretly proposed marriage to her. But the Virgin Queen was well practised in the art of evading such unwelcome proposals without giving too much offence, and his clandestine wooing was of no avail.

Undaunted, The Terrible even suggested a mutual assistance pact under which, if it ever became necessary, he could seek refuge in England and Elizabeth could accept the Kremlin as her own sanctuary abroad, should she be compelled to flee her country! The Queen, however, merely assured him that it would give her great pleasure to welcome the Czar whenever it suited him to be her guest—and to undertake all the charges involved in his entertainment in England. This offer of charity instead of an alliance stung Ivan to reply:

"I had thought thee mistress in thine own house, and free to follow thine own will. I see now that thou art ruled by men. And what men! Mere moujiks! Thyself thou art nothing but a vulgar wench and thou behavest like one. I give up all intercourse with thee. Moscow can do without the English moujiks."

Although Elizabeth chose to ignore the vulgar abuse, the Czar cancelled all concessions to the English companies, confiscated their merchandise and forbade all trading operations. Diplomatic contact between the two countries seems to have been broken off for the next three years. When the two monarchs were on speaking terms again Ivan renewed his efforts to cement an alliance with England. This time, realizing that Elizabeth was not to be cajoled into giving her own hand, the Czar sent over his emissary to win for him one of the Queen's nieces, Mary Hastings, daughter of the Earl of Huntingdon. Ivan's ambassador was under orders to study the girl carefully, to note particularly her face, complexion, figure, indeed all her vital statistics; he was further to collect information about her exact age and her family tree and, above all, he was to bring back her picture. Ivan had rapped out all these instructions to his envoy only a few weeks after he had married for the sixth time!

Again Elizabeth of England outsmarted him. She did more— she made a fool of him, dragging out the negotiations with every kind of ingenious excuse, including at one stage an "apology" to the Czar because she did not think her niece beautiful enough to suit his taste. Ivan swallowed this hook, line and sinker and asked the Queen's envoy for a list of all Elizabeth's nieces, with names, titles—and portraits. Indeed he died still longing and scheming without success for an English alliance. And, considering the titanic struggle with Poland, under her new King Batory, in which he was locked in the closing years of his reign, there is little doubt England's help would have been invaluable.

Ivan's ideas of religious observance were as bizarre as his ideas of international relationships—he believed in redeeming excess of debauch with excess of devotion—and in the suburb of Alexandrov he created the *Sloboda* which was to become infamous in history. The *Sloboda* had all the outward appearances of a hermitage. Within its walls three hundred chosen companions, all attached to the sovereign's person, lived according to a severe rule. They had to wear black gowns over gold-embroidered kaftans and carry out the most complicated religious observances, with the Czar playing the role of prior. First prayers were at midnight, then at 4 a.m. everyone was in church again for matins, at 8 a.m. there was Mass at which Ivan prostrated himself so often that his forehead became a mass of bumps and bruises; at noon dinner was served in the refectory, where the Czar read from some religious book and all food left over was given to the poor. It was after dinner that the debauchery began—everybody sat down to drink and entertainment, to which the ladies were invited....

The stories about the goings-on in and around the *Sloboda* are legion. It is said that in the afternoon Ivan loved to tour the torture-chambers revelling in the anguish inflicted at his command. More than once he himself even played executioner of luckless subjects whom he had condemned to death. But the more regular sport was bear-baiting. Often the bears were set to fight pitched battles, not only with each other, but with human beings. The Englishman, Horsey, whose testimony has already been mentioned, tells of six fat monks, found guilty of rebellion, who were forced to fight for life with six huge bears which ate up five of them, although the sixth managed to survive.

Another historian of the period declares that in winter when the frozen-over river attracted a large crowd, the Czar would let some of his bears loose on the peaceable inhabitants of Alexandrov. All the chroniclers agree that fearful orgies followed the pious exercises at the *Sloboda*—one pastime seemed to have involved the collection of a number of peasant girls who were stripped naked and forced to chase flying poultry while the monks shot arrows at all and sundry. Ivan, who was said to be followed everywhere by a harem, was the leader in the debauches. But after vespers, the Czar would retire to his bedchamber where three blind men waited to put him to sleep by telling him stories.

Perhaps the most dangerous post in all Ivan's Russia was that of Czarina. He is known to have had eight wives in all. The first three died by poisoning. Usually their families were wiped out too. Some were disposed of simply because they became too thin —and the Czar did not like thin women. The first wife bore him two sons and the elder, Ivan, shared most of his father's gross tastes. Indeed, according to the historian Oderborn, he and his father were in the habit of exchanging mistresses.

Of all the crimes crammed into the reign of The Terrible the one that has taken strongest hold on the popular imagination was the murder of this son by his father. There are many versions, with variations, of this dark deed but the most plausible cause was a quarrel over the son's third wife who when pregnant was reproached by the Czar for lack of modesty in her attire. The Terrible is said to have struck her so heavily that she miscarried during the night. When the son tackled the father, Ivan The Terrible in a frenzy hurled a spear at his son and slew him. For many nights after this Ivan is said to have yelled aloud in grief, calling his *boyars* again and again, telling them he was unworthy to continue as their ruler but always pointing out that his second son, Feodor, was too sick in body and weak in mind to succeed.

Ivan sent 5,000 roubles to a monastery for the repose of his son's soul and an equal sum for himself. This was a thoughtful precaution, for his own end was not far off. Horsey tells how in the year 1584, he was invited to the Czar's treasure-chamber where the dying Ivan was fond of lingering among his gold and precious stones. Suddenly the Czar picked up some turquoises and said to Horsey—"See! They change colour, they turn paler. This is because I have been poisoned. They foretell my death!" Then he asked for his sceptre, "made from a unicorn's horn", to be brought to him. The Czar's physician was made to draw a circle on a table and put spiders inside the line. They all died. "Too late!" cried Ivan. "The unicorn's horn cannot save me now." Then he showed Horsey a huge diamond. "It is the most precious of all the Eastern stones," he told the Englishman, "but I have never cared for it. It curbs fury and lust and instils abstinence and chastity . . . I feel ill, take me away. . . ."

On the evening of 18 March he sent for Boris Godounov to play chess with him and was setting up the pieces when he turned faint. A few minutes later he was dead and, although his crown passed into the hands of his idiot son Feodor, the power—and, indeed, later the Czardom—went to Godounov.

The present-day psychiatrist would have little difficulty in diagnosing Ivan The Terrible as an extreme case of paranoia. But it must be remembered that in the Russia of his day the ruler was everything and owned everything, the people were as nothing and owned nothing save through him. This tradition hardly inculcates modesty in a sovereign. Ivan was composed of fascinating contrasts—he was energetic and violent, yet timid to the point of downright cowardice; his pride amounted almost to madness, yet his humility was occasionally grovelling; he was undoubtedly intelligent, yet again and again he was guilty of the most remarkable folly.

Despite his atrocious record of degenerate cruelty and arrogant absolutism, he remains, with Peter the Great and Catherine, one of the most formative influences in Russian history.

Chapter 7

THE MARQUIS DE SADE

How many people who freely use the noun "sadist" or the adjective "sadistic" are aware that the words originate from the name of a notorious French libertine of the eighteenth century, the Marquis de Sade? Of those who do know that, few are acquainted with his erotic writings and even fewer with the details of his debauched life. Are those details worth knowing? If he were just another roué indulging his sexual fantasies in a variety of vicious ways, the answer would be no. But de Sade was much more than this. He was a considerable literary figure with some claims to distinction as a scientific philosopher. What is more important, he put forward a view of the nature of Man which is at once a challenge to the liberal-humanist thinkers of the present day and to those who follow the precepts of Christianity.

There is another reason for taking an intelligent interest in de Sade—the documents, records and correspondence dealing with his peculiar way of life are only now coming to light, after lying buried for almost a century-and-a-half. So the whole truth about a unique and mysterious personality is being unearthed. This is the man who so scandalized his own generation that he, himself, expressed in his Will the hope that "my memory will be wiped away from the minds of man".

His philosophy was hedonistic, founded on pleasure experienced through pain. He argued that pleasure is Nature's indication that we are acting along the lines laid down by our true selves. Therefore all acts which give pleasure must be natural and *good*. Pain produces more visible changes in human beings than does pleasure. The link between inflicting pain and sexual pleasure is almost universal. Most people, through the restraints imposed by religion or convention, lack the courage to pursue their subconscious wishes into the field of action, but whenever

130

individuals develop the courage and the power, they will indulge themselves in these painful pleasures. The ideal state, according to de Sade, is therefore one in which power is *always* accompanied by the pleasurable infliction of pain. He reasoned, therefore, any analysis of human society which ignores man's innate lust for cruelty is false and in the search for absolute truth such delusions must be exposed and destroyed.

Certainly no seeker after truth has done more than de Sade to experience and to catalogue sex perversions and fantasies. He might be described as an eighteenth-century Dr. Kinsey who reported on what he practised rather than on what he heard.

Perhaps because of the disgrace he brought upon his family through two major lawsuits and long imprisonments for depraved conduct, many of his papers were destroyed after his death in 1814. But his police records were methodically filed away, his family *did* keep a trunk packed with unpublished manuscripts and letters, and his correspondence with the de Sade family lawyer has been preserved intact. Thanks to the painstaking and dedicated work of two students of de Sade (Maurice Heine, who died in 1940 and Gilbert Lely, who in 1948 was given permission by the family's present-day representative, Count Xavier de Sade, to avail himself of the family archives) most of the documentation has now been sifted and published.[1] This analysis of the Marquis necessarily leans heavily on that translation for official details of his life.

The Marquis de Sade was born on 2 June, 1740, at the Condé Mansion, which occupied almost all the ground taken up today by the Rue de Condé in Paris, facing the Luxembourg Palace. He was baptized Donatien Alphonse François, names which he later came to dislike—he chose to call himself Louis. His parents were the Count de Sade, lord of the manors of Saumane and La Coste (he became a high-ranking diplomat) and Marie Eleonore, a member of the younger branch of the royal Bourbon family. There is only one record of the Marquis de Sade's childhood years spent with his mother in the Paris mansion and that is autobiographical.[2]

"Allied through my mother with all the grandest in the kingdom

[1] *Vie du Marquis de Sade* by M. Lely, translated by Alec Brown, Elek Books.
[2] The novel *Aline and Valcour.*

131

and connected through my father with all that was most distinguished in Languedoc—born in Paris in the heart of luxury and plenty—as soon as I could think I concluded that nature and fortune had joined hands to heap their gifts upon me. This I thought because people were stupid enough to tell me so, and that idiotic presumption made me haughty, domineering and ill-tempered. I thought everything should give way before me, that the entire universe should serve me, and that I merely needed to want something to be able to have it."

De Sade left the Louis le Grande College, a Jesuit institution in Paris, when he had just turned fourteen and he was granted a certificate of nobility which enabled him to enter cavalry training school—this cost 3,000 livres a year and accepted only young men of the most ancient nobility. Discipline was rigorous. After twenty months de Sade was appointed unpaid sub-lieutenant in the King's own infantry regiment. At seventeen he was granted a commission as cornet (standard-bearer) in the Carbine Regiment of the Count of Provence and took part in the war against Prussia.

"I have no doubt I gave a good account of myself," he writes in *Aline and Valcour*. "The natural impetuosity of my character, that fiery soul with which nature endowed me, served but to enhance that unflinching savagery which men call courage."

At nineteen he was promoted captain in the Burgundy Horse. The National Library of France houses a letter from de Sade to his father, the Count, about this period of his life. It is interesting because it gives some information about the beginnings of his love-life—it was written when the marquis was returning to the army in Germany after a spell of leave in Paris. Here is an extract:

"I rose every morning to run in search of pleasure and the thought of it made me oblivious of all else. I believed myself fortunate the moment I found it, but what seemed happiness evaporated as quickly as my desires, leaving me but regrets. By evening I was desperate and saw my mistake, but that was the evening; with a new day there were my desires back again and back I flew to pleasure. I would quite forget what I had thought the evening before. At the suggestion of a love bout I accepted, thought I enjoyed myself, then saw I had merely committed follies and not enjoyed myself at all in my heart of hearts . . . was it indeed possible that I thought the girls I saw would really be able to afford me pleasure? Alas, does one really enjoy the happiness that one buys and can love-making devoid of delicacy ever be truly heart-felt? Now my pride suffers when I tell myself that they only loved me because I paid perhaps a little more generously than the others."

When the Seven Years War ended and de Sade, then twenty-three, was discharged from the army with the rank of cavalry captain. Under the regulations of that time he was entitled to re-join if in good health, a concession of which he availed himself later. By this time his father's affairs were in sorry shape. The Count de Sade had become a misanthropic hermit, no doubt driven to that state by his son's social conduct, for now the marquis had become a gambler, spendthrift and profligate, hanging around stage doors and frequenting the houses of procuresses. Stories of his excesses were circulating in aristocratic circles in the French capital.

His father decided there was only one cure—to find him a wife. The count chose Lady Renée Pelagie de Monteuil, daughter of the President of the Taxation Court, with a considerable fortune and splendid connexions. Young de Sade raised no objection to his father's proposal, although he was then deep in a torrid love affair with Lady Laure de Lauris. He was still trying to persuade that lady to marry him up to a fortnight before his wedding to Lady Renée! It seems that while he was officially engaged to the one he was unofficially engaged to the other. The real state of his feelings is shown by this extract from a letter written by him to Lady Laure dated 6 April, 1763—a month before his marriage to Lady Renée:

"Perjurer! Wretch! What has happened to those assurances of life-long devotion? Who has prompted this inconstancy? Who obliges you to break the bonds which were to unite us for ever? What becomes of me when I learn that, inspired by great-hearted devotion, you fall on your knees before your parent to ask him to abandon all thought of this marriage . . . you graceless deceiver, you. Afraid to be united to one who adored you! It was the idea of leaving Paris that frightened you: my love was not enough, nor was I the one to inspire constancy in you. Well, you can stay there for ever, monster, born to make my life wretched!"

There is much more to the same effect. Later in this letter, however, there is an odious touch of blackmail when he writes:

"Beware of inconstancy, it is something I do not deserve and, make no mistake, I should be very angry indeed, there would be nothing too awful for me to do in revenge. The little business of the —— [here de Sade uses a slang term for gonorrhea] ought to make you go carefully with me: I assure you I shall not conceal it from my rival, nor will that be the only secret I shall tell him. I swear it, there is no awful length I would not go to."

However, all his threats and persuasions could not make her his bride, so on 1 May at Versailles, honoured by the consent of the king and queen, the dauphin and his consort, sundry dukes and princes, lords and ladies, the Marquis de Sade was married to Lady Renée Palagie with the greatest pomp and ceremony. Four months later he was languishing in Vincennes Fortress, convicted of offences involving excesses committed in a bawdy house. But his fifteen days in prison there by no means deterred him from carrying on his vicious and depraved way of life. In fact there now followed five years of the most furious and dedicated debauchery ever recorded. . . .

In 1764 (de Sade was then twenty-four) Police Inspector Marais warned a notorious procuress to stop furnishing the marquis with girls. It would seem, however, that at about the same time de Sade found a plentiful supply of material for his perverted practises in the Royal Academy of Music, especially among the young ballet dancers. Certainly he was involved in one lurid scandal with an expensive actress, Mlle de Beauvoisin, whom he had the temerity to take down to his country home and tried to pass her off as his wife (whom his country neighbours had not yet seen).

Meanwhile he relentlessly hunted society women who stirred his emotions. To enable him to carry on these multitudinous affairs simultaneously he rented flats and houses of convenience not only in Paris but at Versailles and Arcueil.

Public disgust at the stories—embellished as they passed from one gossiping mouth to the next—of de Sade's lewd behaviour was steadily mounting. On Easter Sunday, 3 April, 1768, it exploded with full violence over the affair of Rose Keller. On this occasion de Sade chose to combine sexual excess with religious mockery. He commemorated the scourging of Our Lord with the ritual flagellation of a thirty-six year old street beggar, Rose Keller.

He picked the woman up in the Place des Victoires in Paris and took her to his love nest in Arcueil. There he put her in a small, dark room on the ground floor, ordered her to undress and tied her, face downward, to a divan upholstered in white and red calico. This done, he put a bolster across her shoulders, then took off his coat and shirt, put on a sleeveless waistcoat, tied a kerchief around his forehead, took a switch and a cat-o-nine-tails and lashed her, silencing her shrieks of terror by brandishing a knife and threatening to kill her. Five or six times he whipped the woman, using the switch and the "cat" alternately. When she craved mercy and pleaded that she did not want to die without having made her Easter confession, he told her that he would confess her himself and returned to the flagellation, pausing only to rub ointment into the weals.

When he had done with her he took her to another room, supplied her with a bowl, jug of water and a towel. He gave her a small bottle of brandy and persuaded her to use the spirit as a lotion for her wounds. Then he locked her in the room. Rose Keller used knotted sheets from the bed to escape from the window into the garden. In the nearest village she stopped some women and told them of her ordeal. They all agreed the man must be a devil and took her to the police.

Based on this, and later experiments of a more complicated character by de Sade, sex psychologists coined the term sado-masochism (or in Greek *Algolagnia*, the enjoyment of pain) for the neurosis which they claim is widely experienced, though often latent, and which has been thus defined by Dr. Eugen Duhren:

"Sadism is the relationship deliberately sought or arising by accident between sexual excitation and the realization of enjoyment (even if only in the imagination) of events that are terrible, of horrible facts or of acts of destruction which menace or destroy the life or the health or the property of man or of other animate creatures. The man who obtains sexual pleasure from such instances may himself be the immediate cause, or may be only the spectator, or even willingly or by force the victim of these agents."

The psychologists tell us that those suffering from this neurosis have only three solutions—suppression (dangerous as this leads to phobias and obsessions), violence (dangerous because anti-social), and sublimation (often by expressing oneself in literature or in art). In the less analytical period in which Sade lived it was simply called bestiality. He was put on trial.

Maurice Heine, who devoted most of his life to a study of de Sade and his works, has this to say:

> "For fifteen years Sade was to be the victim of the most complete liberty of the senses—no convention, moral, social or religious, was to be an obstacle. He came to know a restless, fervent, persecuted sort of existence, above good and evil, triumphant and pitiable by turns. Rebelling against the laws of God and man, he was to combine the pride of the wicked angel and the anguish of the outlaw."

Be that as it may, de Sade was handed over by the criminal court to the High Court. There he was sentenced to be detained "during the king's pleasure" for his treatment of Rose Keller. In fact he was released after a few months' imprisonment on condition he withdrew to his country estate. His noble and loyal wife went with him.

Far from chastening him, this experience seemed merely to whet his appetite and the following year (1769) he was back in Paris, apparently with the king's consent. Three years later he was to reward his wife's devoted loyalty by committing adultery with her younger sister, Lady Anne Prospère de Launay. Discovery of this dastardly intrigue proved too much for his long-suffering mother-in-law and she petitioned for his arrest. The marquis thwarted her by running off to Italy, taking her younger daughter Anne with him!

The Easter Day sacrilege was an outlet for the sadism of the marquis alone, but four years later he was involved in a notorious escapade in which that compulsion was allied to its counter-part, masochism. During a visit to Marseilles with his manservant, Latour, in that year (1772), a rendezvous was arranged at a house in the rue d'Aubagne with four girls.

The marquis turned up dressed in a grey surcoat lined with blue, wearing waistcoat and breeches of marigold silk, plumed hat, sword and gold-topped cane. First he primed two of the girls with aniseed sweets treated with cantharides (popularly known as Spanish-fly extract)—such preparations had been in use in France since the sixteenth century and, indeed, were given great vogue by the Cardinal Richelieu—then he indulged in a number of perverted practices including sodomy, a capital crime in the eighteenth century.

The Marquis also had furnished himself with a cat-o-nine tails and a heather broom with which he commanded the girls to lash him—and with which he in turn whipped them. Further details of the subsequent orgy are unprintable, save to record that knife-cuts on the mantelpiece of that room kept count of the number of blows inflicted on the four girls—they totalled 215, 179, 225 and 240. One girl was later found to be poisoned—the effect of the doctored sweets.

Sexologists who have gone into this case in detail describe it as a "lesson in experimental sexual psycho-pathology" and list some of the perversions practised as "sado-masochism, copro-phily, exhibitionism and voyeurism". It is also abundantly clear from the record of the proceedings that de Sade deliberately set out to repudiate and defy every moral convention.

Lacking the advantages of later discoveries in the field of psycho-analysis, the unsympathetic Royal Prosecutor of Mar-seilles drew up criminal charges against the marquis and his manservant for that day's work—but de Sade had already fled to Italy with his incestuous partner, Lady Anne de Launay. Nevertheless the case was tried at Aix-en-Provence in their absence, and de Sade and Latour were sentenced to execution "for poisoning and sodomy". Both culprits were, however, by this time well beyond the reach of the Provençal jurisdiction, so the High Court had to be content with executing and burning effigies of the marquis and his servant in the Place des Precheurs at Aix.

The marquis and his sister-in-law thereafter indulged their guilty passion for three months in Venice and other Italian towns, but the vengeance of his mother-in-law caught up with him when he returned to the Duchy of Savoy (then the territory of the King of Sardinia) and tried to reside in secrecy at Chambery. He was arrested on the orders of the King of Sardinia, acting on the request of Lady Montreuil. Yet it seems that the grievously wronged wife was able to forgive both culprits, because shortly afterwards she accompanied her sister-in-law to Paris and made several unavailing efforts to visit her husband in prison.

However, in less than a year, the irrepressible marquis had contrived to make a daring escape from his fortress prison. He hid more successfully this time; nothing is known of his movements for eight months following his escape despite an intensive police search for him aided and partly financed by the relentless mother-in-law.

When the furore had quietened down he bobbed up again in 1774 at his estate in La Coste where he joined the marquise and they travelled together to Lyons in the company of a maid, five fifteen-year-old girls as staff, and a secretary who was somewhat older. Inevitably a new scandal involving the five minors blew up. The modern French writer Paul Bourdin, working on a collection of de Sade documents, describes the goings-on with these young girls as "a frenzied witches' Sabbath with the aid of the servants' kitchen". The upshot was that criminal proceedings were begun at Lyons against de Sade, who fled incognito to Florence and later to Rome. The death of his mother, the Dowager Countess de Sade, lured him back to Paris—and his downfall—for in 1777 he was arrested there by the patient Inspector Marais and lodged in Vincennes Fortress. From now on he was to spend more of his life inside prison walls than outside them.

In this new misfortune Sade turned to his ever-loyal wife, urging her to "throw herself at the feet" of Ministers of the Crown to obtain his release. To his implacable mother-in-law, Lady Montreuil, he wrote reproaching her with having, in one fell moment "betrayed every feeling that is sacred, every sentiment of humanity, having a son arrested on the request of his mother". He implored her to have him freed and to give him time to make up for his errors. Nevertheless he stayed in prison for sixteen months before making his second escape. Once more he reached La Coste. This time he was at liberty for thirty-nine days.

When his marquise heard of this she was all eagerness to join "her adored little love whom she loved endlessly" but her mother sternly forbade this, and enforced her embargo by a threat of notifying the authorities. Before they could surmount that difficulty, ten men armed with swords and pistols burst into de Sade's home at four in the morning, bound him and dragged him off to

Vincennes once more. And there, despite all entreaties, threats, vituperation and blasphemy, he was to remain for the next five-and-a-half years, from 1778-84. The first time his wife was permitted to visit him was in 1781—a separation lasting till then four years, five months—and that meeting was in the presence of a police officer. After this visit de Sade was possessed by jealousy and thereafter his letters to her were poisoned with abuse and vulgar obscenity. He seized on a reference, in one of his wife's letters, to his former secretary, M. Lefevre, to imagine him a rival. He wrote to her:

"and it's a rapscallion of that sort, a paltry clodhopper on my estates, a little squirt who has pickled himself in filth, to whom you have recourse to be false to me, is it?"

The most savage manifestation of his insensate jealousy is supplied by his treatment of a drawing of his imagined rival (still in the possession of his descendant, M. Xavier de Sade). All around this drawing the marquis had written the most virulent and explosive remarks, bloodstains smear the paper, and it has been torn thirteen times. One of de Sade's comments runs:

"The woman who solely for either vile vengeance or, perhaps worse still, for the turgid, coarse craving of satisfying her bodily lust, shamelessly gives herself to a valet, to a peasant of the vilest breed, to whom her husband's father gave largesse, that woman, I say, has no longer even the right to be called wife."

This, from a man with his record!

All through this, for her, an agonizing period, the Marquise de Sade answered these vituperative charges with the most touching patience, assuring him again and again of her love and fidelity. But her assurances merely fed the fires of his crazy suspicions, so, to remove even the vestige of an excuse for his humiliating accusation, she decided to withdraw into a nunnery.

The psycho-analysts explain this ungovernable jealousy by diagnosing it as sado-masochism in which the sensuous enjoyment of dishonour (real or imagined) is savoured to the full by a husband who is bi-sexual.

Eventually the fever of suspicion worked itself out of his system, sublimated in part no doubt by his erotic meditations, which helped him to compile his first lengthy work in prison,

120 Days of Sodom. He also turned out plays in verse and prose none of which showed the slightest merit.

Throughout these five-and-a-half years in the Vincennes Fortress, de Sade kept planning for, pleading for, and demanding his release. In 1784 his condition changed—but only for the worse. He was transferred to the Bastille where he was to spend another five-and-a-half years of his turbulent life. As he was originally imprisoned under a *lettre de cachet* on the request of his family (in fact, of his mother-in-law) he had to be supported in prison by his family. At once he complained that the Bastille was much more severe than Vincennes, so eventually he was allowed visits from his wife and access to his books. In the following year (1785) he was able to revise his first major work, *120 Days of Sodom*, which he sub-titled *The School for Libertines*.

By 1789, when the disorders of the mob in Paris were mounting daily—it was the year of the French Revolution—de Sade tried to take advantage of the situation by shouting from his cell window that the Bastille prisoners were being slaughtered and appealing to the crowds below for rescue. He ingeniously contrived to make a megaphone out of a stove-pipe in his cell so that his voice would carry much farther and he managed to attract quite an audience in this way. Without further ado the Bastille Governor had him transferred to another jail, at Charenton. Six men, pistols in hand, tore him from bed, allowed him barely time to dress before bundling him into a cab and getting him away from the Bastille. His cell containing six hundred books, fifteen of his own manuscripts besides his furniture and clothing were sealed up and lost to him.

De Sade began his serious literary work around 1780, when he was forty and in prison. By the time the Paris mob stormed the Bastille and set all Europe alight he had already built up a considerable catalogue which, apart from the *120 Days of Sodom* still to receive its final polishing, included a philosophical novel in four volumes, *Aline and Valcour; Justine* or *the Misfortunes of Virtue* in one volume; *Stories Long and Short* (four volumes); *The Portfolio of a Man of Letters* (four volumes); and two volumes of plays. During the Revolution he made strenuous efforts to have his plays staged but the only audience they achieved was in a lunatic asylum of which he became an inmate. In 1795, as Citizen D. A. F. Sade, he pestered the theatre managers of provincial cities from Lyons to Rouen. Despite his own high opinion of himself as a dramatist, the theatre managers saw his characters as dull and lifeless and the dialogue (much of it in verse) as muddled and uninspired.

In the *120 Days of Sodom* de Sade actually became the first man to classify sexual abnormalities, a century before Krafft-Ebing and Freud specialized in this work. It is also regarded by some intellectuals as a book of outstanding literary merit and of rare philosophical importance. Its form is modelled on Boccaccio's *Decameron* and the introduction leaves the reader in no doubt as to its purpose:

> "Now at once, dear reader, you should dispose your heart and soul to the most impure story told ever since the world began, there being no such book either among the ancients or moderns. Realize that all decent bodily indulgence is prescribed by that *beast* of whom you are always talking without knowing it and which you call *Nature,* that such indulgence in any of its forms is to be expressly excluded from this collection. . . ."

Well aware that his manuscript might be seized as obscene, de Sade performed the diligent task of taking a meticulous copy in tiny handwriting on a roll of paper 13 yards long made up of small sheets stuck end to end. He spent three hours for each of twenty evenings in the Bastille covering one side of this roll, then he turned it round and proceeded to complete the other. Alas for him, after the Bastille was pillaged by the mob he never saw the roll again. Yet it was found after his death—in the very cell he occupied! The roll was eventually sold as a collector's piece at the beginning of this century and in 1904 it was published in Berlin under a pseudonym. Maurice Heine published a three-volume edition of this work between 1931 and 1935.

His philosophical novel, *Aline and Valcour*, was according to the author's note, written in the Bastille, one year before the French Revolution—"the fruit of several sleepless years". It was prohibited in 1815 and again in 1825, not only for its immorality but also because of the advanced social theories it contains. Wicked characters of every kind abound in this work and it certainly shocked even the advanced thinkers of Year III of the

Revolution. There followed *The New Justine,* or *The Misfortunes of Virtue,* published in ten volumes with one hundred obscene engravings and seized by the police a year later. Such was the depravity of this work that de Sade, who was given his liberty when the Revolutionary Tribunal freed all prisoners detained under *lettres de cachet,* was arrested again in 1801, even though he persistently denied authorship. Yet he wrote a sequel to it entitled *Juliette* or *The Prosperities of Vice* which is apparently no less horrible than *Justine.* The Paris police seized and destroyed one thousand copies of this work, too.

Now de Sade was lodged in the St. Pelagie Prison where he was said to have "tried to satiate his bestial passion" on some young louts picked up for rowdiness at the theatre and put in a cell adjoining his. For this outrage he was transferred to the Bicetre Prison, known as "the mob's Bastille", and finally to Charenton Lunatic Asylum where his family paid his board. He was regarded as being in a state of "incessant licentious insanity". Even there his presence caused disgust as the Chief Medical Officer urged the removal of this man "made too famous by his brazen immorality", suggesting that he be transferred to some prison castle "to save the sick minds from the incessant impression made by his profound corruptness".

All attempts to have him removed from this asylum—and there were many—failed and the Marquis de Sade died peacefully there in December, 1814. His son, Donatien Claude Armand, was given the task of making an inventory of his father's possessions and works, being required by the Director of Police to extract these manuscripts "which concern morals or religion". The son, by all accounts a miserable, greedy creature, who had persistently refused to pay for his father's board despite getting his hands on all de Sade's considerable properties long before his death, actually asked the police to burn some of the manuscript and insisted on being present when this was swallowed by the flames. He ignored all but one of his father's last wishes as to the disposal of his remains and had him buried with a plain stone cross without inscription for 65 livres made up of 10 for the coffin, 9 for candles, 6 for the chapel, 6 for the grave-digger, 6 for the almoner, 8 for the bearers and 20 for the cross.

So there passed into history this strange, tortured rebel whose

moral philosophy outraged the royalist as well as the revolutionary, the priest and the pauper alike. His conduct caused his name
to become for future generations a term for unparalleled depravity
and vice, and the record of his astonishing infamy is founded on
a volume of work which remains largely unread and was compiled
during twenty-eight years spent in confinement. Yet throughout
the 150 years since his death his memory has somehow been
kept alive by a dozen or so intellectuals who are prepared to
award him the mantle of greatness both in literature and philosophy. The rest of the civilized world no doubt prefers to accept
the verdict of de Sade's own times and to regard him as a monster
who lived like a libertine and wrote like a pervert.

Chapter 8

CASANOVA

MORAL leper or fascinating rogue? Prodigious liar or honest reporter? Vicious libertine or gallant lover? Literary genius or bombastic fraud? These are some of the questions which have excited the world of letters since the first publication of Casanova's Memoirs—in 1822, a quarter of a century after the death of the author.

Had it not been for this autobiography, the name of Casanova would long ago have passed into obscurity: because of it, his name is accepted in every European language as an automatic synonym for The Great Lover. Whatever the verdict of posterity on Casanova the Man, there can be no doubt that his Memoirs have won a high place in literature as an incomparable record of the century in which he lived.

But it is with the man we are concerned—and to assess him what fairer method can be employed than to take him at his written word; to accept his confessions as true in substance and in fact? As he himself writes as a dedication to his book ". . . why should I not be veracious? A man can have no object in deceiving himself, and it is for myself that I chiefly write".

This appraisal of one of history's most remarkable characters is therefore based on the autobiography itself which Casanova, although a Venetian, penned in French in the declining years of his long life and which he titled *Histoire de ma vie*.

Giacomo Casanova, who came to prefer the French-style Jacques, was born in Venice on 2 April, 1725, the eldest of a family of six. In the first chapter of his Memoirs he traces his family pedigree back to a Don Jacob Casanova, "secretary to King Alfonso of Spain", who was of illegitimate birth and established a tradition for his descendants by running off with a pretty nun the day after she had taken the veil.

The father of Jacques Casanova—let us say his acknowledged

father for even that is in doubt—carried on Don Jacob's tradition by running away from his native Parma to pursue an actress named La Fragoletta. They appeared together on the stage in Venice where Gaetan-Joseph, as Casanova's putative father was known, switched his affections to a shoemaker's daughter, Zanetta Farusi, and one result of their liaison was Jacques. Zanetta became a distinguished leading lady of the stage, but Gaetan-Joseph never rose above the second-rate. Zanetta abandoned her son (who describes himself as an "imbecile up to the age of eight-and-a-half") to her mother, Marzia, who, scorning medical science, handed the boy Casanova over to a sorceress for treatment.

Whether this lady's herbs and incantations did the trick or not, Jacques was cured of all ailments and thereafter had a lifelong interest in cabalistic science which he was to turn to his personal profit again and again. This cure also introduced him to his ruling passion—the ministrations of women; for the sorceress promised him a visit from a beautiful lady who would be very kind to him provided he kept his mouth shut about her. He tells us that on the same night he was awakened by "a dazzling woman with immense hoops, splendidly attired and wearing on her head a crown set with precious stones which seemed to me sparkling with fire". Only he expects us to believe that she came down the chimney!

At the age of nine he was sent to school at Padua. He claims also to have taken a degree at Padua University, then a famous seat of learning, but diligent research has failed to produce any evidence of his having matriculated there. He decided to enter the Church and indeed preached two sermons, but he "dried up" during the second and abandoned that career. Casanova the teenager found himself much more suited to the wild night life of Venice and after one or two daring escapades he had his first taste of prison in the Fort of Saint Andre. His mother at last began to worry about her tempestuous boy and managed to get him into the service of a bishop.

So, in 1743, began his travels, which were to continue for half-a-century and take him to every country in Europe. It was also to be a voyage of non-stop love affairs and when he at length came to anchor in a remote castle in Bohemia, he summed up his undeniable success at the art of love in this way:

145

"In my long and profligate career in which I have turned the heads of hundreds of women, I have become familiar with all the methods of seduction; but my guiding principle has never been to direct my attack against novices or those whose prejudices were likely to prove an obstacle except in the presence of another woman. I soon found out that timidity makes a girl averse to being seduced, while in company of another girl she is easily conquered—the weakness of the one brings on the fall of the other . . . the girl grants some small favour, and immediately makes her friend grant a much greater one to hide her own blushes—before she has had time to think pleasure attracts her, curiosity draws her a little further, and opportunity does the rest."

His first journey from Venice to join his new master, the Bishop of Martorano, in Rome was expensive but instructive. He fell in with a rascally friar who introduced him to a gang of card-sharps. As a result the ambitious Casanova, at the very outset of his search for fame and fortune, found himself cleaned out. Now he had to live on his wits, and very nimble those wits proved to be. His first victim was a rich Greek merchant who traded in wines and minerals. Casanova, making cunning use of his knowledge of chemistry, showed the Greek how to make an amalgam of mercury with lead and bismuth by which the mercury increases its weight by 25 per cent. He deluded the Greek into believing that this was a secret of alchemy and into parting with a large sum of money for a share in the know-how.

During a sea voyage he found himself caught up by quarantine regulations in the harbour of Ancona where he was virtually a prisoner for twenty-eight days. Although locked up in a first-floor suite he managed to catch the eye of a Greek slave in the yard below.

As he reports: "Was it likely that I could feast my eyes constantly upon such a charming object without falling desperately in love?" His problem was how to make advances to her without knowing whether she would reciprocate. He solved this by sealing two envelopes, one containing a blank page, the other a love letter. First he dropped the blank over his balcony to fall at her feet, reckoning that if she picked it up she was interested and if she did not he had given nothing away. As soon as he saw her stoop to pick up the decoy, he dropped the love letter too. This ran roughly as follows:

"Beautiful angel from the East, I worship you. I will remain all night on this balcony in the hope that you will come to me for quarter of an hour and listen to my voice through the hole under my feet. We can speak softly, and in order to hear me you can climb up to the top of the bale of goods which lies beneath the same hole."

At midnight, when his fish had risen to his bait, he lay flat on the floor of the balcony and placed his head against the hole which was about six inches square. He saw her jump up on the bale and her head reached to a point twelve inches from the balcony. Having got her so near he breathed soft endearments to her and persuaded her to put her hand through the hole. He rained kisses upon her hand, then thrust his arm through and caressed her. It was a promising start, he felt, but racked his brains to find a way of taking the affair a stage farther. He told her that he would somehow remove a plank from the balcony if she could devise a way of reaching him. This she did by persuading a servant to build up bales of cotton below the balcony. At last, after a precarious balancing act on the part of the girl, he was able to get his hands under her elbows and drew her up to him. Before he could savour his triumph to the full, the quarantine guard surprised them and Casanova promptly dropped the girl back to the floor below. "Giving vent to my rage," he writes:

"I throw myself flat on the floor of the balcony and remain there without a movement, in spite of the shaking of the keeper, whom I was sorely tempted to strangle. Finally I rose from the floor and went to bed without uttering a word, and not even caring to replace the plank."

Few of his amorous adventures ended so unfortunately for him, however. There was, for instance, the double liaison which he carried on with two nuns at the same time. . . .

The first, whom he initialled C.C. to conceal her identity, was a girl of fourteen with a rascally brother who was imprisoned for fraud. Her father sent her to a convent on the Isle of Murano, off Venice, to get her out of Casanova's clutches. Of course illicit messages passed between them and he attended a taking of the veil ceremony to which visitors were invited so that he could see his beloved and be seen by her. But, as he himself confesses,

147

"with a nature like mine, how could I possibly remain satisfied without positive love?" He paraded at church each Sunday morning for a month so that C.C. might feast her eyes on him through a grille and he reports, with charming modesty, that "all the convent, boarders and nuns, not even excepting the old ones, expected me anxiously—they warned each other of my arrival and watched me take the holy water."

Imagine, therefore, his delighted surprise when a letter is dropped in front of him as he is about to enter a gondola for the return journey to Venice. The letter tells him that "a nun, who has seen you every Sunday in the church of her convent, wished to become acquainted with you". This nun he conceals behind the initials M.M. As she is also the mistress of the French Ambassador to Venice, the Abbe de Bernis, she has many privileges, including the one of slipping out of the convent at night to keep secret trysts with Casanova, apparently with the full knowledge and consent of the Ambassador. Indeed, it seems that the Abbe de Bernis, concealed in a small closet, watched Casanova make love to his mistress, the ravishing nun! Further, the Ambassador has designs on C.C. and arranges for Casanova to spend a night of love with both nuns so that he can do likewise a little later. This episode in the Memoirs certainly throws a blinding light on the manners and morals of the age.

While Casanova was involved in this triangular intrigue, the Venetian Inquisitors were taking a suspicious interest in his activities. The reports of their spies accused him of living on others, of duping credulous persons and of consorting with debauchees with a view to furthering their dissolute habits. He was also condemned as an impostor and a card-sharp, as a womanizer and fortune-hunter. But, despite that formidable catalogue, his downfall was caused by—a poem! One of the Inquisition spies claimed he had heard Casanova recite one of his own poems which was not only obscene but mocked at religion. For this he was arrested on the night of 25-26 July, 1755, and taken to the Leads, that dread prison in the attics of the Ducal Palace from which no one had ever escaped. Casanova caused yet another sensation by organizing an ingenious break-out with a debauched monk named Balbi. This was the way of it:

At exercise in the garret of the prison he picked up an iron bar and hid it under his armchair. Using a piece of marble as a whetstone he made an eight-sided pike out of the bar. Next he fashioned a lamp from a small bowl, using the oil from his salad and a shred from his cotton counterpane as a wick. He got sulphur under doctor's prescription to cure an imaginary ache and a flint on yet another pretext. His home-made lamp allowed him to work in the darkness of his cell for six hours a day to pierce the floor with his do-it-yourself kit. With his escape hatch ready, he fixed the day for the attempt. Alas, on the day before he was moved to another, and more spacious cell!

Such wretched luck might have broken the determination of many a man, but Casanova, undaunted, set to work to plan his break-out from the new quarters. He kept his equipment intact but now he had to bring his adjoining cell-mate, Balbi, into his escape plan. He decided to pass the home-made pike to the monk inside the parchment binding of a large folio Bible which Casanova suggested could be used as a tray for a dish of macaroni. It worked. Balbi was able to pierce the ceiling of his cell next to the separation wall and then made a hole in the ceiling of Casanova's cell through which they might both escape.

Casanova knotted a rope from his bed-sheets and, with Balbi's help, removed the lead plates of the roof (which gave the prison its name). Once out on the roof they were able to squeeze through a dormer window into a room which they found to be unlocked. With the help of their invaluable pike they managed to thread their way from room to room in the Ducal Palace until they reached the main door of the grand entrance stairway. This proved impenetrable, so Casanova gesticulated to men in the palace courtyard that he was locked in. The door-keeper was summoned to unlock the huge main door and the escapers rushed past him to the canal where they leaped into a gondola and got away. With consummate impertinence, Casanova managed to rest overnight in the home of the Chief of Police who was out all night seeking the vanished prisoners!

This is regarded as one of the most ingenious escapes in prison history—so adroit, indeed, that many critics were disposed to doubt it until the records of Venice's archives provided complete confirmation. The escape was on 1 November, 1756.

Casanova paused at Bolzano only long enough to raise funds

from a nobleman whom he had put under his cabalistic spell, then moved on to Munich, Augsburg, Strasbourg—and Paris. There he was quick to note that the Abbe de Bernis, who shared his lewd attachment to the nuns C.C. and M.M., was now Louis XV's Foreign Minister.

De Bernis, who was either remarkably loyal to his fellow libertine or, more likely, susceptible to a hint of blackmail, sponsored Casanova as a financial wizard and that audacious rogue was quick to seize his opportunity by proposing a scheme which would give the ever-needy king "the interest of a hundred million francs". This turned out to be a public lottery and Casanova was made its director. Its avowed object was to furnish funds for the Ecole Militaire but it certainly furnished a lush livelihood for the wily Venetian. Casanova's lottery was, in fact, the forerunner of the present National Lottery of France so he did make more than a literary mark on posterity.

His success with the French Government did not end with the lottery—he became a secret agent and undertook a number of diplomatic missions. Now he had gained entrée into the most elevated social circles in Paris and he was not long in charming the ladies of all ages, the young ones in the usual way and the more elderly with his prowess as an occultist, since the cabalistic science was currently in fashion with the bored aristocracy.

He made a complete captive of the distinguished Marquise d'Urfe and became a boon companion of her ne'er-do-well nephew, the Comte de la Tour d'Auvergne. The ageing marquise, a deep student of the occult, proved rich prey for Casanova who duped her shamelessly and helped himself lavishly to her generous bounty for seven years—he himself quotes her nephew as estimating that he milked her of a million francs during that period. There seems little doubt that he was also her lover. Even he was moved by his conscience as he wrote about their association, commenting:

"Now that I am no longer the victim of these illusions which pursued me throughout my life, I blush at the remembrance of my conduct, and the penance I impose on myself is to tell the whole truth and to extenuate nothing in these Memoirs."

This Marquise d'Urfe owned one of the most renowned libraries in France, begun by an ancestor in the sixteenth century, and including a remarkable section on the occult—indeed many of these manuscripts went eventually to the national libraries of Paris and Vienna. Like so many distinguished people of her day, she imagined that she was on the track of the secret for transmuting base metals into gold through the Philosopher's Stone or a powder of projection, as it was known. Casanova, although admitting that he knew all this was hocus-pocus, nevertheless made use of his facility with the appurtenances of magic to conjure good money out of the purses of the credulous and to give himself an air of mystery and importance.

There was, however, one individual who proved to be more than a match for him in this field, if not in all. This was the extraordinary Count de Saint-Germain, one of the sinister and mysterious figures of the century. He could be called a genuine spellbinder with an almost hypnotic gift of words—even Casanova, who hated him, fell under the magic of this man's voice although he did not swallow his claims to have been born three centuries previously and to possess the power of making diamonds and the knowledge of how to achieve eternal youth. Among Saint-Germain's many accomplishments was alchemy; his research into it was financed by Louis XV himself. The tone in which Casanova writes of this strange personage suggests that he came off second best in their encounters. Mme d'Urfe was also greatly attached to the Count and this, too, may help to explain Casanova's attitude to a more brilliant rival.

Another possible cause of Casanova's jealousy was that Madame d'Urfe had introduced Saint-Germain to Louis XV in the hope of providing that world-weary monarch with a new interest and the magnificent charlatan not only showed the king how to make a large diamond out of several small ones but also deluded Madame de Pompadour into believing that he supplied to her the water of eternal youth. So delighted were the king and his mistress with Saint-Germain's accomplishments (real or apparent) that they gave him the suite formerly occupied by the French hero, the Marshal Saxe.

Casanova's effrontery never took him quite to these heights, but he did convince Madame d'Urfe that he had the power to make her soul pass into the body of a male child born of the mystic union of a mortal and an immortal, that is between an ordinary man and a woman of divinity. Listen to the rascal's excuse for leading her on:

> "If I had thought it possible to lead back Madame d'Urfe to the right use of her senses I would have made the attempt, but I felt sure that her disease was without remedy, and the only course before me seemed to abet her in her ravings and to profit by them.

> "If I had spoken out like an honest man and told her that her ideas were nonsensical, she would not have believed me; she would have thought me jealous of her knowledge, and I should have lost her favour without any gain to her or to myself. I thus let things take their course and to speak the truth I was flattered to see myself treated as one of the most profound brothers of the Rosy Cross (one of the highest orders of magic) as the most powerful of men by so distinguished a lady, who was in high repute for her learning, who entertained and was related to the first families of France, and had an income of 80,000 francs, a splendid estate, and several magnificent houses in Paris.

> "I was quite sure that she would refuse me nothing, and though I had no definite plan to profit by her wealth, I experienced a certain pleasure at the thought that I could do so if I would."

Casanova's extravagance in Paris was boundless. He himself says that he lived like a prince, but he would have had to be Louis XV, bleeding the population of France, to keep up the pace. Instead, he could batten on only a few people so that ruin was merely a matter of time. For instance he set up a business around a process for printing exquisite designs on silk and this led him to engage twenty Parisiennes to paint the designs. Naturally he chose the prettiest applicants and inevitably—but let Casanova tell what happened. . . .

> "The chief expense of my life was incurred in connexion with the girls who worked in my establishment. With my complexion and my pronounced liking for variety, a score of girls, nearly all of them pretty and seductive, as most Paris girls are, was a reef on which my virtue made shipwreck every day. Curiosity had a good deal to do with it, and they profited by my impatience to take possession by selling their favours dearly. They all followed the example of the first favourite, and everyone claimed in turn an establishment, furniture, money and jewels; and I knew too

little of the value of money to care how much they asked. My fancy never lasted longer than a week, and often waned in three or four days, and the last comer always appeared the most worthy of my attentions."

In the year 1760 Casanova, now aged thirty-five, began an Odyssey across Europe which lasted for a quarter-of-a-century, following his whims or, as he himself preferred to put it, his genius—although it is noticeable that his genius moved him on when the law—or an irate husband or lover— was about to catch up with him. Thus he left Paris for Holland, where he had some trouble with bills of exchange and promissary notes. Thence he can be traced to Germany and Switzerland (where he had a long interview with Voltaire), thence to Aix-les-Bains, which he leaves in a hurry "to escape the snares of a couple of dangerous adventurers", he tells us, and to Grenoble where he casts the horoscope for a ravishing young lady and foretells from it that she will become the king's mistress (which she dutifully does); on he goes to Marseilles, Nice and Genoa, having a series of routine amorous adventures en route, so by stages to Florence and a chance meeting with an old love, by then a famous opera singer, who confronts him with the tangible evidence of their old passion—a handsome youth masquerading as her young brother. Again and again in his Memoirs Casanova records his delighted surprise at encountering his offspring in various parts of Europe and, if we are to believe him, none of the mothers bore him any ill-will.

His sojourn in the bosom of his new-found family in Florence was rudely cut short by a peremptory order to get out of Tuscany. He went on to Rome, where he had a mild affair with an innkeeper's daughter, then he visited the Pope, whom he persuaded to intercede with the Venetian authorities (they hadn't forgiven him for escaping from the Leads) on his behalf and promptly bought a winning lottery ticket, using the money to help an artist's daughter to marry the man she loved (Casanova taking care to seduce her first). He sums up this little episode in this remarkable paragraph:

"Before we parted she thanked me for what I had done for her and begged me to believe that, her poverty notwithstanding, she had given herself for love alone."

On to Naples were he was so entranced by the beautiful
Leonilda, mistress of a duke, that he nearly married her (with
ducal blessing). But when he called on her mother he found that
she was yet another old flame and the daughter was his own.
Unabashed, he immediately offered to marry the mother on
condition that the daughter remained with them "as he cannot
bear to be parted from her"! The mother wisely refused, believing that her daughter would be better off with the duke. Casanova
bade them all farewell and returned to Rome.

His erotic wanderings brought him again to Paris, where he
found the devoted Marquise d'Urfe impatiently awaiting the
magical rejuvenation which Casanova had promised her and
for which expectation she was paying dearly. He stalled her with
yet another plausible excuse, extracted still more money from
her and went off to visit his sister-in-law, who was full of complaints against his brother. This "charming woman", as Casanova calls her, told him that his brother—a reasonably successful artist—had no business to marry her, "knowing that he
could not show himself a man".

"Why did you not make the trial before you married?"
Casanova asked her.

"Was it for me to propose such a thing?" she replied indignantly. "How should I suppose that such a fine man was
impotent?"

Casanova tells her that she has two courses open to her—
either to have her marriage annulled, or to take a lover, "and
I am sure," he adds, "that my brother is too reasonable a man
to offer any opposition to the latter course".

"I am perfectly free," she answers, "but I can neither avail
myself of a divorce nor of a lover for the wretch treats me so
kindly that I love him more and more, which doubtless makes
my misfortune harder to bear."

Then follows this remark which illuminates Casanova's
opportunistic character even at the expense of his brother:

"The poor woman," he writes, "was so unhappy that I should
have been delighted to console her, but it was out of the question.
However, the mere telling of her story had afforded her some
solace and, after kissing her in such a way as to convince her that
I was not like my brother, I wished her goodnight."

He had to leave Paris precipitately. (After accusing an adventurer named Santis of stealing a diamond ring, Casanova ran him through with his sword.) His objective was Augsburg. Unluckily for him he made a stop at Strasbourg where he picked up two new friends, one "a pretty woman"—inevitably—and the other her "protector", a man named Desarmoises.

For once Casanova now found himself on the wrong side of a confidence trick. These two swindlers not only robbed him of all he possessed but Renaud, the extremely pretty woman, passed on to him a dreadful disease which all but killed him. However, by taking eighty-six pills containing eighteen grains of manna, he recovered his health—and his buoyant optimism. It must be said that Casanova had an easy-come-easy-go attitude to money and he never wasted much time in bemoaning his ill-luck. As soon as he was on his feet again, he indulged in a double affair with his landlord's daughter and their cook— "they were both young and pretty," he writes, "and I imparted my love to both of them at once, for I had foreseen that, if I attacked them separately, I should conquer neither."

By now Madame d'Urfe in Paris was becoming impatient for her promised rejuvenation and Casanova realized that he could string her along no longer. So back to Paris he went to convince his benefactress that he meant to keep his word to her and make her be born again as a man. To do this he had to seek, in a spot pointed out to him by the spirits, a maiden who was the daughter of an adept in magic and who had to be impregnated by him with a male child. Madame d'Urfe was to receive the child into her arms the moment it was born and to keep it beside her for seven days. After that period she would die with her lips on the lips of the child who would in this fashion receive her "reasonable soul". When this had been done, Casanova had to look after the child until it reached its third birthday when Madame d'Urfe would regain consciousness—"and then I was to begin to initiate her into the perfect knowledge of the great work". Most important, the deluded Madame had to make a will in favour of the child whose guardian Casanova was to be until its thirteenth year.

Casanova chose a ballet dancer named Corticelli to play the role of the maiden—"this new part certainly came as a surprise to her," he comments. Off he went to Metz to meet her, loaded with presents and a hefty credit from the cornucopia of Madame d'Urfe.

Corticelli brought her mother with her because Casanova assured them that they would make their fortunes. He had to coach them for twelve days to make sure they would not slip up with Madame d'Urfe, to whom he wrote that he was on his way back to her with the virgin, last of the family of Lascaris who had once reigned at Constantinople. She replied that she would receive them at the old castle of Pont-Carré, near Paris. When they arrived there on the day appointed the false princess was accorded all honours, given a bed next to Madame d'Urfe's and the "operation" was fixed for the fourteenth day of the April moon. Casanova goes on:

> "On that day we had a temperate supper, after which I went to bed. Quarter of an hour afterwards Madame d'Urfe came, leading the virgin Lascaris. She undressed her, scented her, cast a lovely veil over her body, and when the princess was laid beside me she remained, wishing to be present at an operation which was to result in her being born again in the course of nine months. The act was consummated in form, and then Madame d'Urfe left us alone for the rest of the night, which was well employed . . . afterwards I asked the oracle if Lascaris had conceived. That might well be, for I had spared nothing to that intent, but I thought it more prudent to make the oracle reply that the operation had failed. . . ."

Alas, the phoney princess became a trifle greedy, being eager to get her hands on Madame d'Urfe's jewels, and Casanova had to persuade the Lady Bountiful that their "princess" had been possessed by an evil spirit so that she would disbelieve anything she said and, for good measure, he added he must search for another virgin whose purity must be under the protection of more powerful spirits! To obtain guidance on this new quest, he suggested that Madame d'Urfe write to the moon. Now let him tell in his own words how he arranged for the moon to reply:

> "I had made all the necessary preparations in a room of the ground floor of the house, the letter which was to fall from the moon, in reply to Madame d'Urfe's epistle, being in my pocket.

At a little distance from the chamber of ceremonies I had placed a large bath filled with lukewarm water and perfume pleasing to the deity of the night, into which we were to plunge at the hour of the moon, which fell at one o'clock.

"When we had burnt incense, we sprinkled the essences appropriated to the cult of Selenis; holding the letter concealed in my left hand, with the right I graciously led Madame d'Urfe to the brink of the bath. Here stood an alabaster cup containing spirits of wine which I kindled, repeating magical words which I did not understand but which she said after me, giving me the letter addressed to Selenis. I burnt the letter in the flame of the spirits, beneath the light of the moon, and the credulous lady told me she saw the characters she had traced ascending in the rays of the planet.

"We then got into the bath, and the letter, which was written in silver characters on green paper, appeared on the surface of the water in the course of ten minutes. As soon as Madame d'Urfe saw it she picked it up reverently and got out of the bath with me. We dried and scented ourselves. I told Madame d'Urfe that she might read the epistle which she had placed on a scented silk cushion. She obeyed, and I saw sadness visibly expressed on her features when she saw that her hypostasis (spiritual essence) was deferred until the spring of next year. The genius also said that the Lascaris could now only do her harm, and that she should consult me as to the best means of getting rid of her. . . ."

Once more he had successfully postponed the day on which he would have to do the impossible and made sure of another year's income from his gullible victim.

Casanova was thirty-eight before he made his first visit to England. The magnet for him here was his former lover—a female Casanova, if ever there was one—Therese Imer, who was then masquerading in London as Madame Cornelis, playing the fine lady and organizing subscription balls on a lavish scale, making certain that they had the necessary snob appeal for the London aristocracy. These two Venetian adventurers apparently agreed to operate in the capital together.

It may be of interest to English readers to quote his first impressions of their native land:

"The stranger who sets foot on English soil has need of a good deal of patience. The customs-house officials made a minute,

vexatious and even an impertinent perquisition . . . but I thought
resistance would be useless. The Englishman, who prides himself
on his strict adherence to the law of the land, is curt and rude in
his manner, and the English officials cannot be compared to the
French, who know how to combine politeness with the exercise
of their rights.

"England is different in every respect from the rest of Europe;
even the country has a different aspect, and the water of the
Thames has a taste peculiar to itself. Everything has its own
characteristics, and the fish, cattle, horses men and women are
of a type not found in any other land. Their manner of living is
wholly different from that of other countries, especially their
cookery. The most striking feature in their character is their
national pride; they exalt themselves above all other nations.

"My attention was attracted by the universal cleanliness, the
beauty of the country, the goodness of the roads, the reasonable
charge for posting, the quickness of the horses, although they
never go beyond a trot; and lastly, the construction of the towns
on the Dover road, Canterbury and Rochester for instance, though
large and populous, are like long passages, they are all length and
no breadth."

It was during his stay in London that the curtain came down
on the farce he had played out with Madame d'Urfe as he
received a letter announcing her death owing to an overdose of
a liquid she called "The Panacea". Her will left all her wealth
to the son or daughter that should be born of her, as she declared
she was with child. Casanova was named as the governor of the
child who never was—which annoyed him greatly as he said it
would make him the laughing-stock of Paris.

The cosmopolitan adventurer, however, found London too
much for him—he confesses that his experiences there ended
his career as a devil-may-care, love-'em-and-leave-'em gallant.
The fact is that he proved easy prey for a family of unscrupulous
women—a grandmother, her three daughters and a beautiful
granddaughter known in London as The Charpillon. They
cashed in on Casanova's overweening vanity, on his arrogant
confidence that no woman could for long withstand his fatal
charm. By employing the oldest bait in that form of angling,
repeatedly promising to bite on his hook and always eluding
it, The Charpillon kept him dangling until in the end he con-

templated suicide and actually set out for the Thames with lead weights in his pockets. His futile pursuit of this charmer landed him in Newgate Gaol for beating her up. Here is his description of that experience:

"When I got to this abode of misery and despair, a hell such as Dante might have conceived, a crowd of wretches, some of whom were to be hanged in the course of the week, greeted me by deriding my elegant attire. I did not answer them and they began to get angry and to abuse me. . . ."

Luckily he was quickly bailed out by his tailor and wine merchant. He was so distracted and thwarted by his elusive siren that he bought a parrot for ten guineas and taught it to say in French this sentence: "The Charpillon is a bigger whore than her mother." The bird, it seems, became the talk of London and achieved an article in the *St. James's Chronicle* with the comment that the ladies whom the parrot insulted must be very poor and friendless, or they would have bought it at once but, the writer went on, "the parrot's teacher has no doubt made the bird an instrument of his vengeance and has displayed his wit in doing so; he ought to be an Englishman".

Casanovist researchers have dug up the history of The Charpillon's family (all prostitutes on the distaff side), from the police records of the time. It appears that these disreputable women plied a prosperous trade both in Paris and London. It seems remarkable that a rake of Casanova's experience should have fallen into their clutches but he admits that he could not resist the lure of possessing The Charpillon whom he describes as "a born actress".

Moping around London alone after his shattering experience with these harpies, Casanova went to dine by himself in the Canon Tavern. There he met Baron Stenau who invited him to join his mistress, "an alluring English woman", and himself at a table. After the meal they played dice and the baron lost a hundred guineas. The baron left, ostensibly to get the money, and Casanova took advantage of his absence to seduce the mistress. Baron Stenau returned with a bill of exchange for £500 drawn on a reputable banking house in Cadiz and said he was having difficulty getting it discounted. Casanova not only volunteered to have the bill paid and send the baron the balance but also bought his mistress from him for ten guineas. Alas, his London luck did not change, for he contracted venereal disease from the mistress, which nearly cost him his life, and the bill of exchange turned out to be a forgery, which would have cost him his neck had he not fled to France.

Feeling that he had exhausted his welcome in the west Casanova now turned his face eastwards. So to Berlin where he seems to have found favour with Frederick the Great, thence to Russia, where he had three interviews with Catherine the Great in her summer garden on the River Neva, and to Poland where, after a promising start, he antagonized the nobility, fought a duel with Count Xavier Branicki and eventually was given twenty-four hours to leave the country by King Stanislas. On these non-stop travels he seems to have repeated again and again the bizarre experience of being welcomed by the distinguished people of each country he visited only to be hounded out by the police. This happened in Rome in 1745, Paris in 1759, Cologne, Stuttgart and Florence in 1760, Turin in 1762, Warsaw in 1766, Vienna and Paris in 1767, Madrid and Barcelona in 1768. Clearly, at forty, he was a marked man in almost every big town in Europe.

After his expulsion from Spain, Casanova was cured of his wanderlust and longed to return to his native city, Venice, still unhappily barred to him because of his notorious escape from the Leads. For five years he travelled up and down Italy, bringing all the influence he could to bear on the State Inquisitors to grant him amnesty.

Back at Ancona where his Odyssey had begun so long before, he indulged in a backward glance . . . he writes:

"When I thought it over it was quite a shock to find that this was thirty years ago, for thirty years is a long period in a man's life. What a difference I found between my youth and my middle age! I could scarcely recognize myself. I was then happy, but now unhappy; then all the world was before me, and the future seemed a gorgeous dream, and now I was obliged to confess that my life was all in vain. I might live twenty years more, but I felt that the happy time was passed away, and the future seemed all dreary. I reckoned up my forty-seven years, and saw fortune fly away . . .

these are the thoughts of declining years and not of youth. The young man looks only to the present, believes that the sky will always smile upon him, and laughs at philosophy as it vainly preaches of old age, misery, repentance, and, worst of all, abhorred death. . . ."

At last, in September, 1774, the Venetian consul brought him the long-awaited news that the newly-elected Council of Ten and the three new inquisitors had granted his pardon. He was free to return to his own city. His final sojourn in Venice lasted eight years but it is not described in his Memoirs which break off abruptly (and characteristically) with the words "Three years later I saw her again at Padua"—he is writing of an old lover —"her daughter had become a charming girl and our acquaintance was renewed in the tenderest manner."

The chronicle of these years compiled only recently from outside sources leaves little room to doubt that this veteran roué, card-sharp and swindler became a secret agent for the Venetian Government and made reports to the Inquisitorial tribunal on (of all things!) the corruption of public morals!

Whether his own hypocrisy sickened him or whether once again he went too far, the fact is that, at fifty-eight he left Venice and became a wanderer—through the Tyrol to Austria, Holland, Belgium and eventually to Paris where he suffered, for him, the greatest indignity of all—to be ignored, even by the police! He found himself confronted by that last desperate expedient for such men as he—to look for employment. In Bohemia he fell in with a young nobleman, Count Waldstein-Wartenberg, whose interest in the occult gave Casanova a chance of making an impression. The result was an invitation to visit the count's ancestral castle at Dux, near Teplitz—a visit which was to last, with short breaks, until his death fourteen years later. Here Casanova compiled his *magnum opus*, six volumes on human science, philosophy and political wisdom which were destined to gather dust, unread. Here, too, he elaborated the biographical notes he had made during his colourful life-time and, as he worked, thoroughly enjoying the unbridled licence and worldly-wise cynicism which he allowed himself in this "distraction" from his more serious labours, he had all the while the conviction that his Memoirs would never be published.

His last years were spent in the library at Dux where he grumbled incessantly about the food, about slights to his position. The sad fact is that libertines should die young. When the end came for him, on 4 June, 1798, at the age of seventy-three, his final words were: "I have lived as a philosopher and die as a Christian."

Strange to reflect that his memorial is one of the most divertingly scandalous books ever published and that, because of it, the name of Casanova will endure so long as there are men and women left to make love.

Chapter 9

ADOLF HITLER

THE very mention of Adolf Hitler's name never failed to produce a spasm of apprehension or anger in the English-speaking world from the day he burst on to the world stage in 1933 until he fired his last shot—into his own mouth—on 30 April, 1945. Throughout the Second World War—history will call it Hitler's War—that name was, to his enemies, synonymous with evil. Yet to the Germans he led it spelt at first Hope, Glory, Victory and at last despair, ruin, defeat. Now that almost a score of years have passed since his final gesture in a Berlin underground bunker closed the most momentous period of our times, it is possible to put the man in perspective, to submit him to cool-headed analysis, perhaps even to reach a verdict on his significance as weighed in the scales of human values.

Like those other towering figures of revolution, Napoleon and Lenin, Adolf Hitler approached his destiny with such crushing disadvantages that if he had made a reputation even in his own district it would have been remarkable. For such a man to tyrannize first all Germany and then most of Europe staggers belief.

Hitler sprang from country stock rooted in a peasant community sixty miles north-west of Vienna—he was not even a citizen of the Fatherland he was to speak about with such emotion. His father, Alois Schicklgruber was legitimized by his grandfather's declaration and the name was altered in the baptismal register to Alois Hitler. The son was never known by any other name than Adolf Hitler—despite the favourite taunt by Allied war-time propagandists who packed as much contempt as they could into the name Schicklgruber.

Adolf's father was a cobbler who "got on"—he became a minor Customs official. Adolf was the third child of his third marriage. His half-sister Angela was the only relation with

163

whom he kept up any sort of intimacy. Indeed Angela's daughter, Geli Raubal, was the only woman he every truly loved—and his love brought her a tragic and untimely death.

Although the Nazi myth-makers have done their best to prove that their Führer was a born leader, there is no evidence that Adolf distinguished himself in any way as a boy. What did demonstrate itself early in his life was ruthless determination to get his own way over his father, who wanted him to become a civil servant. Hitler tells in *Mein Kampf* how he thwarted parental authority by refusing to work at any subject in school except those that interested him. He hoped to be an artist but failed to get a School Leaving Certificate and later was rejected by the Vienna Academy of Fine Arts. He tried to switch to architecture, but here again could not gain admission as a student.

When his mother died in 1908, Adolf Hitler found himself alone, penniless and without a trade. Thirty years later Der Führer broke his journey to Vienna (on his way to declare the Anschluss) to lay a wreath on his mother's grave.

Hitler himself has described his early years in Vienna (from 1909-13) as the unhappiest of his life—"the years in which I had to earn my daily bread, first as a casual labourer, then as a painter of little trifles". Even so, he glosses over much of the evidence now available about that period of his Kampf. For instance, he omits to mention the nights spent on park benches and in cafés, or his spell in doss-houses which lasted, according to Konrad Heiden who pierced the evidence together, from 1908 to 1913.

According to the records of the Vienna police court, Hitler sued another inmate of the doss-house, a tramp named Hanisch, for cheating him out of a small sum. Indeed Hanisch's description of his first meeting with Hitler is also on record:

"There sat next to me a man with nothing on except an old torn pair of trousers—Hitler. His clothes were being cleaned of lice, since for days he had been wandering about without a roof and in a terribly neglected condition."

Surely, in all recorded history, there has never been a success story equal to this—from doss-house to Reich Chancellery.

Until the outbreak of the First World War Hitler scratched a precarious livelihood in Vienna, and later in Munich, by drawing crude advertisements and posters. He seems to have been lazy and moody, with a marked distaste for regular work but capable of bursts of activity—a strange amalgam of ambition and indolence. He read a lot, but as a dabbler and not as a student. He used the public library to burrow into religious history, occultism and yoga. Even at this time his few acquaintances noticed his vehemence in airing his pet "hates"—the greatest of these being the Jews. Indeed his remorseless hatred of the Jews provides a monotonous theme for all his adult life: he never stopped excoriating them from his first soap-box to his last will and testament.

Of these early days Hitler was to write:

> "A view of life and a definite outlook on the world shaped in my mind and became the granite basis of my conduct at that time. Since then I have extended that foundation very little, I have changed nothing in it. Vienna was a hard school, but it taught me the most profound lessons of my life."

Certainly he applied these lessons throughout his subsequent career as rabble-rouser, politician, statesman, dictator and war leader. The doss-house taught him to trust no one, to lie convincingly, to play astutely on fear, greed and envy. Politics added other ingredients—how to fan the lust for power in his fellow men, and, above all, how to use all these weaknesses for his own unscrupulous ends. The career of Adolf Hitler offers a blistering commentary on the statesmen of Europe during the 'thirties—that, although having greater advantages of birth and breeding, their public morality rose no higher than that of an occupant of a Viennese doss-house.

His years in the gutter produced in Hitler no feeling of kinship with the depressed members of the working-class of his time. He had nothing but contempt for their efforts to improve their lot by combination either in trades unions or workers' parties. He indignantly refused to associate himself with these efforts and persistently scorned the status of a working man. He preferred to believe that the Social Democratic Party was a secret weapon of "World Jewry".

He tells in *Mein Kampf* of his first sight of a Jew . . . "One day, when passing through the Inner City" [of Vienna]:

> "I suddenly encountered a phenomenon in a long caftan and wearing black side-locks. My first thought was: Is this a Jew? I watched the man stealthily and cautiously, but the longer I gazed at this strange countenance and examined it section by section, the more the question shaped itself in my brain: Is this a German? For the first time in my life I bought myself some anti-Semitic pamphlets for a few pence.
>
> "Was there any shady undertaking, any form of foulness, especially in cultural life, in which at least one Jew did not participate? On putting the probing knife carefully to that kind of abscess one immediately discovered, like a maggot in a putrescent body, a little Jew who was often blinded by the sudden light."

Here began an obsession that grew by what it fed on and which was to culminate in the most blood-curdling policy ever undertaken by an allegedly civilized nation—to exterminate the Jewish race. According to the figures given at the Nuremberg Trials of the major Nazi war-criminals, of the 9,600,000 Jews living in Europe at the outbreak of Hitler's War, 60 per cent were exterminated—5,700,000 Jews were missing from the countries in which they formerly lived, and of that total more than 4,500,000 could not be accounted for by the normal death-rate or by emigration, nor were they included among the displaced persons.

Hitler believed that inequality was an absolute law of Nature. He despised the fundamentals of a democratic society—freedom of speech, Press and Parliament. His megalomania was chronic —even as a jobless, half-starved pauper he never wavered in his belief that he was one of nature's superior beings.

One must seek an answer to the question: how could a man like this, whose political thinking was crude and unoriginal (his views were picked up from the lower levels of the nationalist and anti-Semitic newspapers and magazines of his doss-house days), how could such a man achieve world eminence in our sophisticated and civilized society? And the answer is that he used his undeniable gift of oratory to create a mass-movement by means of which he could exploit every twentieth-century technique with complete ruthlessness, to play on the emotions and weaknesses of mobs, to put over the Big Lie and ultimately to apply with remorseless thoroughness the classical precepts of tyranny.

The First World War was a godsend for Hitler, as for thousands of other shiftless nondescripts who could find no niche in their society. Yet it is claimed that, when he left Vienna for Munich in 1913, he did so to escape military service for the Hapsburg State. He failed to report for his army duties, was traced to Munich and ordered to present himself for examination in Linz. He sent an ingratiating reply, pleading poverty and asking to be allowed to report at Salzburg, thus reducing his travelling expenses. This was conceded, he turned up for his examination—and was rejected on grounds of poor health.

When the Germans marched into Austria in 1938, he ordered the Gestapo to make a thorough search in Linz for his records of that period—and he was furious when they failed to produce them. An Austrian politician astutely held on to them and later made them available to Josef Greiner for his book, *The End of the Hitler Myth*. Greiner had shared a room with Hitler during his Munich stay.

Nevertheless, of the declaration of war by Germany following the assassination of the Archduke Ferdinand at Sarajevo in 1914, Hitler writes in *Mein Kampf*: "For me these hours came as a deliverance from the distress that had weighed upon me during the days of my youth. . . ." He addressed a formal petition to King Ludwig of Bavaria seeking permission to volunteer, although an Austrian, for a Bavarian regiment. The request was granted and Hitler was enrolled in the 16th Bavarian Reserve Infantry Regiment. Throughout the war he served as a runner between company and regimental headquarters. It was a dangerous enough job and kept him at or near the front for four years.

Hitler won the Iron Cross (Second Class) in December, 1914, and was awarded a cross of the First Class in 1918 when holding the rank of corporal. Many jibes, of course, were hurled during the Second World War at "the upstart corporal" but it is clear that he carried out his soldiering duties bravely and conscientiously and there is no evidence that he ever sought promotion to a higher rank. Apparently he was a soldier apart, receiving no letters or parcels from home and showing no interest in leave or women. He himself often referred to the "stupendous impression produced on me by war—the greatest of all experiences".

He emerged with one burning conviction, that physical force by itself can only be defensive, but allied to "a new spiritual doctrine" (his word for it was *Weltanschaung*, or "world view") it must prove victorious. It was to take him far along the road to fame—and, finally, to infamy. Out of this conviction came the idea of moulding a new movement which would win over the masses by means of propaganda on a massive and un-scrupulous scale. Hitler played up for all it was worth his own dual rôle as a man of the people and an ordinary soldier of the First World War. Although he could never have achieved his fantastic power over the great mass of the people without propaganda, it is also true to say that, without his own tremendous will-power and belief in himself, he would have remained a mob-orator.

With the war behind him Hitler, now thirty, unheard of and unconsidered, went relentlessly in pursuit of his destiny with a set of fixed ideas and prejudices—hatred of the Jews; contempt for democracy, internationalism and peace; an intolerant nationalism; a rooted belief in authoritarian forms of govern-ment, and in force as the instrument of a new world order. All he needed was a chance to put his ideas into practice. The chance came with the confusion and disintegration of the German Empire which followed the disaster of defeat in war. It is undeniable that Hitlerism could never have succeeded simply through propaganda and the ingenuity of Nazi campaigning methods had it not appealed to the mood and desires of a large proportion of the German people.

This can be demonstrated by the sensational rise in the Nazi vote in the Reichstag Elections from 1928, when Hitler was regarded as a crackpot Bavarian agitator, to 1932 when they became the most popular party in Germany. In 1928 they polled 810,000 votes; in 1932 it rose to 13,745,000. In those four years Hitler's programme had captured the middle-class parties, the Nationalists, and the young people voting for the first time.

Although Hitler was an out-and-out revolutionary, he achieved power for his party and himself by constitutional means backed, of course, by the strong-arm tactics of what amounted to his private army, the S.A. (*Sturm Abteilungen* or Storm Troopers). He launched his revolution, perfectly legitimately, *only after* he won power in 1933, although his accession to the office of Reich Chancellor was the result of a shabby political deal with the "Old Gang" of German politicians whom he had never ceased to attack with his usual soapbox vehemence. Only after supreme power inside Germany was his did the full extent of his megalomania reveal itself. He was not in the slightest degree interested in the administrative work of government, only in advancing his own power. Thus, although he bore final responsibility for the manifestations of his régime he left his party bosses—Goering, Goebbels, Himmler and Ley —to run Germany as they saw fit, under his general policy direction. Each of these men set about building up his own empire—which was all right with Hitler, just so long as they remembered that *he* could have no equal.

Perhaps the most astonishing feature of the Hitler era— 1938-45—was the refusal of Britain and America to take him seriously as a world figure. To most people in the English-speaking communities he remained a figure of fun, a cartoon character distinguished by a wandering lock of hair, a smudgy moustache and preposterous, strutting mannerisms. It seemed impossible that such a comic creation could bring our kind of world to ruin and destruction. Even during the darkest days of the war the hard-pressed British people, in and out of uniform, were ready to laugh at Hitler's reported antics and sayings, although by that time no one any longer underestimated the deadly menace of Germany's armed might.

Yet by any test which the decent and civilized man would apply, Adolf Hitler was the embodiment of wickedness. His fiendish policy of race extermination would not have ended with the Jews. There is plenty of evidence from the life of Heydrich that the Slav peoples were next on the list; a beginning was to have been made with the Czechs and then slaughter was to have moved eastward to Russia! This man was prepared to bring about the annihilation of scores of millions of his fellow human beings to perpetuate in power his so-called master-race. Yet Hitler did not even have the excuse of extreme patriotism. When all was lost, he would not accept defeat but preferred to sacrifice millions of his own soldiers rather than his own vanity. He saw in the sufferings and defeat of the German people only their betrayal of himself.

Was Hitler "a man possessed", as many distinguished diplomats believed? Did he himself genuinely believe that he was a chosen instrument of Fate ("I go the way Providence dictates with the assurance of a sleepwalker," he once said), or was his whole performance bogus, a ruthless exploitation of the hypnotic effect his eyes and voice had on others? These are the fascinating conundrums set by this strange and sinister figure. Considering it in the nineteen-sixties, with the passions aroused by the living Hitler now thoroughly cooled, the answer may well be that he cynically exploited his influence on others to such effect that he was deluded by his own myth. He began to believe in his own magic and, in the end, was destroyed by his imagined "invincibility".

He dreamed of a vast empire embracing all Europe and much of Asia, of breeding biologically pre-selected élite, and establishing a New Order of blood and iron to take the place of the crumbling liberal world of the past century. This meant reducing to abject slavery whole nations and entailed the extermination of entire races, but such was the bent of his disordered imagination and to that his treatment of the Jews, the Poles and the Russians bears brutal testimony.

Although in his early years he appeared gawky and awkward, he trained himself to play the part of Adolf Hitler with such thoroughness that he became a consummate actor. He had the ability to absorb himself utterly in his rôle, convincing himself of the truth of all he said—at the time he said it. He was able at will to develop what seemed to others to be uncontrollable rages; then his face changed colour and became swollen with fury, his voice rose to a high-C scream, his arms gyrated wildly, his fists thundered a tattoo on table or wall—then suddenly the fit was over, he smoothed his hair, tidied his collar and his voice became normal.

He had other attributes of the accomplished actor. When he

wanted to win someone over he could display great charm and exercised a gift of personal magnetism to an almost irresistible degree. But when he meant to frighten he could switch on the most brutal and threatening language. Take his meeting with Kurt von Schuschnigg, Federal Chancellor of Austria, at the time chosen by Hitler to grab his native land. Hitler was waiting on the steps of the Berghof, his mountain retreat in Bavaria, when Schuschnigg arrived. Hitler at once led him to his study for a private talk before lunch. Schuschnigg began to make some polite remark about the view when Hitler brushed it aside and launched into a tirade about the course of Austrian policy. Schuschnigg's attempts to defend himself were shouted down. Unless Schuschnigg accepted all Hitler's demands at once he would settle matters by force. Hitler did not detail these demands but went on:

"Think it over, Herr Schuschnigg, think it over well. I can only wait until this afternoon. If I tell you that, you will do well to take my words literally. I don't believe in bluffing—all my past is proof of that."

The indignant monologue lasted two hours, then Hitler led his guest in to lunch and throughout the meal was charm itself. There were two of Hitler's generals at the table.

Hitler's simplification of diplomacy into "Take-my-terms-or-take-the-consequences" was so successful over Austria, backed by the well-tried Nazi methods of inflated grievances, hysterical threats and strong-arm incidents provoked by his Storm Troopers, that there seemed every inducement to try it on again. He did—and the next prize was Czechoslovakia.

Throughout these self-induced crises, Hitler showed his utter contempt for the civilized world with its respect for law, its concern for the rights of small nations and its abhorrence of the settlement of disputes by force. The year 1938—the year of his annexation of Austria and the Sudetenland, the year of the shameful Munich Agreement which dismembered Czecho-slovakia and bought time for Britain and France to prepare themselves for war—faced the entire Western world with a problem which most people assumed had been solved for ever, the problem of dealing with an unscrupulous and destructive megalomaniac. The undisputed leader of a powerful nation was prepared to lie, to cheat, to invent, to browbeat, to bully, to blackmail or to fight to overcome all opposition to any demand; every concession to him became a prelude to his next demand. He showed the twentieth century, which prided itself on its emancipation from primitive instincts, how hollow were fine words and noble ideals backed by no determination to defend them by force of arms. He brought ignominy to those who appeased him and augmented the power of another ideology as ruthless as his own. Hitler left the world a fearful legacy.

His racial prejudices are, of course, well known, but his megalomania extended in all directions. He believed that he could have been a great artist or architect—his views on art were held with the same opinionated dogmatism as his views on international affairs—and, as usual, he would tolerate no contrary opinion. He passionately detested all forms of modernism—hence his Exhibition of Degenerate Art held in Munich in 1937 alongside his hand-picked exhibits of German art which revealed his pronounced preference for the classical. Always on his desk was scrap paper for his idle sketching.

His taste in music was limited and bigoted—Wagner, of course, some of Beethoven, and in light music his fondness for Lehar's *The Merry Widow* caused much amusement among his detractors. He was a film fan and never missed a Garbo picture.

As an architect manque, he liked to rebuild. After he came to power he reconstructed the Chancellery and his house in Bavaria, on the Obersalzberg—the famous Berghof. He loved spaciousness—big rooms, thick carpets and tapestries. This apart, his tastes were simple and changed little after his ascent to greatness: he enjoyed fast cars, cream cakes, sweets, flowers and dogs. And he relished the company of pretty women. For their part many women were fascinated by his hypnotic personality. During the war, when extreme vilification of our arch-enemy was fashionable, his sex life was the subject of all manner of tittle-tattle—he was impotent, he was a pervert, he was a syphilite and so on. The undeniable fact is that no woman had ruled his actions and decisions. On all known evidence he showed real interest in only two women—his niece, Geli Raubal, and Eva Braun, whom he married on the day before he committed suicide with her.

Geli's mother, Angela Raubal, took the girl with her when she went to keep house for Hitler on the Obersalzberg in 1925. Geli was then seventeen, attractive and unaffected, with ambitions to be a singer. For the next six years she became Hitler's constant companion. There is little doubt that Hitler fell deeply in love with this girl twenty years younger than himself. He was inordinately jealous and refused to allow her any sort of life of her own. He turned out to be a domestic tyrant as well as a national and international one. She was not allowed to go to Vienna to have her voice trained and she was forbidden even to strike up a friendship with any other man. It is also alleged that she was repelled and disgusted by the nature of the demands Hitler made upon her. Whatever the truth of that charge, she was found shot dead in Hitler's flat in Munich on 18 September, 1931. The inquest verdict was suicide. No motive was suggested. It has been said that Hitler himself pulled the trigger in a passion of jealousy.

Whether he was responsible, directly or indirectly, for her untimely end, Hitler collapsed under the shock of it and for weeks moped alone, refusing all callers. For the rest of his life he never spoke of her without emotion; her room at Berghof remained as she left it, her picture hung in his room in Berlin and Munich and was decorated with flowers on the anniversary of her birth and death. All this could have been proof of his abiding love or, as the cynics believe, of unforgettable remorse. The answer to that riddle died with Hitler.

His other favourite, Eva Braun, has had much more of the spotlight than Geli Raubal. The daughter of a working-class Bavarian family, she too was twenty years his junior. She met Hitler while she was employed in the shop of his photographer, Heinrich Hoffmann. After Geli's death she became his mistress —Hitler provided her with a little villa in Munich, a car and an allowance. Eventually—in 1936—she was installed in the Berghof as Hausfrau and sat on Hitler's left hand at lunch. This affaire was managed with the greatest tact—he rarely allowed her to appear in public with him in Berlin and she was ordered to stay in her room during major occasions, receptions and official dinners. Eva Braun was at any rate unswervingly loyal to her Führer and he seemed to become sincerely fond of her.

She was a woman of very few pretensions and made no attempt to play the confidante or the intellectual. Her interests were commonplace, mainly sport, animals and clothes; she liked trashy romantic novels and films. She also enjoyed dancing and smoking, but she had to do both in secret for Hitler disapproved. Eva was certainly subjected to the same petty tyrannies as Geli. Twice she too attempted suicide (or pretended to), which caused Hitler great trepidation, since he was most anxious to avoid a second scandal of this sort.

Did Eva Braun bear Hitler any children? If she did, positively no proof exists and it seems extremely unlikely. She certainly deserved an Iron Cross (First Class) for Hitler must have been an appalling partner to live with. Always the egotist, shrouded in his own greatness, vindictive to a degree, pursuing mean and spiteful vengeance even in trivial matters, incapable of generosity of spirit, consumed with jealousies, he cannot have been every woman's ideal man. He was not noted for his sense of humour except that he took malicious pleasure in the misfortunes of others and could not stand a joke against himself. He was incapable of feeling compassion, regarding mercy and pity as base human weaknesses. Men had to be hard and ruthless at all times if they were fit to belong to the Master Race. A man, you might think, that not even a mother could love.

Perhaps the most striking aspect of Hitler is the way in which the other important figures of his time underestimated his political acumen before his 1938 coups. His fellow-dictator, Mussolini—the young Hitler regarded him as the greatest states-man of the age—referred to him after their first meeting as "that mad little clown" and "a dangerous fool". This proved to be a naïve appraisal. Although in almost every sense uneducated, Hitler possessed considerable intellectual power. He was convinced that mankind had evolved to a high level through struggle and that the law of nature was the eternal victory of the strong over the weak. The ability to seize superiority by force is determined by race, and all that mankind had achieved, wrote Hitler in *Mein Kampf*, had been the work of the Aryan race.

In each nation only a part could be described as Aryans, the élite which stamped its ideas on the whole population (in Germany the Nazi Party in general and the Storm Troopers in particular). Hitler opposed the concept of "race" to the democratic belief in the equality of man before God; to the idea of personal liberty he opposed the superior claims of the *Volk* which is permanent, as the individual is transitory. By this manufactured philosophy he could justify both the right of the German Volk to trample on inferior peoples such as the coarse Slavs, and the right of the Nazi élite to stamp out all opposition in Germany. Such half-baked ideas were not original thinking but the frightening thing about Hitler was the will-power he showed in translating such fantasies into realities.

Never was Hitler's real character more thoroughly exposed than in the vengeance he exacted from Yugoslavia in 1941 when he chose to assume that little nation had dared to cross the purpose of mighty Germany, then all-conquering. A group of Yugoslav officers, rebelling against their government's slavish subservience to the Axis, carried through a successful coup d'état in Belgrade on the night of 26-27 March. Without waiting to find out whether this coup was short-lived or, indeed, whether it materially affected his plans for a campaign to sweep the British out of Greece, Hitler decided on the complete destruction of the nation "for its insolence". By 5 April—ten days after the coup—Hitler ordered his bombers to wipe out the Yugoslav capital. More than 17,000 people perished in the Belgrade bombing raids in what Hitler officially called "Operation Punishment".

It was this same insufferable and overweening arrogance in his character that brought him to disaster in Russia. The successful campaigns of 1939 and 1940 convinced him that the German armed forces under his direction were invincible. He would listen to no warning against his plan to invade the east. He was certain that the war in Russia would be over in three months at the outside; accordingly, he refused to take precautions for a winter campaign. "We have only to kick in the door," he told one of his generals, "and the whole rotten structure will come crashing down."

The ruthlessness of his method of conducting this war horrified his military chiefs. His directive was that the recognized rules of war would not apply to this campaign. He laid it down that the food-producing areas of Russia were to supplement German Europe's supplies not only while the war in the East lasted, but

175

afterwards too. It would be difficult to unearth a more calculated example of man's inhumanity to man than an official German memorandum summarizing plans for "Barbarossa" (the operational title for Hitler's onslaught on Russia) which begins:

> "The war can only be continued if all the armed forces are fed by Russia in the third year of the war. There is no doubt that, as a result, many millions of people will be starved to death if we take out of the country the things we need."

Another German document states that "many tens of millions in the industrial areas will become redundant and will either die or have to emigrate to Siberia".

Just as his policy for the war in the East condemns Hitler as an inhuman monster, so his repeated treachery to his friends and personal associates convicts him of the most debased wickedness. The case of Ernst Roehm will serve to illustrate the selfish way in which Hitler sacrificed those to whom he owed so much to gain his own ambitious ends. Major Roehm's support was invaluable to the Nazi leader during his early days of struggle. This army officer, of considerable ability, exercised great influence in the bitter underground of political conspirators, among First World War veterans, and numbers of secret Defence Leagues in the disintegrated Germany of the nineteen-twenties, all of which provoked such a rich breeding-ground for the Nazis. His was the organizing genius which built up the S.A.—the political strong-arm squads on whose backs Hitler rode to power.

In 1934 Chancellor Hitler gave him a seat on his Cabinet. A letter from Hitler to Roehm at the beginning of that year was couched in terms of the warmest gratitude, thanking him for his "imperishable services to National Socialism". A few months later, on the morning of 30 June, Roehm was dragged from bed, taken to a Munich prison and, by order of Hitler, shot as an alleged ringleader of a *putsch* which bore all the evidence of a Goering-Himmler invention. The purge which followed allowed Hitler to dispose by execution of all the able men who could be regarded as rivals.

So much for Hitler's international morality, so much for his personal friendship. What of his patriotism? He never tired of telling his vast audiences of how he devoted all his waking moments to his beloved Germany. When all was lost and he was facing death and the annihilation of his régime, Hitler lived out the last days of April, 1945, in the Berlin bunker with the sound of the Russian guns booming in his ears, heaping reproaches on everyone but himself. He stormed against Goering, against German officers who did not observe his "No Retreat" orders literally, against the German people, but not one word of regret, not a sign of remorse did he give for sacrificing millions of his soldiers when all resistance was hopeless, for his own errors in preparing for a quick war in Russia, in ignoring all expert opinion and trusting only to his own infallibility, his "intuition".

His last message to his people included one characteristic piece of deceit. He chose the coward's way out of his responsibilities by committing suicide, he did not lead the remnants of the Nazi faithful to a hero's death as he expected his own officers to do; the text of his Will and Political Testament dictated in the early hours of 29 April, deliberately conceals this shameful betrayal of the armed forces and the nation.

Picture the scene in the Chancellery air-raid shelter, buried 50 ft. beneath the ground and built in two storeys covered with a canopy of reinforced concrete, as the wickedest man of our time realized that his hours were numbered. Hitler and Eva Braun had a suite of six rooms in the lower of the storeys. This was split into eighteen small rooms and known as the *Führerbunker*. Hitler had a bedroom and a study, the sole decoration of which was a portrait of Frederick the Great. Eva had a bedsitting-room, a bathroom and a dressing-room. Goebbels and his wife occupied four rooms on the upper floor, Martin Bormann and his staff and the various service chiefs were in shelters built nearby. Non-stop air raids, the awareness that the hated Russians were in their capital, nervous prostration, despair and desperate fear—above all the presence of a man who was not only ill but on the edge of insanity: all these factors created an atmosphere which can be described only as sepulchral.

Yet there was Hitler, who by this time had lost all grasp of events, calling conference after conference, keeping up the delusion that victory could still be snatched from utter defeat. Then, on the night of 26 April, the Russians began shelling the Chancellery. The *Führerbunker* shook as masonry crashed into the courtyard. Even Hitler could delude himself no longer. On Saturday evening the final blow—a Reuter message—reached Hitler. It disclosed that Himmler had been in communication with Sweden's Count Bernadotte as a go-between to negotiate peace terms with the Western Allies. Hitler went berserk. That Himmler should betray him was the most bitter of all possible blows. Even at that late hour his thoughts turned to revenge. He called in Goebbels and Bormann. He lashed out orders to arrest Himmler at all costs.

He could count on but one human being to remain true—Eva Braun—and she should have her reward. So, between 1 a.m. and 3 a.m. on 29 April, Hitler married Eva. The ceremony was performed according to civil law by one of Goebbels' staff and took place in the map-room of the bunker. Goebbels and Bormann were present as witnesses. Then the bridal party returned to their suite, where they were joined by the Goebbels, Martin Bormann, Hitler's two secretaries, his adjutants and his cook. While champagne was being passed round Hitler retired to a private room with his secretary, Frau Junge, to whom he dictated his Will and Political Testament.

Some hours later on the 29th, news reached the bunker of the fate of Mussolini and his mistress, Clara Petacci, who had been shot on the shore of Lake Como, their bodies taken to Milan and hung upside down in a public square. Probably this decided Hitler—he would not be put on public exhibition after death. Now he began systematic preparations for taking his life. First he had his alsatian dog, Blondi, destroyed. Then he assembled his staff and walked along the line saying farewell. He gave Bormann a last order for his successor, Doenitz—"Proceed at once and mercilessly against all traitors." He lunched at 2 p.m. Then his chauffeur was ordered to send 200 litres of petrol to the Chancellery garden. Hitler fetched Eva from her room and they said farewell to the Goebbels for the second time. Hitler and Eva returned to their suite and closed the door. A few minutes later a shot was heard. The group outside went into the suite. Hitler was lying on a blood-drenched sofa—shot through the mouth, Eva lay by his right hand poisoned. It was 3.30 p.m., ten days after Hitler's 56th birthday.

So perished a tyrant whose dreams of grandeur were insatiable.

Chapter 10

RASPUTIN

To the last Czar of all-Russia and his neurotic half-English wife the tall Siberian peasant-mystic with the sonorous voice and the strange hynotic eyes was "Our Dear Friend". To his enemies, and they were many among the great personalities of Court and Government in St. Petersburg, Grigori Efimovich Rasputin with his unkempt beard and filthy black fingernails was "The Holy Devil" and "possessed of the devil", as he certainly was in the medieval sense of that term.

Wickedness takes many forms. Evil does not necessarily involve the monstrous deeds of a Nero or the massacres of a Genghis Khan. But, if abasement of the most noble and holy instincts and their exploitation for the gratification of a perverted creed's sexual lust be evil, then Rasputin must rank with the wickedest men of all time. By utilizing the phenomenon of his mystic powers to suggest that he was the human manifestation of divinity itself he seduced and ravaged hundreds, if not thousands of women, from princesses to prostitutes. In doing so he convinced nearly all of them that they had achieved "spiritual rebirth through sin".

Even today Rasputin remains an historical enigma. Whether he was a satanically inspired mystic or nothing more than a peculiarly cunning religious charlatan, he made a major contribution to the fall of the House of Romanov; and to that Russian Revolution which has exercised such a profound influence on human history in the half-century since his murder. For in these years immediately prior to the momentous events of October, 1917, Rasputin was in many respects the real ruler of Czarist Russia.

Yet the sly monk mystic-cum-satyr was not wholly evil. He brought peace and comfort to a tragic child, the sorely-tried heir to the Russian throne condemned to a miserable existence

179

by the haemophilia (bleeding disease) which he had inherited from his English royal forebears. To other humble souls Rasputin was a simple lovable man who brought them nothing but good. He was corrupt—and yet gave his goods to help the poor.

Neither friends nor enemies were able to analyse his extraordinary powers. But both concede them. Some claimed it was all due to hypnotism—but that seemed only part of the answer. There was certainly something oppressive in his kind, gentle, but at the same time sly and cunning, glance from his small still blue eyes. But even without looking at him people felt helpless under the domination of the powerful will which he seemed able to transmit by some unexplained power of telepathy. Even men who hated him, such as the French Ambassador of the day, could recognize this power and loathed it.

In women he produced something akin to religious madness. When he halted before them they experienced a thrill of ecstasy as though from some supreme religious experience. They became convinced that in the small unmoving eyes of the greasy Asiatic peasant before them they could see the Holy Ghost itself. They felt that his touch transmitted to their sinful bodies the grace that was in him; his kisses and embraces sanctified them as though, as in classical legend, they had intercourse with Jove himself.

This extraordinary person was the son of a Siberian village carter from the village of Pokrovskoe in the administrative district of Tobolsk where he was born in 1872. As a child "Grisha", as he was known to the family, was a wild, unruly and sometimes alarming boy. Even in his earliest years he had a curious interest in anything religious. In winter when curled before the great stove and immersed in the family holy book of pictures and verse he seemed transformed into a different being. It was not until he was twelve, however, that Grisha first gave a hint of these mystic qualities which in later years would make him the real ruler of the Czar and of Russia.

In some boyish escape Grisha and his elder brother fell into the nearby River Tura. His brother died from pneumonia. Grisha survived, much changed. He seemed in a permanent fever and soon lapsed into a semi-coma. He was moved to a bed in a dark corner behind the stove. One evening he lay there half-conscious while a group of angry peasants discussed who had stolen a horse from a nearby stable. Suddenly the boy jumped from his bed, leaped on the back of one of the most respectable peasants at the gathering and accused him of horse stealing. A secret check was made. The half-delirious boy was proved correct. Early next morning the superstitious Siberian peasants made the sign of the cross on the Rasputin door; clearly Grisha was "possessed".

His experience, however, produced little sign of grace. Young Rasputin became notorious as one of the most disorderly, drunken, and lecherous youths of the district. In his late teens he married, but it made little difference to the dissipated life he led. One day, however, when striding behind a plough he had a vision. He believed he saw the Virgin Mary in the sky amid a choir of hundreds of angels. He told no one except his plough-boy companion—but he was convinced that God had some special design for him.

In due course Grisha followed in the footsteps of his father and became the village carrier. He carried goods and passengers in one direction as far as the provincial capital of Tobolsk, and in the other to the monastery town of Verkhoture at the foot of the Urals. It was one of the passengers, whom Grisha drove to the monastery town, who brought about the revolution in his life. At that time Grisha was twenty-three years of age.

The passenger was a young monastic novice bound for the Verkhoture monastery. As they drove, novice and carrier discussed God and the Church. The young seminarist was astounded at the knowledge of the simple peasant. He tried to persuade Rasputin that he must not waste such gifts, and went on to expound a doctrine curiously at variance with that taught in the Russian Orthodox Church. This joyful doctrine maintained that even a sinful man could enjoy heavenly bliss if he would but follow the tenets of a mysterious "true faith in God".

Rasputin was enthralled. By the time he reached the monastery he had agreed to stay and join the half-monastic, half-agricultural community. Although considerable efforts were made to conceal the fact, it took Rasputin only a few days to discover that the brothers at Verkhoture were sharply divided—into jailers and prisoners. Soon he realized that the monks under supervision were open or secret adherents of heretical creeds—chiefly members of the "Khlysty" sect or "The People of God" sent to the monastery to be weaned from their heresy. This strange sect, founded two hundred years previously, drew its strength from a Freemason-like mystery. To protect its truth from profanation its members were ordered zealously to observe the externals of the Russian Orthodox "false faith". Their own rites were reserved for strange orgiastic festivals celebrated on Saturday nights in lonely barns or obscure peasant homesteads.

Little by little Rasputin learned the fundamentals of the "Khlysty" creed—that the Lord had re-appeared over and over again in the form of a Russian peasant; that wherever "The People of God" assembled the Holy Ghost descended among them and chose the worthiest as the earthly envelope so that Christ could become again incarnate. Henceforth the Siberian carter had but one aim—to achieve perfection according to the belief of "The People of God".

As soon as he had acquired as much of the doctrine as he felt was necessary Rasputin visited an anchorite who lived in the vicinity. To Rasputin's astonishment, after he had confessed his sins the saintly old man told him "Rejoice my son for the Lord has chosen you. Leave your wife and children and go forth and wander until you hear the earth speak. Then and only then return to the world."

For the next few years Rasputin lived a life of vagabondage wandering hither and thither across western Siberia. As he wandered he availed himself more and more of his sect's belief that marriage is intolerable and must be replaced by "marriages in the spirit" blessed not by a priest but by God himself.

As he wandered from village to village the monk-mystic made contact with the secret communities of "The People of God" and was initiated into the Saturday night orgies of the sect. As the years passed he discovered that the "Khlysty" dogma provided unusual opportunities for combining his powerful sensual lusts with his mystical ambitions.

In the usual pattern of the orgies, after preliminary hymn singing and liturgical chanting, pairs of men and women started to dance in time to the singing. Gradually excitement grew. When a state of ecstasy was reached the believers knew that the Holy Ghost was descending upon them. A peasant man and woman became "transformed" into Christ and the Virgin Mary. Round them the sectarians huddled weeping and trembling with rapture. Thereafter dancing was resumed. It quickly became wilder until at last it was completely unrestrained. The peasants bared their bodies to their waists and the "christ" flagellated them with a staff of fecundity. In a blasphemous representation of Christ throwing off mortality the sectarians discarded all their clothes. Some had convulsions. The lights went out. Women fell upon men and embraced and kissed them passionately. Then in "sinful encounter" the "People of God" rolled on the ground and copulated regardless of age or relationship. Only in this mad intoxication, they believed, was earthly consciousness and self will completely extinguished; for in "sinful encounter" the earthly ego lost influence and only the will of the invisible spirit prevailed.

It was during these orgies that Grigori Efimovich Rasputin first learned to understand the real meaning of the peculiar mystery of "rebirth through sin"; from thenceforth he was convinced that the only path to true submission and humility was through sinful encounter—through the casting away of the final barriers and the deepest self abasement in carnal sin.

For years, as he wandered through the Siberian borderlands, his family heard of Rasputin only by rumour. From time to time came reports that he had been seen deep in a forest surrounded by a troop of pretty girls. When their devotions were ended they danced and sang while Rasputin kissed and fondled his "sisters". When the dance reached a delirium the "prophet" shouted: "Abase yourself through sin—try your flesh." Of the forest orgies which followed the Siberian peasants dared speak only in whispers.

At last, after years of vagabondage, Rasputin, dirty, unkempt and looking like an old man, appeared at the door of the now substantial family home in Pokrovskoe. Abjuring all family life, he descended to the cellar. There, stretched out on the clammy stone floor, he mortified the sinful body and did penance. Long hours of groaning and lamentation were punctuated by brief bursts of jubilant psalm singing. At first his family thought he was mad. So overwhelming, however, was the power of his strange personality that soon they, too—his old father, his wife, and his three children—were induced to take part in his heretical devotions.

They in turn were joined by one villager after another who came to scoff and stayed to pray. Soon there was a steady stream of visitors to "the prophet", he made a particular impression on the girls and young women of the village. When they returned to the light of day after "communing" with him in his cellar their cheeks bore a delicate flush such as only love can bring to the face of a woman.

Only the venerable village priest was unimpressed. This saintly old man determined to beard the false prophet in his cellar. Watched by a huge crowd the priest entered the dungeon. A few minutes later the old man crawled out and took to his heels like a whipped cur. He was certain that he had narrowly escaped from the clutches of the anti-Christ himself. The priest reported the affair to his ecclesiastical superiors and a commission, headed by the local bishop, appeared in Pokrovskoe. They ordered that all who had communed with Rasputin must give evidence. First the pretty girls were heard in complete privacy. To the consternation of the commission they had nothing but the highest praise for the "holy Grisha". With glowing cheeks one after another stated he was "truly holy". Other peasants told the same story. Rasputin they asserted served God in deep contrition.

The bishop became furious. He sent a policeman to interrogate the alleged saint. But the local custodian of the law was also a peasant. After a few minutes in the cellar he reappeared shouting, "Father Grigori forgive me for my sins." He reported to the commission that he had seen nothing suspicious. The bishop decided that there was nothing to be done beyond keeping Rasputin under surveillance.

Within a fortnight the fame of the wonderful new "starets", as he was called, had spread beyond the confines of the district of Tobolsk. His persecution by the authorities merely increased that fame.

Three weeks after beginning his penance Rasputin suddenly appeared at the door of his home. With slow and dignified steps he approached a crowd of peasants who had quickly gathered. To a man they bowed down and, as he blessed them, kissed his hands, kissed the hem of his kaftan and cried, "Father Grigori —our Saviour."

As he blessed them Rasputin told them: "I am come to preach to you the message of salvation through sin." Followed by a huge crowd he slowly made his way to the river. There he again blessed all the peasants and dismissed all except his women disciples. Then encircled as always by pretty girls "the saint" took the road into the forest—and disappeared from Siberia.

Some time later a Siberian *muzhik*, reported to be widely honoured as a holy man among his own people, sought lodging in the monastery attached to the St. Petersburg Academy of Theology. At first the young theologians, with the condescension of their kind, talked down to him as yet another rural religious curiosity come to see the sights of the capital. To their amazement they found that "Father Grigori" was more than a match even for the best of them. As discussion waxed fiercer the group was approached by a small saintly man, their rector Father Feofan, who was also confessor to the Empress.

Father Feofan was much impressed by the "Siberian starets" and gently put a few questions which Rasputin answered clearly and pertinently. The old archimandrite then asked about sin. At once the hitherto peaceful Rasputin launched into a tirade and denounced the Gospels. "How can you drive out evil without repentance," he shouted, "and how can you repent if *you* have not sinned?"

Father Feofan began to answer in his soft gentle manner. Unheeding Rasputin continued to shout him down. The rector began to stutter and stammer and became confused. As he looked at Rasputin's eyes everything around him appeared blurred. His body began to tremble.

Suddenly Rasputin stopped. The sinister look disappeared from his eyes. Father Feofan recovered, and, as was his custom, began to bless his pupils before retiring. When he approached Rasputin the archimandrite's hand fell back; he whispered, "Little father, *you* must bless me." Father Feofan was much troubled. He could not deny that the Siberian peasant seemed

185

better able than he, himself, was to explain the scriptures.

Had this Siberian *muzhik* some divine intuition? Or was he an emissary of Satan sent to confuse the pious and the holy? Father Feofan decided to summon his close friend Bishop Hermogen first thing in the morning. The archimandrite had just started to explain his strange experience to the bishop next morning when Rasputin broke into the room. "Is that your bishop?" he asked pointing at Hermogen. Rushing forward he then embraced both men and kissed them three times, so boisterously that they became somewhat alarmed.

From the outset Bishop Hermogen liked Rasputin. He was delighted with his homely, and often coarse, peasant language and what seemed his obvious sincerity. Unlike the others the cynical and worldly churchman did not succumb to the strange influence of "the new saint". But as a militant servant of his Church he was quick to recognize the uses to which this strange personality might be put. The bishop decided to use Rasputin for his own political ends.

Within a few days the bishop presented the "starets" in person to the Central Committee of the True Russian People, a powerful and dangerous association of extreme political reactionaries devoted to the maintenance of autocratic power in the hands of a suitable advised Romanov Czar. There were some sceptics among the members of the Committee. But Rasputin, radiating the strength of his great personality, silenced all critics. The meeting ended inevitably in complete success. That evening Bishop Hermogen set out to induce his friend Father Feofan, to bring "Father Grigori" to Czarskoe Selo, the palace where the Czar and his family lived in almost complete seclusion—and with almost no contact with the millions of Russians over whom they enjoyed autocratic power.

The Czar Nicholas II and his wife "Sunshine"—formerly Princess Alexandra of Hesse and a granddaughter of Queen Victoria—remained deeply in love throughout their married life. But as the years passed and one tragedy after another overtook Russia the Czarina became ever more neurotic and the Royal couple gradually cut themselves off even from the rest of the Royal Family. Nervous even before her marriage, the Czarina had been quick to sense the anti-German feeling of the

Russian court, led by the Dowager Empress, born a Danish princess and the sister of Queen Alexandra.

Following the birth of four daughters in succession her failure to produce a male heir to the Russian throne caused the Czarina gradually to give way to superstition. In desperation she took advice from a succession of soothsayers and clairvoyants ranging from a quite genuine Tibetan naturopath to a slobbering epilectic "wonder-idiot". When at long last she gave birth to a boy, Alexei, she discovered to her horror that he suffered from haemophilia, the bleeding disease passed on by Queen Victoria through her granddaughters to their male issue. As soon as the Czar and Czarina were certain of the illness of their heir they abandoned formal Court life altogether and withdrew into their immediate family circle. The Empress became seriously ill with an acute nervous complaint which caused severe abdominal pains. Soon her only friend was Anna Vyrubova, daughter of a former head of the Imperial Chancellery, whom the Czarina had first met when she acted as a temporary lady-in-waiting. The Royal Family's only private outings were to Anna's little house two hundred yards from the palace where they spent much of their time. It was to Anna that the Czarina confided her fears, her worries and her doubts about her son—and the future of Russia.

When Rasputin reached Russia the Czarevitch Alexei was seriously ill, suffering from an internal haemorrhage caused by a knock received at play. The Czarina had begun to despair of the little boy's life when from two other members of the Royal Family, the Montenegrin-born Arch-duchesses Stana and Militsa, she heard of the wonderful holy man discovered by Father Feofan.

Rasputin, through the introductions of Father Feofan, had already become a regular visitor to the palaces of the two grand-duchesses. Stana told the Czarina that on the previous evening he had said: "Tell the Empress to weep no more. I will make her little boy well again and once he is a soldier he will have red cheeks."

At first the distraught mother scarcely took in what she was told. Then she appreciated that here was new hope. Here was a new "friend" who might save Alexei's life. She developed an overwhelming desire to see this strange "Father Grigori". She said she would speak to the Czar that night. At dinner her fourth daughter Anastasia (later to be the subject of one of the great mysteries of the twentieth century) spoke about the new holy man and was full of his deeds. The Czar became interested, and the Royal couple decided that they could do no harm by sending for Rasputin.

Two evenings later the most minute precautions had been taken to bring Rasputin to Czarskoe Selo unostentatiously, he was admitted through a side entrance. The Czar was trying to calm his wife, who was tense at the prospect of the coming interview, when suddenly the door opened and Grigori Efimovich, the Siberian peasant, in a long black kaftan, his beard untidy and his hair unkempt, entered the Czar's study. With a beaming smile Rasputin walked forward. Without any ceremony he embraced the Czar and his wife giving each a smacking kiss on the cheek. Utterly amazed but saying no word the Czarina led the way to the nursery of the Czarevitch. Softly Rasputin entered. He fell on his knees before the sacred ikons in the corner and prayed in a low voice. Then he turned to the bed where the royal child lay pale as death, his little face twisted with pain and his knees held stiffly against his chest.

Rasputin made the sign of the cross and started to speak. Alesha, as the Czarevitch was known to the family, opened his eyes and stared in wonder at the queer stranger with the huge beard who smiled at him.

"Don't be afraid, Alesha," said the stranger in his pleasant deep voice. "Look, I have driven all your horrid pains away," he continued as he stroked the little invalid all over his body. "Nothing will hurt you any more. Tomorrow you will be well again and just you wait and see what fun we'll have together."

Gradually the small boy began to brighten. Soon he was listening intently to a story of Rasputin's boyhood pranks in Siberia. He was so interested that he began to pull himself up in the bed to see his visitor better.

"Be careful," said the anxious mother hovering in the background. "Leave me alone, mama," said the boy as he pleaded with Rasputin to tell him another story. It was only when Rasputin promised to come again the next evening that the little prince lay down contented and went to sleep, for the first time for many nights.

Father Grigori did indeed return the following night and for many nights thereafter. Soon the gauche Siberian peasant and the heir to the Imperial throne became fast friends. By this time Father Grigori was fast friends also with the Czar and Czarina, each of whom he greeted every evening with a kiss. He became indeed a member of the inner circle of the Russian Royal Family, and often with the Czarevitch in his dressing-gown on his knee, told them about the life of the Siberian peasants and of his own wanderings through Russia.

The four daughters of the Czar were enthralled by the "starets". The two elder ones took his advice on their love affairs with young Guards officers. The Czar himself began to make notes in his diary of his talks with "Grigori the man of God from the Tobolsk government".

Rasputin's visits to Czarskoe Selo did not go unobserved. The whole court and Russian government were soon aware of the appearance of the new miracle worker, and of his influence over the Royal Family.

The first to attack him openly was the governess of the Czar's daughters. She protested that during his evening visits Rasputin went into the bedrooms of the grand-duchesses, who usually were in bed, to bless them. She persuaded their father to ban Rasputin from his daughters' bedrooms. Meanwhile a flood of gossip and scandal swept through St. Petersburg. It was widely rumoured that on one of his early visits to the palace he had raped the nurse of the Czarevitch. She complained to the Czarina and was met not only with disbelief but with a reproof for being fanciful.

The success of Rasputin at the Russian court aroused the enthusiasm of the extreme right-wing reactionaries who had first set him on the road to Czarskoe Sela. Soon he was the guest at innumerable aristocratic dinner parties at which his political supporters gave themselves the luxury of drinking tea with the new redeemer and discussing everything from theology to politics with him.

Rasputin's visits to the palace gradually became less frequent. The Czar had become worried about the scandals revolving around his name: he and his wife preferred to meet Rasputin at the nearby cottage of Anne Vyrubova. The Czarina, like her Royal friends, had become convinced of his holiness from the first minute she had looked into his cold blue eyes. She believed that he was an ambassador of God sent to protect the House of Romanov, to which she was devoted. When repeated rumours of Rasputin's dissolute life reached the Czarina she refused to be shaken in her belief in the holiness of her "dear friend". When shown evidence of his orgies she described them as "temptations of the devil" from which he had emerged victorious. Indeed, like thousands of other women in St. Petersburg, the superstitious Czarina was infatuated with Rasputin, although there is not the slightest shred of evidence to suggest that her passion had any other basis than in religion and in a very genuine thankfulness for what he had accomplished for her ailing child.

Within a few months, however, the fantastic sexual life of the miracle worker had become not only the main subject of scandal in the capital, but the subject of an ever-growing dossier of the secret police, whose agents kept an almost nonstop watch on his activities. There is no question about the veracity of these reports. Secret agents were stationed on the stairway to his flat; when he became bored he often invited them in to gossip and drink. In the years that followed these agents made literally thousands of reports on the women with whom the "starets" had sexual relations: they included princesses, famous actresses, the wives of ministers and generals and many impecunious seamstresses, servants and peasant women—all were the same to Rasputin. There were innumerable reports of his orgies with gipsy girls— which were observed by agents who climbed up to the windows of the inn where he organized his debauchery. Sometimes there were even amusing titbits, such as the incident when Rasputin appeared at an aristocratic party in nothing but his shirt.

Apart from the concourse of women with whom he spent his nights there was an almost constant court of female admirers to be found all day in the big dining-room of his apartment. Tensely they waited for the saviour to appear. Sometimes he appeared drunk, sometimes sober, sometimes with his clothes ruffled and the clearest indications that he had had a girl on his knee. It made no difference to the faithful. As he appeared they crowded round, caressing and kissing his filthy beard until he had blessed each one of them. Then he would sink back on the sofa between two of his closest disciples. As he ate of the food piled up on the table he talked unctuously of God and salvation or retailed some coarse story about any minister or ambassador of whom he disapproved. When he was replete he withdrew into his Holy of Holies, a small private room in his own quarters where he received new initiates and petitioners.

As he disappeared those who had already had "communion" with the "starets" whispered together and nodded their heads. Some had peculiar smiles on their lips. They knew the secrets of the bare little room with its iron camp bed, the ikons with the ribbons, the framed texts of scripture, and the autographed photographs of the Czar and Czarina. When he was closeted with a woman no one was allowed to enter. Only if a telephone call came from Czarskoe Selo—as they often did—would his maid-servant knock quietly at the door and summon him to talk with his Royal friends.

It was in the "Holy of Holies" that the initiation of novices into the new doctrine of "redemption through sin" took place. And it was after each "initiation" that Rasputin decided which women should become members of his circle of "intimates". Many young girls left the mysterious room with happy radiant faces. But there were those who rushed out, their dresses disarranged; some were weeping, some grossly insulted and livid with fury, some hysterical and shrieking. The police agents had to be summoned to get rid of them. Not everyone was ready to be "redeemed through sin". As Rasputin explained, in some of them the "devil of pride was too strong to let them take the true path of humiliation".

Some of the outraged women went to the police and accused Rasputin of rape. The police chief carefully noted the charges and passed them to all interested departments. There they were read with a mixture of prurience, admiration and envy. But no one had the slightest intention of taking legal proceedings against the "dear friend" of the Czar and his wife.

However, it was not very often that Rasputin's advances met with blunt refusal. Many high society women boasted that he had honoured them with his love. On one of the rare occasions after one young novice had rebuffed him and been ejected from the Holy of Holies with much bad language and some violence, she was asked by a married woman: "But how can you refuse anything to the saint?"

Pertinently the novice answered: "But does a saint need sinful love—what sort of holiness is that?"

The reply explained much of Rasputin's amorous success, "Everything he touches he makes holy". For many women found in Rasputin the fulfilment of two apparently irreconcilable desires, religious salvation and the satisfaction of their carnal appetites.

Since Rasputin's friendship with the Romanov Family shielded him from police action, whatever scandalmongers might say had no effect and gradually this strange man became the most powerful individual in Russia.

It was not only women who thronged to Rasputin's ante-chamber. His apartment received a steady stream of top-level visitors, ministers, bankers, diplomats and men of affairs, all taking counsel or, more probably, doing discreet deals with Father Grigori.

For with the same rapidity that it had been rumoured that he was a new saviour, word passed from mouth to mouth that the miracle man had a sound business sense and was amenable to bribes. For a suitable gift he was only too willing to exercise his influence: he could obtain a military commission, organize a highly valuable commercial concession, secure release from imprisonment, in short he could influence favourably anything that involved a discreet word in the ear of the Czar or his immediate entourage. Moreover, Rasputin was not unkind: news spread among his poorer admirers that Father Grigori did not always *insist* on a present. He never forgot he was a Siberian peasant and was ready to be friendly and kind to the insignificant among his petitioners, indeed often he openly robbed the rich to help the poor.

In the earlier years of his sojourn in St. Petersburg Rasputin was circumspect. He made no attempt to exert any influence beyond that on his Royal patrons, and that was by no means constant or assured at all times. As time passed he realized that both the Czar, and still more the Czarina, were clay in his hands. He began to change his methods. The corrupting effects of unchallenged power came into play. Presently ruthless and unscrupulous abuse of supreme autocracy was added to his other malevolent influences on Russian life. By the end of the first decade of the twentieth century Rasputin was not only the most evil but without question the most powerful man in Russia.

In 1911 he showed his hand openly for the first time. In the face of solid opposition from the higher councils of the Orthodox Church he forced through, with Royal backing, the appointment of a simple and virtually illiterate peasant as bishop of his home See of Tobolsk. Though this defeat of the princes of the church gave him great satisfaction, it cost him the support of the reactionary "True Russian People", who had been his original sponsors at court. In the intervening years his relations with the reactionaries had steadily deteriorated, for, as though conscious of the ferment of Russian ideas following the abortive rising of 1905, Rasputin's viewpoint had instinctively moved towards the left. He remained an authoritarian but with tendencies towards radicalism. Although a devoted monarchist Rasputin declared publicly that the sovereign must be honoured by the humblest class *on whom the power of the Czar fundamentally rested*. In consequence of his radical speeches and utterances the reactionary clique withdrew its support, and after a time attempted to overthrow him. For a time he was in a very insecure position.

Now Rasputin made a pilgrimage to the holy places of Eastern Christianity, Kiev, Constantinople and Jerusalem, which further raised his esteem in the eyes of the Czar and Czarina. By this time he had become a problem to successive Russian governments, which had been quick to observe how real power was passing into the miracle worker's hands.

The Prime Minister Stolypin, before he was assassinated in Kiev in 1911, had complained to the Czar about the "dissolute peasant". But the Czar was unsympathetic and the problem was still unsolved when Stolypin died. His successor, Kokovsov, had a violent antipathy to Rasputin. He tried at first to persuade the "starets" to depart by offering him a fortune. Rasputin bluntly refused. "If Papa [the Czar] wanted him to leave" he would go willingly. Otherwise he stayed. The Prime Minister then addressed himself to the Czar. Nicholas dismissed the whole thing with a wave of the hand. "These critics are idiots," he said, "*I* know Rasputin."

The Czar, however, was not as entirely infatuated as was his wife. In the most considerate way he asked Rasputin to go back to Siberia for a time. Rasputin acceded to the Czar's request, but he held a trump card. When the Royal family was on a hunting trip in Poland the Czarevitch started an internal haemorrhage. Symptoms of blood poisoning appeared. When his mother tried to soothe the sick child he opened his eyes and pleaded for "the little father". Secretly the Czarina told her friend Anna to send a telegram to Rasputin asking him to pray for her son. Next morning came an answer from Siberia "God has lent an ear to your prayers and your tears. Do not be despondent. Your son will live." On hearing what Grigori had said the boy rallied. A few hours later the fever disappeared. Soon he was well enough to return to Czarskoe Selo. Then the Czarina at once had her "dear friend" recalled to court.

Some years later, at the beginning of the First World War in 1914, the Czarevitch, by now a big boy, bumped his nose against the window of the Royal train. This started bleeding which would not stop. The Czarevitch was rushed home and Rasputin was summoned. On his arrival Grigori made the sign of the Cross over the invalid and then told his mother: "Give thanks to God. Once again he has granted life to your son."

Under strong pressure from his ministers and advisers the Czar did from time to time put up some resistance to Rasputin's demands. After this incident, however, Rasputin's conceit became intolerable. He returned home to tell his friends: "The Czar will think twice about disregarding my advice in the future." He also made a prediction: "So long as I live the Imperial family will also live; when I die they also will perish." As history was to prove, this was a curiously accurate prophecy.

In the years immediately before the outbreak of the war Rasputin's power became almost unchallenged. He controlled the appointments of ministers whose "souls he examined" personally before the appointment was made. One Prime Minister, Boris Stuermer, was his personal protégé; the appointment of Khvostov as Minister of the Interior was held up for a considerable period because he had been rude to Rasputin. This had occurred when the latter made a trip to Nizhni-Novgorod to inspect the candidate and cabled to Czarskoe Selo: "The grace of the Lord is in Khrostov—but for the time being there is something lacking."

At heart Rasputin was a Christian pacifist. He strongly opposed the Czar's tendencies to become involved in the Balkan wars. When in the summer of 1914 war again seemed imminent, the "starets" forcibly expressed to his Royal "friend" the opposition of the millions of Russian *muzhiks* like himself who would suffer personally the horrors of war. At the beginning of August, when war did break out, Rasputin was in hospital suffering from a stab wound inflicted by a woman whom he had failed to convert to the doctrine of salvation through sex. In later years he constantly asserted that he would have been able to stop Russia entering the war "but for that damned woman". Even from his hospital bed he sent the Czar a telegram exhorting him to preserve peace at any price.

As he had been unable to stop Russia getting into the war Rasputin thereafter devoted all his energies to preventing and ameliorating military abuses. In this he enlisted the support of the Czarina who, when her husband was at the front, sent a stream of telegrams to her husband urging him to accept "our friend's" views. By 1915 Rasputin was actively interfering in the plans of the Russian High Command. He warned the Czar against the great offensive in Galicia but the High Command prevailed against him. The subsequent disaster proved the soundness of Rasputin's view of strategy. A year later he urged that Brusilov's great offensive should not be pushed too far; he said that it had already achieved its purpose.

"Our friend is much disturbed," wrote the Czarina to her husband, "that Brusilov has not listened to advice to stop the advance—and now he says we have more pointless losses."

Some of Rasputin's military counsel might well have achieved favourable results for it consisted mostly of sound common sense. But by the autumn of 1916, following vast losses at the front, the political temperature of Russia was rising to fever heat. During the two years since the start of the war the effective civil government of Russia had, for all practical purposes, consisted of an unholy trinity headed by Rasputin. Its other two members were Khvostov, the Minister of the Interior, and the police chief, Belitski. They met regularly at a series of "fish suppers" given for Rasputin by the political adventurer Prince Adronnikov and his mistress. These functions, at which Rasputin guzzled vast quantities of fish with his bare hands, became regular political institutions. Indeed most of the important affairs of state were settled on these occasions by the peasant-monk, the minister and the policeman.

By the early autumn of 1916, their alliance had begun to wear thin. The rapidly-deteriorating political situation made it imperative to call a meeting of the seldom-summoned Russian Parliament, the Duma.

Rasputin was strongly opposed to such a course. He knew that most of the sitting would be taken up with attacks on himself and his untrammelled power. So Khvostov attempted to trick Rasputin into going on a tour of inspection, his intention being to summon the Duma during Rasputin's absence. Rasputin ostensibly agreed; he took a gift of 500 roubles to pay for the trip. Weeks later he was still in St. Petersburg. In the end Khvostov lost patience. He inquired when Rasputin intended to leave. Rasputin blandly informed him that he had no intention of going anywhere. Accompanied by the police chief Khvostov walked out. When they reached their car Khvostov muttered to his colleague: "Believe me, dear Stefan Petrovich, we'll have to make away with that rascal."

Thereafter the murder of Rasputin became the main pre-occupation of Khvostov. Various plans were formulated and abandoned for one reason or another. Then the minister and the police chief started to double-cross each other. Incriminating documents reached Rasputin, the Prime Minister Stuermer and Anna Vyrubova. They passed to the Czarina. Both Khvostov and Belitski were sacked. Rasputin's former friends Father Feofan and Bishop Hermogen were also in one of the plots. They were exiled.

Rasputin was quite untroubled. He knew all about the plans for the masked men in the motor car and the bottles of poison. From his knowledge of the mutual hate and suspicion among the various contending parties and police forces he felt secure.

By now he had come out openly in favour of a negotiated peace to end the war with Germany. He had thrown down the gauntlet to the Allies, who became highly alarmed. His open enemies included the French and British Ambassadors, the latter the influential Sir George Buchanan who enjoyed a privileged position owing to the affectionate relationship between the Czar and his cousin King George V.

It was at this point that a fabulously rich, and rather ineffective aristocratic dilettante, Prince Felix Yusupov, who was married to a niece of the Czar, decided to intervene.

Prince Yusupov had long regarded Rasputin with the utmost distaste, especially after he had watched the "starets" paw and slobber over a pretty girl named Munia, who had been the fiancée of his deceased brother. Yusupov, after much heart searching, therefore decided to murder Rasputin. He was fortified in this resolve by what he heard from his friends on all sides, even from the Royal Family itself, from ministers and high officials and from generals at the front.

Everywhere he went Yusupov heard stories of the shameful and dissolute life of the "peasant chancellor", of his interference in the highest functions of the State, and of his disgraceful orgies. Yusupov also shared the view of all influential Russians of that time, that the fate of the monarchy itself was at stake. In little more than half a year the accuracy of that belief was to be but too apparent.

What political encouragement Yusupov received is still uncertain. Through his wife, the Princess Trina, he was aware that, at the instigation of the British Ambassador, powerful members of the Royal Family were pressing the Czar to dismiss Rasputin. It is significant also that from the outset Yusupov enlisted as a fellow conspirator his closest friend, the effeminate playboy Grand Duke Dmitri Pavlovich. The presence of a member of the Imperial Family in any plot would effectively prevent any subsequent police action. He also enlisted a number of other conspirators. Among them were the Duma deputy Purishkevich, who had recently made a violently anti-Rasputin speech; the deputy's assistant on a hospital train, the Polish-born Dr. Lazoverts; a cavalry officer named Sukhotin, and Yusupov's own valet, Nefedov.

Satisfied with his own idealistic motives and the personalities of his fellow conspirators Yusupov proceeded to make preparations for the assassination of the most hated man in Russia.

He recalled that when he had first met Rasputin at the home of his brother's fiancée Munia, the "starets" had obviously been attracted to him. With the help of the girl therefore he agreed to have tea with Rasputin a few days later. As soon as Rasputin entered the room he rushed up to the Prince and embraced him fondly. Yusupov had the greatest difficulty in concealing his disgust and was almost physically sick. But he did his utmost to put on a show of friendliness and admiration for the "starets".

Yusupov was disgusted also by the arrogance and conceit of Rasputin who talked disparagingly of the Royal couple, of several important Russian personalities and added: "I have only to bang my fist on the table to get everything I want. That is the only way to deal with you Russian aristocrats."

Yusupov said nothing. Manfully he endured Rasputin's caresses. When they parted they agreed that they must meet again soon. Next morning Yusupov had a call from Munia. Rasputin wanted to meet him again, and, having heard that he could sing gipsy songs which were an especial delight of the Siberian peasant, he was to bring his guitar to the next meeting.

Yusupov suddenly realized that here he held the key to the assassination of Rasputin; he had only to exploit the gipsy songs and the guitar to speed up their friendship.

At the next tea party a few days later Rasputin showed even more devotion to his "little friend", as he dubbed Yusupov. Presently he agreed to visit Yusupov at his own home, the vast family palace on the Moika. The pretext for the visit was that Yusupov's wife, the Grand Duchess Irina, wanted to meet the "starets". Actually the beautiful young princess was in the Crimea at the time.

Yusupov told Rasputin that his wife felt ill and would like him to give her "treatment". Rasputin was enchanted by the idea. He had long sought a personal meeting with the beautiful princess. So he gladly accepted an invitation to visit the Yusupov palace on the evening of 16 December. He seemed to have not the slightest suspicion of the plot on his life, although normally he was cautious and highly suspicious.

For the scene of the crime the plotters had chosen a large underground room in the Yusupov palace from where no screams or shouts could be heard. As success lay in pretending that the room had been lived in, Yusupov and his valet moved some fine pieces of furniture from the rooms above and luxuriously equipped the cellar with carpets, curtains and other expensive furnishings. The preparations took the better part of a day, but by the evening of the sixteenth the room looked extremely comfortable. The servants were ordered to lay places for six and provide tea, cakes and wine. When the domestics had withdrawn the plotters made their final preparations. They disarranged the furniture to give the impression that several people had just taken tea. Then Dr. Lazoverts went into action. Removing the top layer of a number of small chocolate cakes he spread potassium cyanide, with which he had armed himself, on the lower halves. The upper portions were restored and the poisoned cakes laid out on a plate. As a reserve the doctor put poison into several glasses of wine standing on a tray. All that remained was to secure the victim. Yusupov had undertaken to perform that mission. To prevent anyone from knowing what was going on Dr. Lazoverts acted as chauffeur of the field-grey Yusupov limousine.

Rasputin, who was excited about his invitation to the Yusupov palace, dressed himself with great care. He was still preparing when he had a sudden visit from the new Minister of the Interior, whom he had appointed to replace Khvostov. The Minister warned him of a plot against his life. When Yusupov arrived to pick him up Rasputin told the prince: "I hear that some wicked people want to murder me—but they won't succeed; their arms are not long enough."

Yusupov was almost overcome at the thought of enticing a defenceless man to his own home to murder him. Then he recalled his "patriotic duty" and escorted Rasputin to the waiting car.

When they entered his home they could hear the sound of a gramophone coming from a first floor room. Rasputin asked if there was a party. Yusupov told him that it was his wife entertaining a few friends. But first said Yusupov they must go to the dining-room and have a cup of tea. Quite unsuspecting,

Rasputin followed his host downstairs to the alleged dining-room. Yusupov poured out tea but had not the courage imme-diately to offer Rasputin the poisoned chocolate cakes. First he gave him some harmless pink ones. Only after that did he pluck up courage to hand Rasputin the plate of poisoned cakes. As always Rasputin devoured one after another. Yusupov had been told that the effect of cyanide was almost instantaneous, yet Rasputin went on talking as though the chocolate cakes had been as harmless as the pink ones.

In desperation Yusupov went to the tray of wine glasses. He asked if the "starets" would care to sample some of the famous Yusupov wine from the family's Crimean estates. With obvious relish Rasputin gulped several glasses—all heavily impregnated with poison. He seemed to get glassy-eyed—but otherwise there was no marked effect. As though drunk he slid to the floor. Yet he was quite conscious, and with a smile begged Yusupov to play the guitar and sing some of the gipsy songs which he loved.

Completely incredulous, Yusupov peered at the apparently half-drunk Rasputin. Was this some superman that he could consume without ill effect enough poison to kill a large group of ordinary people? Rasputin was cheering up. So there was nothing for it. Yusupov played and sang to the man into whom he had just poured several fatal doses of cyanide.

By now the conspirators upstairs had become uneasy. They began to call to Yusupov. Rasputin wanted to know what was happening. Yusupov said it was only his wife's friends, but that he would go and see. Half demented he rushed upstairs, told the other plotters what had happened, and seized a revolver. Returning to the cellar he fired every shot it contained into Rasputin. . . .

Some time after midnight a passing policeman heard shots coming from the courtyard of the Yusupov palace. He went to the scene and was met by the prince himself, who said that one of his guests had got tipsy and fired off his revolver. Soon after-wards, however, the prince's steward came for the policeman and escorted him to a private room. There he was confronted by a man in uniform who said he was a member of the Duma. This man announced that "the notorious criminal and national danger Rasputin" was dead. He warned the policeman to tell no one. The policeman, however, did report the circumstances to his superiors.

In the morning the Yusupov palace was searched. A trail of blood was found leading from the basement to the courtyard. Yusupov explained that the blood came from a dog which had been shot by a friend—and the carcass of the animal was indeed seen in the courtyard.

About noon two watchmen found a golosh and bloodstains in the centre of the Petrovski Bridge. The ice was broken and divers were sent for. After two days' search they found Rasputin's body. His legs and arms had been bound with ropes and the corpse showed numerous bullet *and knife* wounds. One arm was out of the rope and the lungs were full of water. *Rasputin had been still alive* when he was thrown into the icy river.

On learning of the news of the murder of her "dear friend" the Czarina alternated between despair and a desire for revenge on the members of the Royal Family who had taken part in the plot.

Rasputin was buried on 21 December in the Royal park at Czarskoe Selo in the presence of the Czar and Czarina and their four daughters. In the meantime a fierce struggle had broken out within the Imperial family over the fate of the two Royal conspirators, the Grand Duke Dmitri and Prince Yusupov. Both had taken refuge in the Grand Duke's palace, to which the police had no right of access. The Czar announced his intention of punishing them without mercy. But his brothers and uncles came to the rescue of the two young men. The struggle reached its climax in a violent altercation (it was heard several rooms away) between the Czar and the Grand Duke Alexander Mihailovich. The Czar threatened vengeance, but as usual he vacillated. In the end the Grand Duke Dmitri was sent to Persia and Yusupov banished to a distant estate.

Three months later, after the Czar had been deposed at the time of the March revolution, rebel soldiers broke into the Royal park at Czarskoe Selo. They tore open Rasputin's grave, seized the coffin and carried it to an adjacent forest. There a great pyre was built. On that pyre the decomposing body of the "starets" was lain and soaked in petrol. Then the last relics of a strange and wicked man were destroyed utterly in roaring flames.

Chapter 11

STALIN

JOSEPH VISSARIONOVICH DJUGASHVILI, known to history as Stalin, was officially declared one of the world's wickedest men on 25 February, 1956. His accusers were his erstwhile close collaborators and subsequent successors, Nikita Khrushchev and Anastas Mikoyan, of the Supreme Praesidium of the Soviet Union. The full extent of his fantastic evil, until then only rumoured, was revealed in detail to the twentieth congress of the political organ which he had once dominated, the Communist Party of the Soviet Union.

The man who in the previous three decades had been adulated as everything from "Stalin the Great, the greatest man of all time" to Winston Churchill's "great war leader" was suddenly shown to have been one of the most monstrous tyrants of history. He was dubbed "The New Satan". In the subsequent years of de-Stalinization the man who could speak most frankly, the Yugoslav Communist rebel Milovan Djilas, called Stalin "the greatest criminal known to history". That fearsome accusation is justified by the mysterious "disappearance" of twenty-five million human souls from the Soviet census returns during the years of Stalin's rule; but it is not necessarily the final judgment.

Future historians may well take a more objective view and modify some at least of the judgments of the de-Stalinization period. For, despite the vast and terrible amount of human misery for which Stalin must accept ultimate responsibility, he was not, at the outset of his career, an evil man. On the contrary, at the beginning of this century the aim of Stalin, then a young Socialist agitator, was to improve the lot of millions of his fellow countrymen. And, whatever the cost, Stalin certainly did achieve great things for Russia. Without him and his controversial policies Russia might well have succumbed to Hitler and the Nazi hordes who swarmed into the Soviet Union in 1941.

Stalin himself was perhaps the most notable victim of the monolithic Communist system which he did so much to create. His political career is perhaps the supreme twentieth-century example of the famous dictum of Lord Acton: "Power tends to corrupt . . . absolute power corrupts absolutely." It was that absolute power gathered into his own hands by Stalin during long years of dissimulation and intrigue, of terror and brutal murder of his closest associates, which corrupted him, and in the end transformed him into the megalomaniac monster of his last years.

Stalin was not a Russian. He was the grandson of Georgian serfs liberated from bondage a few years before his birth on 21 December, 1879, in the small Caucasian town of Gori, not far from Tiflis. He was the fourth but first surviving child of a poor Georgian cobbler, Vissarion Djugashvili, and his equally humble wife Ekaterina. She survived, in the elastic-sided boots and sober black garments of a peasant woman come to town, as Babushka Keke (Grandma Kate) to see her son "Soso" become autocrat of all Russia.

Little is known of the childhood of little Soso (Georgian for Joe). He grew up among the squalor and poverty into which he was born. His father was a drunkard. For years before he died (at which time Soso was ten) Vissarion had contributed nothing to the family upkeep. His mother therefore was forced to work as a charwoman. At the age of seven Soso became ill with smallpox which left his face pockmarked. He was ill a second time with an infection which developed into an ulcer on the left arm. When he recovered he was unable to bend his left arm, so acquiring an infirmity curiously similar to that of another European autocrat, Wilhelm II, last Emperor of Imperial Germany.

Like other peasant women before and since Ekaterina Djugashvili thought the Church offered the best prospects for young Soso. By some means she succeeded in having him enrolled as a pupil of the ecclesiastical school at Gori when he was nine. He was a moderately diligent pupil, although sulky and quick to take offence. After five years he entered the well-known Orthodox Theological Seminary at Tiflis, the principal seminary in Georgia, to train as a priest.

This institution instilled in him characteristics which he never lost. The strict barrack-like régime imposed by the ecclesiastical tutors was a façade behind which was a veritable breeding ground for the exciting new ideas then seeping into Czarist Russia. Soso found in the seminary many other youths with humble backgrounds similar to his own. Within a few months he was deep in "subversive books"—they ranged from the works of Victor Hugo to those of Darwin—obtained somehow from the local library. Time after time Soso was found reading forbidden works and sent to the punishment cells for varying periods. Soon he was one of the principal rebels, yet it was some time before the Orthodox masters penetrated the smug, hypocritical façade of young Djugashvili, who appeared to be one of their best students.

His fellow students did not find him an easy colleague. Easily incensed when his arguments were challenged successfully, he would nurse a grudge against an opponent and seek to revenge himself by malignant gossip and slander.

By the age of seventeen he had made the acquaintance of Marxist and other left-wing authors. A few months later while still a student at the seminary he joined a clandestine socialist organization in Tiflis. He was given the task of directing workers' political study groups. Soon he was accepted by men much older than himself as a guide and leader. With an impudence and hypocrisy for which he was to be notorious in later life he continued to deceive the monks without the slightest scruple or qualm. An atheist and bitter opponent of the Russian Orthodox Church, he continued to study as though his only aim was to become a priest of the Church. This double life could last only so long. At the end of May, 1899, he was expelled—ostensibly because he failed to attend an examination. In later life he claimed he was turned out for "propagating Marxism".

He had no job. On his expulsion from the seminary a few months before his twentieth birthday he therefore became a full-time agitator and started to dabble in left-wing journalism. He lived from meagre collections taken at workers' meetings, small earnings from writing and circulating illegal leaflets, holding clandestine meetings and organizing demonstrations officially forbidden by the Russian authorities in Georgia.

During the same period he adopted the name of "Koba" by which he was known in the revolutionary left-wing movement for years to come. In 1901 at the age of twenty-two he became a member of the Social Democrat Committee in Tiflis. He was now a recognized leader of the left-wing movement in Georgia. Almost inevitably he was arrested a year or so later.

Russian prisons in those far-off Czarist days were the real universities of the left wing. They provided forums for debating societies, some of whose members subsequently achieved international recognition. Koba plunged into this strange intellectual life. He disciplined himself to eat little, rise early, work hard and debate furiously until, at the end of 1903, he was for the first time deported to Siberia.

The great doctrinal debates of the pre-1917 Russian Social Democrat party are now a part of the theology of world communism. In prison and in exile Koba followed the course of these debates—most of them in Western Europe—with intense interest. Gradually he came to be recognized as a follower of the extreme left wing, or Bolshevik, section of the party. This was the radical wing dominated by an obscure Russian émigré in Switzerland named Vladimir Ilyitch Ulianov. Under the name of Lenin he was to become known as one of the greatest political minds of all time.

Koba was already a convinced Leninist when he escaped from Siberia to reach Georgia in time for the strikes which followed "Bloody Sunday". This was the occasion in 1905 when the Czar's cossacks massacred a thousand Russian workers in St. Petersburg. In the revolt which followed a key rôle was played by another young Russian extremist who was to become one of the principal actors in the Stalin drama. He was a brilliant Jewish demagogue Lev Davidovitch Bronstein, better known in later years as Trotsky.

For most of the years between the "general rehearsal" of 1905 and the Russian revolution in 1917 Koba remained in Russia itself and was a comparatively obscure but devoted lieutenant of Lenin. Most of the other future Bolshevik leaders were at that time overseas.

Koba met Lenin personally for the first time at a Bolshevik conference in Finland towards the end of 1905. Thereafter he was a paid Bolshevik official with all the failings of his kind. He was narrow and sectarian, authoritarian, arrogant, and completely crooked in anything which would secure the Bolsheviks' political ends. His normal stocks-in-trade were falsification and denunciation; he was to continue to use them when he became communist dictator of Russia. Even in exile—he was deported in all six times and escaped on five—he was never able to make a real friend, a characteristic which remained with him throughout his life.

He took no share in the intellectual work of the Party but was the "hatchet man", always involved in operations of a risky nature and particularly in those involving physical violence. Apart from the famous raid in the Caucasus, which secured 250,000 gold roubles for Bolshevik subversion, Koba was active in counterfeiting bank notes, in raids on prisons and indeed in anything dangerous and violent.

These gangster-like activities were interrupted by brief visits abroad, of which the most notable was to a conference in London. He lived then at 77 Jubilee Street, just off Commercial Road in Stepney. There for some strange reason he became a great favourite of the Cockney children who, unable to pronounce "Soso", christened him "Sausage". His peculiar sense of humour appealed to his British acquaintances, who long remembered his attempts to speak elementary English.

It was Koba's record as the Bolshevik man of action which was responsible for Lenin co-opting him as a member of the Central Committee of the Bolshevik Party—at a party conference held in a café in Prague in 1912. This made Koba one of the top men in the Bolshevik revolutionary movement. He decided to ape Lenin and adopted the pseudonym of "Stalin" —Man of Steel. When the Russian Revolution broke out in March, 1917, Stalin was in luck. He was one of the few members of the Central Committee of the Bolsheviks actually in Russia. He rushed back from his Siberian exile to St. Petersburg, now renamed Petrograd, and by pure chance became one of the top Bolsheviks in the capital.

At once he seized control of the Party newspaper *Pravda*, which was being edited by an ultra-left-wing student related to the famous composer Scriabin. Under the name of Molotov this man would be Stalin's *alter ego* during the next forty years.

Stalin's intellectual gifts were not adequate for guiding the policies of the main organ of the Bolsheviks at the most critical period in its history—when it was in violent opposition to the Provisional Government which had been set up on the Czar's abdication. Some of the editions issued under his editorship caused stupefaction. They led to demands for his removal. When Lenin arrived in Russia a few weeks later, Stalin was only too glad to resume his rôle of the party's practical man. Trotsky too arrived back in Russia and in the months preceding the Bolshevik revolution in October he and Lenin dominated the Bolsheviks and in the end secured supreme power.

In the next five years when the names of the great ones of the revolution (Lenin, Trotsky, Zinoviev, Kamenev and Bukharin) were on everyone's lips Stalin remained a comparatively obscure figure operating underground like a mole. But Lenin had been quick to observe that among so many political and intellectual giants Stalin was the man with the greatest administrative ability. It was as administrative chief clerk of the Party that Lenin made him a member of the Political Bureau and of the Revolutionary Committee of the Party.

This was the period of the Russian civil war and of the Allied anti-Bolshevik intervention inspired by Churchill and Clemenceau.

On several occasions Lenin sent Stalin on missions in the field. Only where the crisis could be solved by violent repressive measures (usually the ruthless shooting of any opposition by police) was he successful. In the strictly military field his intervention usually proved a failure. He certainly contributed to the forced withdrawal of Trotsky's protégé, the future Marshal Tukhachevsky, in a great battle in front of Warsaw. In later years there was violent argument about the activities of Stalin and his friend, the former Caucasus oil man who became Marshal Voroshilov, at the town of Tsaritsyn, later renamed Stalingrad and now called Volgograd. Most objective authorities agree with Trotsky that Stalin's operations were well-nigh catastrophic. He was recalled by Lenin after a strong telegram of warning from Trotsky—a telegram that marked the beginning of what has been described as "the greatest hate in history".

In Moscow, where he worked under the watchful eye of Lenin, Stalin was much more successful. Gradually he acquired one post after another. He became Commissar for Nationalities and a member of the Organizational Bureau set up at his own suggestion to relieve the much pressed Politburo of day to day administration. Stalin already had begun to appreciate that the real road to power lay in gathering the whole administration into his own hands.

In March, 1922, Stalin became General Secretary of the Communist Party of the Soviet Union at its second congress. This post he was to retain for the rest of his life. Lenin, who nominated him for the job, considered it no more than a minor cog in the internal administrative machine. The post, however, was to prove the key to everything that followed. Once again Stalin had superb good fortune. A few weeks after his appointment Lenin suffered a stroke.

The impact of Lenin's stroke on the Soviet leadership was profound. The master mind was suddenly withdrawn. Stalin, with that peasant slyness which never deserted him, was quick to appreciate what no one else at that time did realize—that Lenin was a dying man and *that the succession was wide open*.

The monolithic structure of the Bolshevik administration created by Lenin seemed tailored for a Stalin take-over bid. He had only to invoke the mystic concept of "the Party" to silence all criticism and opposition. The General Secretary set to work with the weapons of which he was already a master—intrigue, cut-throat bargaining, police pressure and vilification of his rivals. Within a few months he had worked his creatures and his lackeys into most of the key appointments of the party. He was well on the way to getting complete control.

It was a virtuoso performance which Lenin (who had previously predicted that Stalin would cook some spicy dishes for the Party) realized as soon as he got back to his office at the beginning of September. He was appalled at the changes which had taken place in his absence. All around him Lenin could sense a vague but unmistakable sense of fear, the source of which, he soon established, was the General Secretary's office. Perhaps partly on this account, he suffered a second stroke in the middle of December, 1922. After a week he recovered sufficiently to deliver a series of notes to his secretary. This was the long suppressed and equally long rumoured "Lenin testament", of which the existence was publicly admitted only at the time of the twentieth Party congress in 1956.

To the amazement of his disciples, who saw the testament just after Lenin's death, he said that the two ablest members of the Bolshevik leadership were Trotsky, which was obvious, and Stalin. Lenin added: "In becoming Secretary Comrade Stalin has concentrated immense power into his own hands . . . and I am not convinced that he will always use it with prudence."

Just after writing that Lenin made one sensational discovery about Stalin. Five days later he added an amazing postscript.

"Stalin is too rude and that is a fault . . . which is intolerable in the office of General Secretary. Therefore I propose to the comrades *to find a way to remove Stalin from that position* and to appoint another man . . . more patient, more loyal, less capricious, more polite and more attentive to the comrades. This circumstance may seem an insignificant trifle but I think from the point of view of preventing a split and from the point of view of the relations between Stalin and Trotsky . . . it is not a trifle, or it is such a trifle as may acquire decisive significance."

Lenin certainly took action to sack Stalin. Early in March, 1923, Lenin made a frontal attack on Stalin in *Pravda*.

The following day, as a result of gross impertinence by Stalin to Lenin's wife Krupskaya, Lenin had a sharp exchange with the General Secretary. He then dictated a letter breaking off all personal relations with Stalin. And he began to take practical steps to limit Stalin's power.

Once again Stalin had superb good fortune. On 9 March, in the midst of these moves, Lenin had a third stroke from which, although he lingered on until the beginning of 1924, he was not to recover.

Lenin had not been alone in observing Stalin's sly bid to seize supreme power. Other important Bolsheviks headed by Trotsky had also noted the crafty manoeuvres of the General Secretary. Stalin was quick to realize his isolation. With characteristic guile he played on the long-standing jealousy of Trotsky felt by the two veteran Bolsheviks, Zinoviev and Kamenev. They formed a powerful triumvirate which, as all three were members of the Politburo and held other key appointments, had a virtual stranglehold on the official Party machinery.

Trotsky and his allies, in contrast, hampered themselves by clinging to the monolithic concept of the Party laid down by Lenin. A radical step towards democracy within the Bolshevik movement would almost certainly have overthrown Stalin and his two allies, but this was not taken. Another important factor was that by the second half of 1923 the Russian Communists were beginning to weary of constant revolution and the almost superhuman exertion which it demanded. Bolshevism was settling down. It was falling more and more into the hands of the bureaucrats thrown up by the revolution and of these Joseph Stalin was the supreme example.

The Stalin-Trotsky feud grew ever more bitter, for Trotsky was a formidable opponent. It was reaching new heights when in January, 1924, Lenin died. Trotsky, who had been ill, was recuperating in the Caucasus. Again fate seemed on Stalin's side, for all Russia regarded Trotsky as Lenin's inevitable successor. Stalin, as General Secretary, seized his opportunity; he took over all arrangements for the funeral. In his self-appointed rôle of chief mourner it was Stalin who by implication appeared as Lenin's successor.

When, with Stalin as principal pall-bearer, Lenin's embalmed body was carried into the crypt of the Mausoleum in Red Square, the first step had been taken towards the creation of that curious cult of Leninism, which owed more than a little to Stalin's ecclesiastical background. Stalin was to exploit that cult to his own advantage in the years to follow.

Lenin's widow, Krupskaya, who knew full well the real relationship between the dead man and Stalin, protested violently at this attempted deification of Lenin; she started to attack Stalin in public without restraint. However, Stalin now was the master. He turned on the woman on whom, when he was a mere nobody, he had poured flattery. According to what Khrushchev revealed to the twentieth Party congress in 1956, Stalin threatened that if Krupskaya made any more public speeches he would prove publicly that she was not Lenin's legal wife. No stratagem that served his ends was too low for the General Secretary.

With the death of Lenin and the ensuing disputes within the Party leadership, more and more power fell into Stalin's hands. He grew more arrogant and more intolerable.

Zinoviev and Kamenev began to realize that they had been exploited by a man who was more astute than themselves. The triumvirate collapsed. At the Party congress at the end of 1925 Zinoviev and Kamenev openly broke with Stalin; they accused him of abandoning Socialism. Stalin was indifferent. He had packed the congress with his supporters and it faithfully accorded him an enthusiastic vote of confidence. Zinoviev and Kamenev lined up with Trotsky and his allies. Stalin, threatened by this left-wing alliance, proceeded to make a new alliance with right-wing elements. He lined up behind him the Party's great theoretician, Bukharin, and the Bolshevik veterans Tomsky and Rykov.

Trotsky always tended to underestimate Stalin's guile. In the next two years the opposition provided by him and his allies proved no match for the Machiavellian tactics of the General Secretary. On the tenth anniversary of the Russian revolution they played into Stalin's hands. In the midst of the general rejoicings they staged a protest demonstration through the streets of Moscow. For the first time Stalin used force. He mobilized the police against Trotsky and the other opposition leaders. The demonstration was broken up brutally. The banners and placards were violently torn down and destroyed. Many of the demonstrators were arrested. A week later Trotsky and Zinoviev were expelled from the Bolshevik Party, and a week or two afterwards this was ratified by a Party congress at which all the 1,500 delegates were carefully-picked Stalin stooges.

Stalin now took a decisive step on the road to supreme authoritarian power. For the first time he used repression against his political opponents—the fathers of the Revolution. Trotsky and thirty of his leading associates were deported to Central Asia in the classic Czarist manner. Many less well-known members of the opposition were simply thrown into prison. Trotsky was finished. From Siberia he passed to Turkey, to Norway and then to Mexico.

The day that Trotsky was deported Stalin publicly humiliated Zinoviev and Kamenev. They were compelled openly to admit their errors, to denounce Trotsky and to ask for Stalin's pardon. Their opposition had collapsed. Stalin was striding forward in the footsteps of Ivan the Terrible. As yet, however, there was still a little opposition to be overcome. That took only a few months more.

Between 1922 and 1928, under what had been called the New Economic Policy, the Russian peasants had been permitted to carry on a certain amount of free enterprise. Trotsky had predicted that this would lead eventually to a major social crisis. At the very moment he was deported he was proved right. In that month the supply of grain to the urban areas of Russia was short by two million tons.

Stalin, who had contemptuously dismissed Trotsky's warnings, now took over the basic policies of his bitterest foe. He forced the Party congress to adopt the "First Five Year Plan". This right-about-turn in economic policy caused a major showdown with his allies Bukharin, Rykov and Tomsky. They in turn had already begun to realize that they were his dupes in the battle for personal power. As yet they were members of the Politburo. But by a palace intrigue in which Stalin used some veiled threats to win over the wavering Voroshilov and Kalinin, the three "allies" were isolated. The secret police, by this time directly under Stalin's control, was used against the rank and file opponents of his policies. Stalin terrorized the opposition. Within six months Bukharin, Rykov and Tomsky also had "admitted their errors". A decision of the Central Committee, which was inspired by Stalin, deprived them of all their offices. From that moment the Politburo and the Central Committee consisted only of "yes men".

Four days before Christmas, 1929, Stalin's fiftieth birthday was celebrated with a demonstration of fawning adulation and sycophantic servility unparalleled since the days of the most fearsome tyrants of history.

Some months before that Stalin had given the signal for one of the bloodiest and most terrible chapters of modern history. Faced by the problem created by the failure of the peasants to deliver sufficient food to the cities, Stalin decided to collectivize the farms. There were about twenty-five million peasants in Russia, of whom about a third lived barely above starvation level. At the other end of the scale were five million fairly well-off peasant farmers or "kulaks". Stalin gave the order "liquidate the kulaks". The millions of so-called "middle peasants", with the traditional conservatism of their kind, were just as opposed as the "kulaks" to any interference from the State.

Within a short time rural Russia was in a state of pandemonium. The overwhelming majority of the peasants faced by Stalin's order rose as a mass to defy his policies. Squads of Communist "commandoes" were sent throughout the Russian countryside to enforce the policy. Many of them according to official reports were "killed at their posts". They were backed by militant trade union officials, who were nothing more than Party lackeys, and the formidable forces of the Soviet secret police. The drive to collectivize the farms developed into a military operation and even into civil war. Some of the brutal police officers wept when they had to surround rebellious hamlets and villages with machine guns and then to mow down hundreds of the peasants who had defied Stalin's orders.

Vast numbers were murdered where they stood. Equal numbers were deported to remote areas of arctic Siberia. Yet they took their revenge. Some years later famine stalked through the Soviet Union. Stalin himself revealed certain grim facts; of the thirty-five million horses in Russia in 1929 half had been slaughtered by 1933; of almost the same proportion of cattle a total of thirty million were slaughtered in the same year; and vast tracts of land on which the crops had been burned lay untilled.

The human toll was even more sensational. According to a statement by Molotov to a Party congress, of the 5,618,000 "declared kulaks" in 1929 there were only 150,000 left in June, 1934.

"Five and a half million kulaks," admitted Molotov, "have been liquidated." How many died in Stalin's enforcement of collectivization will never be known. The total was certainly in millions. Even as early as 1931 Molotov admitted with appalling frankness that over 1,100,000 had been deported to Arctic forests where they were employed on tree felling operations.

As Stalin mercilessly enforced his terrible policies, even his lackeys on the Politburo and the Central Committee began to murmur in private. His young second wife Nadia Alliluyeva, daughter of a Leningrad workman who had sheltered Stalin in 1917, began to doubt the wisdom of her husband's policies, to which she at first had been whole-heartedly devoted. The terror and misery began to prey on her mind. One night in November, 1932, at a gathering in Voroshilov's home attended by other members of the Politburo, she spoke her mind. That was too much for Stalin. In front of their friends he poured out vulgar abuse on his wife. She walked out. Later that night she was found dead. Reports circulated that she had committed suicide. But there have been rumours that Stalin murdered her in a fit of drunken fury.

She left him two young children, a boy, Vassili, and girl, Svetlana, to whom he remained devoted. He also had had a son by his first wife, a Georgian peasant girl who had died in childbirth many years earlier.

Stalin, despite the mass murders which he ordered, never forgave himself for Nadia's death. Members of his police guard who escaped to the West after his death reported that in his later years he frequently went to her grave in the Kremlin gardens at six o'clock in the morning and sat in front of it brooding for half an hour.

Throughout the collectivization drive and the war on the "kulaks" Stalin in public maintained a mask of unruffled calm. Only once did he seem on the point of breakdown. One unofficial account of a meeting of the Politburo alleged that after a murmured admission of the murder of his wife, Stalin continued: "Maybe I have become an obstacle to the Party's unity. If so I am ready to go." The members of the Politburo looked at each other in acute embarrassment. What could they say to the man who was their lord and master? There was a deadly silence broken by Molotov who said, "Oh stop it. Hold your tongue, you *have* got the Party's confidence."

Despite his poker-faced demeanour, the war on the peasants did bite deep into Stalin's soul. He was not as hardened to terror then as he was to become a few years later. During the Second World War he frankly admitted to Churchill that the stress of carrying out his collectivization policy had been much greater than anything he had experienced as a result of the Nazi attack on Russia.

"It was all very bad and difficult," he said, "involving ten million people, but it was necessary."

He carried out the industrialization of the Soviet Union with the same ruthlessness as had been used when he collectivized the farms; tens of thousands of Russian workers who opposed his plans were shot for "sabotage".

By the beginning of the thirties he had realized not merely that Russia faced the possibility of war, but that she could fight such a war only if she were a modern industrial state. At whatever cost in human life and suffering he decided to modernize Russia. He tyrannized 160,000,000 people across the face of the world from the Baltic to the Pacific. His tyranny penetrated to every single facet of their existence. Not only did he hold the power of life and death in his hands, he interfered in the most obscure matters. He forced Russian historians to falsify and rewrite history to glorify his own part in the Revolution. He insisted that the literature should echo his own arid and cumbrous quasi-religious style. Architects were forced to conform to his appalling mid-Victorian taste. Sculptors, musicians and all other artists were encased in a Stalinist straightjacket.

Stalin, himself, was a weary, monotonous speaker. He had always been reserved and with increased age it became more marked. He had few social gifts beyond an inordinate capacity for hard liquor and a love of playing cruel practical jokes. As years passed he became the Hermit of the Kremlin, partly because he liked it that way and partly because he felt safe only in his own part of the Kremlin surrounded by the four hundred members of his personal guard. Even then there are alleged to have been over three hundred attempts to assassinate him either in Moscow, at his *dacha* outside the capital, or, more usually, at one of his holiday villas in the Crimea or the foothills of the Caucasus.

As he advanced into his fifties, however, two traits which had always been integral parts of his character, prudence and distrust, became more marked. It was the second of these which formed the basis of the most sensational period of Stalin's career, the later years of the thirties when, as one authority has written, "The Gods were athirst".

215

As Stalin overcame one group of opponents after another and battered down all opposition to his forced collectivization and industrialization policies, he became obsessed with a psychopathic fear of enemies, both real or imaginary. He saw danger to his absolute rule in everything and everyone—even among the Politburo, where his handpicked stooges waited anxiously upon the slight nod with which he gave decisions.

In the "civil war" against the peasants he had made the cynical discovery that fusillades brought little or no echo. Thereafter Stalin applied the same methods to the highest personalities of Party and State. No one, not even his most trusted collaborators, was safe.

The signal for a notable massacre was given by the assassination in Leningrad in December, 1934, of one of Stalin's bright young men, Kirov, by a youthful "oppositional Communist". Stalin rushed to Leningrad and personally interrogated the murderer. Mystery still surrounds the facts. There have been suggestions that even Kirov had begun to oppose his master's methods. And at the Party Congress in 1956 Khrushchev said there was strong evidence that Stalin was personally involved in the murder of Kirov. Whatever the truth Stalin used the murder of Kirov as an excuse for a general massacre. More than a hundred of the top members of the Communist Party in Leningrad were shot on Stalin's personal orders.

An equal number went to forced labour. Among the rank and file hundreds of thousands were deported to Siberia. There were no trials. On Stalin's orders suspects were merely brought before an officer of the secret police and sentenced. That was the start of five years of slaughter. As his fear of assassination and overthrow grew Stalin's venom knew no bounds. He struck not only at real opponents but rooted out the very environment which had produced them. Anyone who might have collaborated or been associated with one of his opponents to the *nth* degree was exterminated.

Little by little Stalin carried out one of the most horrible machinations in human history. First he humiliated the surviving leaders of the Russian Revolution by forcing a long series of recantations; then after pushing them in and out of prison he dragged them into the dock in the great trials of 1936-38 to exculpate themselves; thereafter they had been led to praise him he sent them to their deaths. This was the nauseating period of great "purge trials" the secrets of which still remain unrevealed.

Stalin's firm determination to eliminate every single member of a potential alternative government to his own can clearly be seen by the bare details of the main trials:

1. *The Trial of the Sixteen:* Zinoviev, Kamenev, and fourteen other top Party members, after confessing to most unlikely crimes were condemned and executed in August, 1936.

2. *The Trial of the Parallel Centre:* Radek, Sokolnikov, Piatakov and others followed the lead of the first group in admitting almost every conceivable crime at their trial in 1937. Although many were sentenced to long terms of imprisonment no one was executed.

3. *The Trial of the Twenty-one:* Rykov, Bukharin, Rakovsky and other surviving leaders of the Revolution were put in the dock in March, 1938, along with the former secret police chief Yagoda who had arrested Kamenev and Zinoviev. With one exception (Rakovsky, who was saved by the intervention of French Communist friends) all were executed.

The most significant trial, however, did not concern the founding fathers of the Revolution, but the heroes of the civil war. This trial held in June, 1937, was the only one held in camera. Marshals Tukhachevsky and Yegorov and a number of senior army commanders were tried, nominally for espionage. The real charge was that they had attempted a coup d'etat against Stalin. And in this case *the charge was true.* The Army High Command, wearied of the years of Stalin terror, along with leading Communists, had, indeed, planned a coup d'etat.

When arrested the conspirators had been on the point of seizing Stalin at a meeting of the Politburo and disposing of him. A military government would have then taken over. In the purge that followed approximately four hundred generals, nearly sixty per cent of the Soviet army commanders, and five hundred other senior officers were shot.

Even that represents but a small part of the purges. For during these years the following were either executed, committed suicide, or disappeared without trace:

Five out of seven presidents of the last Central Committee.

Nine of the 11 ministers of the Soviet Union in office at the end of 1936.

Eight of the 13 ministers of the Ukrainian Republic and seven of the 13 ministers of the White Russian republic.

Forty-three out of 53 of the secretaries of Communist Party Central organizations.

Ninety per cent of the leading foreign Communists in Russia (notably members of the famous Comintern).

A majority of the *high command of Stalin's secret police.*

Seventy out of 80 members of the Soviet War Council.

Forty-two per cent of all directors of metallurgical, mining and engineering plants.

Thirty-five per cent of other executives in these industries.

The majority of the directors, managers, of textile plants.

This list refers only to the more sensational events in the so-called "bullet in the nape of the neck offensive".

On a lower level there also was another slaughter of what has been called the anonymous subaltern officials. Probably this ran into hundreds of thousands. In most cases these officials were executed for "sabotage" of Soviet administration.

Khrushchev gave some of the inside story of the Stalin reign of terror in his famous speech to the twentieth Party congress in 1956 that has never been officially published by Russian sources. As early as 1934, Khrushchev revealed, Stalin had ordered his secret police to use torture to obtain confessions. "Beat them—and beat them again" he told his police thugs. "After Kirov's death," continued Khrushchev, "he ordered the secret police to speed up the executions. He used mass terror and torture to secure confessions."

Even top-level officials of the secret police were not safe from Stalin. In 1936, according to Khrushchev, while Stalin was on holiday in the Crimea with Zhadanov, he sent a peremptory telegram to Malenkov (then his personal assistant): "Yagoda (the head of the secret police) is useless. Arrest him and replace him by Yezhov."

Yezhov, in turn, was arrested a year or two later and replaced by Stalin's fellow-Georgian and boon companion, Beria, who survived until three months after Stalin's death.

Khrushchev revealed that Stalin kept sending Malenkov tele-grams that "the opposition must be physically annihilated . . ." that was his favourite phrase.

"By using secret police as his private instrument," continued Khrushchev, "Stalin liquidated untold numbers of Party com-rades on trumped-up charges. Many thousands of honest and innocent Communists died as a result of the falsification of cases."

Altogether, said Khrushchev, *three-quarters of the leading personalities of the Party were purged by Stalin.* And by deci-mating the Soviet High Command he seriously weakened Russia at a critical moment in her history.

So vast and terrible was the extent of the Stalin reign of terror in the decade after 1929 that the full toll of human suffering and death can be measured only statistically. In these years in Russia a minimum of one million were slaughtered, according to Western experts who have examined the large amount of official Soviet information which has since become available. That is only a part of the total. In the same period *at least another sixteen million perished.* Half of that total died in the great famine; the other half died by administrative murder in the terrible forced labour camps in the Arctic and Siberia. The Russian public has recently been told some of these facts for the first time through the medium of semi-factual novels. They give a total of seventeen million dead in one decade through the evil of a single man. Russian statistics show that during that same period no fewer than another eight million souls were *still alive* in the unbelievable conditions of the Stalin terror camps. Taking no account of normal population growth, that accounts for a total of twenty-five million human souls "miss-ing" from the population of the Soviet Union in 1939. Even Stalin himself on his own figures could not explain where fourteen million of that total had gone.

The statisticians have discovered also that in a single year Stalin's murders exceeded by twenty times the total number of people officially executed by successive Czars in their pro-grammes of repression *in a century.* For political massacres committed against his own people Stalin easily beats even Hitler's record; there is no comparison in the whole of recorded history. In addition, as a result of his deportations, *one Soviet citizen in every fifteen had become a convict.*

By the beginning of 1939 Stalin's thirst for blood had been quenched. At a Party congress (the first for five years) he announced "we shall have no further need to resort to the method of mass purges". By that time the only survivors of the Central Committee of 1917 were Stalin himself, the fabulous Alexandra Kollontai, who was in the comparative safety of the Soviet Embassy in Stockholm, and Trotsky.

The epilogue to the drama of the prewar Stalinist terror took place far from the Kremlin, on the other side of the Atlantic on a sunny afternoon towards the end of August, 1940.

Trotsky was a great author in his own right as well as one of the founders of Soviet Russia. He was working on his brilliant denunciatory biography of Stalin when he was struck in the head with an ice axe. He died a few hours later. His murderer was a special agent of the Stalinist secret police. He had been sent across the Atlantic on the personal orders of Stalin to "physically annihilate" the last surviving member of the Bolshevik opposition. Stalin had extended his crimes from his own people to the international stage.

Unlike Lenin and Trotsky, Stalin was incapable of appreciating the basis of international diplomacy. With clear signs of a growing conflict among the European Powers, Stalin was free to choose between an alliance with the Western Powers, as his Foreign Commissionar Litvinov urged, or an alliance with his ideological enemy but fellow dictator Adolf Hitler in Germany. The Western Powers certainly gave Stalin little encouragement. Yet when, on the night of 23 August, 1939, Stalin in the Kremlin signed a pact with the Nazi Foreign Minister Ribbentrop some confusion and a little consternation could be detected among other leaders in world Communism. Stalin knew very well that, by this cynical betrayal of everything for which the Bolshevik revolution had stood, he had freed Hitler for the time being of the threat of a two-front war. He had set the stage for the Second World War.

Within a fortnight Stalin had demonstrated his political amorality by complete abandonment of the basic tenets of the original Bolsheviks. In mid-September, in accord with a secret agreement with the Nazis to partition Poland, he ordered the Red Army to occupy the eastern part of that country.

By the same secret protocol the Baltic States and Finland were accorded to the "Soviet sphere of influence". Within months Stalin had donned the mantle of a new ruthless Russian imperialist. To each of the three democratic Baltic States he despatched one of his most trusted aides, backed by his secret police. They were ordered to overthrow the existing democratic governments and establish Communist administrations. Within days the three Baltic States had disappeared. They became Soviet provinces. Hundreds of thousands of their inhabitants were either shot or deported to eastern Siberia.

There followed one of the most outrageous of all war crimes. At this date there can be little doubt that it was Stalin who ordered his police general Ivan Serov to murder thousands of Polish officers interned in a camp at Katyn. Believing the crime would remain unknown for ever the bodies were interred in the surrounding forest.

Throughout the spring months of 1941 Stalin was warned from all sides that Hitler was about to disown the Soviet-Nazi pact and attack Russia. Stalin dismissed all warnings as Western propaganda and continued to deliver war material to the Germans. Then at dawn on 22 June, 1941, the German Wehrmacht invaded Russia. Soon troops of the German Army discovered the mass graves at Katyn.

Stalin at first could not believe that the Germans were attacking Russia. He still trusted Hitler. On the morning of 22 June when reports of the first German attacks reached the Kremlin he gave orders that the Russian troops should not fire back. According to Khrushchev in 1956 he said it was nothing more than "ill discipline on the part of some German troops". As a result of Stalin's stupidity the Red Army and Air Force suffered serious losses along the frontier. Soon three great German thrusts had penetrated deep into the Soviet Union.

In the Ukraine, which was under the heaviest attack, there was a desperate shortage of rifles. Khrushchev phoned Stalin from Kiev for more weapons and asked to speak to him personally. Malenkov answered the telephone. He said that Stalin was not there. Actually Stalin was sitting beside him but was apparently frightened to tell Khrushchev that there were no rifles available for him.

By the beginning of December, 1941, Hitler's central army group had driven across the Ukraine and reached the terminus of the Moscow trams only a few miles to the south-west of the city. In fact the Germans could see the towers of the Kremlin in the distance. At this stage Stalin and his secret police panicked. His thugs fled and the "liberated" Muscovites virtually revolted —something which, in the postwar years, Stalin was never to forget. According to Khrushchev, Stalin, himself, also fled. As he went he moaned that "we have lost everything that Lenin created". But if Stalin lost his nerve, those who had survived his purge of the Soviet Supreme Command did not. Under the command of the later Marshal Zhukov the Red Army halted the Germans. Then in the great winter campaign of 1941-42, slowly drove them back.

With Moscow safe, Stalin returned to his office in the Kremlin and adopted the role of Generalissimo. As had been proved in the civil war a quarter of a century earlier, he had no flair for military operations.

Stalin's dabbling in tactics on the Eastern front inevitably led to catastrophe. In the great battle of Kharkov he ignored the advice of the Soviet General Staff. Russia suffered a serious reverse. A whole German army group escaped, and nearly 500,000 Russians were killed. Yet Stalin tolerated no failure in others. After a retreat near Rostov he descended on the headquarters of the retreating formations. The secret police who accompanied him shot the commanding generals and their staffs out of hand. These individual and personal military massacres were repeated at various points until victory was achieved in 1945.

With the turn of the tide after the battle of Stalingrad in the winter of 1942-43 Stalin became an international hero. He was honoured throughout the Western world as the commander-in-chief of the gallant Red Army.

He received Churchill and other Western statesmen in the Kremlin when periods of surly boorishness alternated with cordial invitations to convivial drinking parties in his private apartments in the Kremlin.

In 1945 he made a trip outside the Soviet Union for the first time for many years. Accompanied by a battalion of personal bodyguards he met Churchill and Roosevelt in Teheran. On the eve of the defeat of Germany he again met them at Yalta in the Crimea at the beginning of 1945. And two months after the German surrender he appeared in the German capital to confer with the British and American leaders at the Potsdam conference.

When the Germans had penetrated into the Soviet Union in some areas a number of the non-Russian inhabitants, chiefly Muslims, had collaborated with the invaders. Once the Germans had been driven back Stalin took swift punitive action:

1. In 1943-44 he ordered the deportation of the whole Kalmuck people (descendents of Genghis Khan's Mongols) to Siberia.
2. Early in 1945 he decreed the liquidation of one of the constituent parts of the Soviet Union, the Chechen-Ingush Autonomous Republic. The inhabitants were deported at at few hours' notice to Arctic Siberia.

In both these deportations, and other smaller ones, unnumbered thousands died as they were trundled by train across thousands of miles of Eurasia in open cattle trucks whatever the weather.

At a dinner for some of his European satellite leaders given in the Kremlin in April, 1945, Stalin became drunk and hysterical. This was to happen often in his later years. On such occasions his basic character quickly showed itself. He got up, hitched up his trousers like a peasant about to provoke a fight, and shouted: "The war will soon be over. We shall need another fifteen to twenty years . . . and then we shall have another go."

* * *

It was at that time that the then comparatively insignificant Yugoslav partisan leader Djilas saw Stalin in the Kremlin. This is what he saw:

"An ungainly dwarf of a man passed through the gilded and marbled imperial halls and a path opened before him; radiant admiring glances followed him, while the ears of courtiers strained to catch every word. And he, sure of himself and his works, obviously paid no attention to all this.

"His country was in ruins, hungry and exhausted. But his armies and his marshals heavy with fat and medals, and drunk with vodka and victory had already trampled half Europe underfoot, and he was convinced that they would trample over the other half in the next round.

"He knew that he was one of the cruellest, most despotic figures in history. But this did not worry him a bit for he was convinced that he was carrying out the will of history."[1]

After the war, according to Khrushchev, Stalin became ever more capricious, irritable and brutal. His persecution mania reached unbelievable dimensions. He took an almost fiendish delight in humiliating his closest associates in public. At a dinner in the Kremlin for foreign Communists in 1945 he selected Khrushchev whose short rotund figure fascinated him as the butt of what Stalin thought was fun. As he became more and more drunk Stalin shouted at Khrushchev: "*Khol, Khol,* dance the *gopak.*" (*Khol Khol* is a derogatory Russian term for a Ukrainian, while the *gopak* is a complicated Ukrainian folk dance involving intricate footwork.) For a man of Khrushchev's build and age it was a torture to dance the *gopak.* Yet none could with impunity cross Stalin. "So I danced it," Khruschev told the twentieth Party congress a decade afterwards.

Within a few months of the defeat of Germany Stalin had imposed Communist or near-Communist satellite regimes on all the countries occupied by the Red Army: Poland, Rumania, Bulgaria, Eastern Germany, and it seemed on Yugoslavia. Within a year or two Czechoslovakia had been added to his Communist empire through a characteristically sordid coup d'etat in which one of Stalin's most faithful international friends, President Benes, was forced from office. Wherever the Stalin writ ran the secret police terror followed. Now it was not only Russia which suffered. From the heart of Europe to the far confines of Asia millions of men, women, and children suffered intolerable cruelty; very many died in concentration camps which were as bad, and quite as numerous, as those of Hitler.

At first his non-Russian victims were Socialists, trade unionists, Christians, intellectuals and simple workers who merely believed in liberty and justice. Many once had thought that

[1] *Conversations with Stalin* by Milovan Djilas (Hart Davis 1962).

Stalin shared their views. In addition tens of thousands of amazed and completely despairing non-political victims were deported without apparent reason by order of Stalin's police. Presently thousands who heartily supported Stalin, Communists themselves, were added to the vast but still unnumbered total of Stalin's postwar victims. Veteran Communists, like Slansky in Czechoslovakia, were tried and executed on absurd charges. Even Stalin's one-time crony, the Bulgarian Communist leader Dimitrov (hero of the Reichstag fire and ex-president of the Communist International) almost certainly was murdered on Stalin's order.

Of this nightmare period towards the end of Stalin's life one authority on postwar Russia has written:

"To set against (his) manic flights or the dazzling almost Italian volatility were periods of black depression. Then the gay impulsive killer who allowed himself to be adulated because it was convenient to be adulated and sometimes amusing, who killed because he was a natural killer, out of anger, out of sadism, malice, convenience, megalomania or boredom, all according to mood—then this extraordinary creature became morbid and paranoiac with the results we all know."

Within a year or two of the end of the war even members of the Politburo (the Praesidium as it became) went in fear of their lives. Some of Stalin's kindred spirits such as the detached, inscrutable Molotov, are said to have pleaded for a promise that he would never arrest or execute them. Their fears were not without reason. By 1949 Stalin's paranoia had reached such an advanced stage that he did begin to murder members of the Politburo itself. At the beginning of that year one of the Soviet vice-presidents, Nikolai Voznesensky, head of the State Planning Commission, had serious differences with Stalin on economic planning. One day he failed to appear at a meeting of the Politburo. He was never seen again. Without the knowledge of the Politburo Stalin had had him shot. Thereafter the whole Praesidium went in terror. On one occasion Bulganin told Khrushchev that he had been summoned to Stalin's *dacha* outside Moscow and did not know whether he was going to a banquet or to prison.

Molotov was soon removed from the office of Foreign Minister and placed under house arrest, while his wife was imprisoned for a considerable period. Sons of various members of the Praesidium, including those of Mikoyan, were sent to prison. Stalin's own son, Vassili, however, was permitted to live a life of open debauchery. For years his apartment on one of Moscow's main boulevards was the scene of lavish orgies, with all the classic touches including naked girls dancing on the table. It was not until Vassili was found hopelessly drunk in a Moscow gutter that Stalin took action. Then Vassili was reduced from the rank of lieut.-general to colonel in the Red Air Force and his entertainment allowance was severely cut. Stalin's daughter, Svetlana, a quiet, domesticated girl devoted to her father, was forced on two occasions to break off marriage to the son of a leading Soviet figure because of her father's distrust of everyone around him.

Stalin's own personal life was even worse than that of his son. In the years after the war Stalin, like his boon companion Beria, developed a "Lolita" complex. Former members of Stalin's personal guard who deserted to the West have told of how Beria used his police to pick up forcibly pretty under-age girls off the streets for the satisfaction of his own lust and that of Stalin. If the minors refused they were threatened with deportation and the extermination of their families.

Khrushchev admitted this to the twentieth Party congress when he described "revolting details of Stalin's sexual aberrations".

"In Stalin's later years," said Khrushchev, "his sexual obsessions degenerated into sadism against young girls. A number of minors and other girls (procured for him by Beria) disappeared."

His fellow Georgian Beria was the only person Stalin even half-trusted. In the summer the pair would depart together for their native Caucasus to drink themselves silly, to cook *schashlik* on an open spit, and to stage elaborate "Lolita" orgies on their estates.

By 1952 Stalin was quite mad. He even believed that his life-long friend, Marshal Voroshilov, President of the Soviet Union, was a British spy. And he began to make plans to "physically annihilate" various members of the Praesidium: it is said that he had in mind Molotov, Malenkov and Khrushchev whom he suspected, possibly correctly, of plotting against him. Probably he also developed a strong anti-Jewish attitude. At any rate that is suggested by a "plot" which has remained one of the most enigmatic happenings of Stalin's last days. It was at the beginning of January, 1955, that Stalin announced that a number of leading Soviet doctors (most of whom were Jewish) had been arrested for plotting against high members of the Party and the Army. They were also accused of murdering several Soviet leaders, among them Zhdanov, who had died some years earlier.

What happened thereafter is known only from rumours; one version was alleged to have been given by the famous Soviet writer Ilya Ehrenburg, himself a Jew, to Jean Paul Sartre.

Following the doctors' plot Stalin is reputed to have summoned a meeting of the Praesidium. He announced that he had decided to deport all the Jews in the Soviet Union to concentration camps in the Arctic. Mikoyan and Molotov are reported to have protested strongly emphasizing the inevitable hostile reaction abroad. Voroshilov went further and said that Stalin's proposal was criminal. It was the same policy which had aroused the whole world against Hitler. Kaganovitch, himself a Jew, tried to offer a compromise. He urged that a special committee of the Praesidium should investigate the doctors' plot, but that the decision to deport the Jews should be dropped. All members of the Praesidium, with the exception of Beria, supported Kaganovitch's suggestion.

Stalin was in a fury at this unexpected and unprecedented opposition to his will. He became apoplectic. Then Mikoyan, along with Molotov the oldest serving member of the Praesidium, showed that they had come prepared for a showdown. He warned Stalin not to attempt any foolishness and added:

"If we do not leave your office freely within half an hour the Army is ready to occupy the Kremlin."

Beria, seeing the turn of events, withdrew his opposition to Kaganovitch's proposal.

Stalin completely lost control of himself. He went red, then purple and started to shriek. Before he could say more than a few words he dropped on the floor suffering from a stroke.

It is alleged that Beria then jumped up and started to dance round Stalin shouting: "Joy . . . Joy . . . we are free at last, the tyrant is dead."

Stalin's daughter was sent for from his private apartments. She came in and bent down to kiss her father—and Stalin opened one eye.

Immediately Beria became hysterical. Dropping on his knees he begged Stalin's forgiveness. . . .

That story may be apocryphal. All that is known for certain is that on the night of 1 March, 1953, the world was suddenly astounded to learn in an official Kremlin announcement that Stalin had suffered a cerebral haemorrhage. Four days later came the announcement of his death. Whether he had in fact died a week or so earlier, or whether he was murdered by some of the members of the Praesidium, must remain a subject of conjecture.

Some days before the announcement of Stalin's fatal illness a brief report was issued in Moscow of the sudden death of the commander of his personal bodyguard. His personal secretary also disappeared and has never been heard of since.

Khrushchev may have given a clue when he denounced Stalin as a "mass murderer and a torturer" to the twentieth Party congress in 1956.

"With the fabricated doctors' plot in the last weeks of his life," said the new chairman of the Praesidium, "*Stalin was preparing to plunge the country into a new reign of terror*."

Did the Praesidium decide that *the Stalin terror must end*?

Chapter 12

"LUCKY" LUCIANO

IN February, 1962, there died peacefully, in the all-forgiving city of Naples, a man whose life reads like the scenario of one of Hollywood's more melodramatic gangster-thrillers. His funeral did nothing to dispel that illusion. The corpse was that of "Don" Salvatore Lucania, much better known to the world of international crime as Charley "Lucky" Luciano. Among the mourners were leaders of the most notorious secret society in the world, the Sicilian-American Mafia or Black Hand, of which Luciano had been the European Grandmaster for more than a decade.

He had been more. From the time of his expulsion from the United States in 1946 until the time of his death Luciano had also been "European President" of an international organization with ramifications as widespread in crime as the Comintern's in international politics. Luciano was the undisputed boss in the Eastern Hemisphere of "Dope International", the greatest conspiracy in the history of international crime. For fifteen years Luciano had directed and controlled the vast illicit trade in dangerous drugs, from the Middle East through Italy and France to the eastern seaboard of North America. He had produced profits on a scale unknown to any other trade in the world—and in the process he had killed, mutilated and brought unbelievable misery and suffering to thousands of drug addicts from the Levant to New York's East Side. "Lucky" was a brilliant, gifted, and completely evil man.

Salvatore Lucania, like every other *Capo Mafioso* or Mafia chieftain on both sides of the Atlantic, was born in western Sicily —in the small town of Lercara Friddi in 1897. His birthplace was in the heart of that grim and barren corner of Italy's southernmost island where a one-time resistance movement against French invaders had been transformed into the blackmail-and-murder secret society which even today remains a major problem for the Italian authorities.

Salvatore's father was a hard-working labourer at the local sulphur pits. When the boy was nine his father had saved enough to take the family to America, the land of promise, in that great wave of Italian immigration to the United States at the beginning of the present century. Inevitably, with the Sicilian immigrants went the Mafia.

The Lucania family, like thousands of other poor Italians, found refuge and shelter with Sicilian relatives in the slums of New York City. Within a few months Salvatore had acquired a Brooklyn drawl and was completely at home in the toughest section of New York, the Lower East Side around Brooklyn Bridge. By the age of fifteen he was a pickpocket, petty thief and a knife-carrying thug. A year later he was a runner for one of the principal dope peddlars in the area. Then he was caught carrying a parcel of heroin and spent six months in a reformatory with others of his kind.

Conviction was the surest road to success in the Lower East Side underworld and a period in a reformatory was the equivalent of matriculation. As soon as he came out young Salvatore Lucania asked to be allowed to join one of the toughest gangs of the district. The gangsters had for long had an approving eye on the young man. Small for his age, the lad nevertheless stood head and shoulders above the other young thugs with whom he consorted. He was quick with his peculiarly delicate hands and feet—perhaps an inheritance from some unknown far-off French aristocrat—and obviously he could use his head to great advantage. The gang accepted his application without demur.

The quiet and curiously restrained young criminal had also attracted the attention of a potentate of the underworld far above the level of ordinary Lower East Side gangsters. This was Guiseppe Masseria, who had a formidable record of crime extending back to the beginning of the century. He was especially interested in Salvatore for two reasons:

1. His family had been well-known in Sicily—and that was fundamental.
2. He had the supreme Mafia virtue—steely self-control.

Unlike their close neighbours, the noisy and volatile southern

Italians, the true Mafiosi of western Sicily are grim, cold and undemonstrative men. And even as a teenager Salvatore Lucania had a poker face. His cold, unblinking eyes showed nothing at all—and only the slightest flutter of his hands gave a clue to what was passing in his mind. He stood out as something exceptional in the Lower East Side.

Salvatore deplored violence or the use of firearms—if he could achieve the same objective by negotiation, mediation, intimidation or any other method conceived by his acute brain. He believed in order; and he succeeded in dragooning the young hoodlums around him into accepting that well-organized and disciplined racketeering was infinitely more lucrative than their former haphazard hit-and-run methods.

Salvatore, indeed, was a natural leader. He would have risen to the top of any occupation—criminal or otherwise—which he had cared to select. He moved from the world of petty crime to large-scale racketeering as personal assistant to Masseria, who was *Capo Mafioso,* leader of the Mafia.

By the early twenties "Lucky", as everyone in the New York underworld soon called him, was chief of staff to the *Capo Mafioso* and a power behind the throne in the New York Grand Council of the Mafia.

The combination of Masseria's experience and prestige with "Lucky's" rationalization of crime proved formidable. These were the days of prohibition and of the crimes which it bred. Though Salvatore did not approve of violence if other methods could be used, he would not tolerate disobedience or unbridled opposition. After the partnership had chalked up a total of more than a hundred murders in the course of business Masseria was established as criminal czar of the New York underworld with Luciano as heir apparent. But for business as well as personal reasons "Lucky" preferred to be a backroom boy. He strongly favoured "tidy organization" and a tight chain of command.

Backed by the prestige and authority of the elderly *Capo Mafioso,* Luciano branched out into new fields with all the initiative and enterprise which were a feature of his make-up. He was sure that the days of prohibition were numbered. The Mafia, therefore, must have new business outlets. He extended the brotherhood's activities to what were to become its principal fields of operation—organized gambling, juke boxes, chains of brothels, large-scale dope peddling, and "protection" rackets among the trade unions dominating the New York waterfront, chief among them the garment industry and the wholesale food markets.

In this drive for new outlets his associates were two other young Sicilian-Americans, Giovanni Doto, better known as Joe Adonis, and Alberto Anastasia, who would find a place among the immortals of organized crime (and his own death) as President of Murder Incorporated.

The *Capo Mafioso*, however, was worried. The old Sicilian did not approve of all of these new-fangled ideas. The big-business approach was alien to him, and, he claimed, to the Mafia. With all the authority of a *Capo Mafioso* he said so. His three young henchmen refused to obey. The old man started to use his power to sabotage their plans. Open guerilla warfare started inside the higher councils of the Mafia, as had happened in the past in Sicily. There was a traditional method of resolving such a situation. A *Capo Mafioso* whose initiative had been impaired by age could retire in honour. Thereafter he would be respected as an elder statesman of the brotherhood. Should he prove difficult, however, he received a warning. Traditionally, it took the form of the assassination of one of his closest associates. In 1930 one of Masseria's bodyguard was murdered in an ambush. But the old man was stubborn. He took no heed.

In April, 1931, therefore, Luciano invited Masseria to dinner in one of the best Italian restaurants in Coney Island. Like many others of his nation, Masseria enjoyed his food and his wine. The dinner lasted a long time. When at last the two men were alone Luciano excused himself and went to wash his hands. Unquestionably, he was in the men's lavatory when three men suddenly appeared behind the chair of the *Capo Mafioso*. They emptied their revolvers into him—and disappeared

At the sound of the shots Luciano dashed out of the washroom. For once his grim, austere countenance showed grief. His master had been murdered. The police arrived. None of the waiters could give the slightest description of the three assailants. All confirmed that Signor Lucania had been in the lavatory when the tragedy occurred. As in all Mafia crimes, no one knew anything. This was a traditional Mafia execution. By the rules of the brotherhood *Capo Mafioso* had been "condemned" by a meeting of the Grand Council for failing to accept the warning. By these same historic rules he could die in only one way—suddenly, when full of good food and wine.

Luciano now became *Capo Mafioso* in succession to his master. His rise in the world of crime in the next few years was spectacular but characteristically discreet. He abjured vulgar, flamboyant methods such as were employed by Capone—who, in any case, as a Naples-born Italian, had been a *parvenu* in the higher councils of the Mafia.

Within a few years Luciano had revolutionized the Mafia. When he took over it was still the traditional Sicilian murder-cum-blackmail Black Hand. He Americanized it. He decided it must go into business in a big way. He built it up into one of the greatest crime syndicates in history, just as other men had built up General Motors, Standard Oil and the other monuments to American commercial enterprise.

The report of the Kefauver Commission in the early fifties and the sensational discoveries made by the American police when they accidentally stumbled on a meeting of the Mafia Grand Council at Apalachin, Upper New York State, in late 1957, show that Luciano's "new look" Mafia is as formidable today as it ever was.

The Mafia apart, there were other powerful criminal organizations in New York and throughout the United States. The most important in the early thirties were those led by such notorious criminals as Meyer Lansky, Lepke Buchalter and Longy Zwillman. Luciano was clever enough to form working arrangements with these groups, which eventually led to the alliance which Senator Kefauver has christened "the American National Crime Syndicate". After many months of investigation the Senator wrote that "The Mafia is the cement that binds organized crime together." It was Luciano who, at a key moment, bound the Mafia together.

Luciano staged one other revolution in the American world of crime. He radically changed both the manners and the dress of America's top gangsters. After the sartorial extravagances of the Capone period Luciano set the fashion with beautifully-cut pinstripe suits, expensive but discreet shirts and ties, and hand-made shoes. It has been rumoured that, like other foreign potentates, he ordered them from Savile Row. His manners became equally impeccable. Acting and looking the part of a great Latin "Don" he established himself in a millionaire's suite in the Waldorf-Astoria Hotel under the name of Mr. Charles Ross. The meetings of his Crime Syndicate held in the lounge of his suite were certainly conducted in as serious and as restrained a manner as comparable meetings of great American corporations held elsewhere in the same building.

Within a few years Luciano dominated Tammany Hall and all the pernicious influence that flowed from that den of political corruption. No racket in New York City, or in a big area around, could be started without the not-always-gracious permission of Mr. Ross—whether it were gambling, trade union "protection" extortion, or prostitution. The last he took as a matter of course. The Mafia had always been in the brothel business. For generations *Mafiosi* had been brothel keepers and undertakers in western Sicily.

As a youth in the Lower East Side Luciano had sometimes been both a tout and a pimp. He knew all about the business. When he rose in the world he realized that a well-organized chain of high-class brothels can be quite as lucrative as gambling, extortion and similar operations, although it can never equal the fantastic returns from really large-scale international dope peddling.

From the Waldorf-Astoria, at the height of his influence, Luciano controlled at least 200 "madams", while well over 1,000 girls paid him a cut of their earnings, which totalled £2,500,000. His operational methods were not as restrained as his personal manners. The girls who refused to pay were beaten and slashed —just as they were in London twenty years later by the Messina brothers, *who were Mafia subordinates of Luciano*. Luciano had the utmost contempt for "dumb broads" as he called them. "Whores is whores," he once said on a tapped telephone, "and they ain't got no guts." Unfortunately for "Lucky" some of them did have guts.

Not only did Luciano use the girls as a source of income. He delighted in their personal company and constantly used his business enterprises to supply his private harem. He thought nothing of making telephone calls and doing business with his chief assistants in their presence. That was his undoing.

For a long time Luciano regarded himself as above the law. With his important political friends, who drew their percentage from his various criminal enterprises, he believed that no politically-appointed district attorney would ever dare to interfere with his operations.

By the mid-nineteen-thirties, however, New York had become outraged by its big-time multi-millionaire gangsters and their rackets. A young special prosecutor was appointed by the outraged citizens to try to clean up the city. His name was Thomas E. Dewey. It did not take him long to discover that much of the organized crime in the city stemmed from the Waldorf-Astoria apartment of Mr. Charles Ross. Some of the "dumb broads" who had been Luciano's personal guests were persuaded to talk. Mr. Dewey started to build up a case based on Luciano's control of organized prostitution in the city.

The legal authorities, and certainly the redoubtable Federal Narcotics Commissioner in Washington, Dr. Harry Anslinger, would have preferred to pin Luciano on illicit narcotics distribution. But then, Luciano never personally handled or even saw an ounce of cocaine. His white slave operations were much easier to prove.

To his complete astonishment Luciano was arrested and indicted for the crime of compulsory prostitution. To his even greater astonishment he was found guilty on sixty-two different counts. He was sentenced in the New York Court of General Sessions to imprisonment for thirty to fifty years. Judge McCook, who passed sentence, echoed the opinion of all decent Americans when he said: "You are one of the most vicious criminals who ever appeared in this court."

Luciano disappeared into a New York State penitentiary near the Canadian border known as "Little Siberia". There he became a legend to the other convicts. The guards, too, were intimidated; later, one was to say " 'Lucky' practically ran the place".

"Lucky" was still lording it over convicts when the United States entered the Second World War—against Italy, among other Axis states.

The Mafia suddenly became of military importance. It directly controlled the Italian dock workers in New York harbour and exercised great influence over the rest of the waterfront labour. At the beginning of 1943 Churchill and Roosevelt at the Casablanca conference decided to invade Sicily, the Mafia homeland. One plan called for a landing in the north-western corner of the island. American secret service officers made contact with the top Mafia "dons" in New York. It soon became obvious that only Luciano had the authority to give the necessary orders. There followed an interlude in the Luciano biography which even now has never been completely explained. He was moved to a prison much nearer New York City. There in the latter half of 1942 and the early part of 1943 he took part in mysterious conferences. They were attended by his lawyers, by the cream of the New York Mafia underworld headed by his fellow "don" Francisco Castiglia, better-known to the police as Frank Costello, and unidentified American Intelligence officers.

Luciano was much more of an American than an Italian although he had retained his Italian nationality. It is generally believed that he aided the American war effort in two ways:

1. By preventing sabotage by members of the Mafia in New York docks and other ports.

2. By helping to enlist the Sicilian Mafia as underground agents to prepare the way for the troops of General George Patton when they invaded Sicily under Field Marshal Alexander's command in the summer of 1943.

No one has ever given the facts. Even Senator Kefauver during his inquiries was unable to pry the appropriate secret files out of the Pentagon. It is an undisputed fact, however (as the Nazis admitted after the war), that all efforts to persuade the Italian dockers in New York to commit sabotage proved singularly unsuccessful. It is also a fact that in the weeks immediately before the Allied landing in Sicily the Mafia co-operated by providing guides and secret hideouts for Allied spies on the island.

In 1945, Luciano's lawyers appealed to the New York State Parole Board for clemency. The hearings took some time as everyone, including Luciano, shut up like a clam when wartime operations were even mentioned. At long last the Board came to the conclusion that "Lucky" *had* aided the Allied war effort and it was decided to deport him. It was customary in such cases to deport non-American criminals if they had served a substantial portion of their sentence. Luciano had been in prison for nine years; moreover, he was still an Italian citizen. The American authorities generally were inclined to the view that once home in his native Sicily "Lucky", as they called him, would settle down to live quietly on his very substantial ill-gotten gains. By 1946 Luciano's erstwhile prosecutor, Mr. Dewey, had become Governor of New York. He shared that view.

Luciano was removed from the penitentiary where he was held to Ellis Island to await deportation. His departure was fixed for February, 1946. The Mafia high command did not intend to let their chief go without due honours being paid. So before the Liberty ship *Laura Keene* sailed there took place in New York Harbour one of the most sensational gatherings ever seen.

As the ship raised steam for the voyage to Italy numbers of expensively-dressed men, all carrying union cards describing them as "stevedores", crowded up the gangway from a New York pier. Most of the great personalities of the New York underworld were there: Alberto Anastasia, the youthful associate of Luciano; "Socks" Lanza; Meyer Lansky, representing the Mafia's criminal allies; and even the "Prime Minister of the Underworld", Frank Costello himself, the man who had largely taken over in New York when Luciano went to prison.

For hours before the arrival of the leaders of the American National Crime Syndicate crates of caviare, smoked salmon, and other delicacies, and cases of every kind of beverage from Italian wine to Scotch whisky had been carried aboard. Last of all came the guest of honour, saturnine, greying Luciano, escorted by a posse of Federal guards who had been ordered to bring him across the river from Ellis Island.

As Luciano strode up the gangway, bowing and waving, like a Hollywood idol, there were shouts from the dockside of "You'll be back, Lucky", and "Keep punchin', boss". These came from picket lines of hoodlums drawn up parallel with the ship to keep back newspaper reporters and cameramen who were trying to record this historic occasion in the annals of crime.

Once aboard the s.s. *Laura Keene,* Luciano soon showed that a decade in an American penitentiary had done nothing to deprive him of his fire.

"Stand aside," he told the Federal guards in whose charge he was supposed to remain as long as the ship was in United States territorial waters. "Keep out o' this . . . if y'know what's good for ya."

The warders protested. They were met with sinister threats of "Forget it—get out" from Frank Costello and the other criminal nabobs massed in the tiny passenger saloon of the Liberty ship.

The Federal Guards, poor fellows, had to live. The Mafia party went on for hours. It was the climax and (some American officials were naïve enough to believe) the conclusion of one of the greatest criminal careers of all time.

There is little doubt, however, that the expulsion of Luciano from the United States marked a turning point in the operations of the New York Mafia. It now extended its operations to an international scale, for the real beginning of the great and terrible post-war "Dope International" was the day that "Lucky" Luciano stepped ashore at Naples. From that moment he was the motivating mind behind the intercontinental enterprises of the fantastic dope peddling criminal co-operative.

As soon as he reached Italy Luciano went through the technical formalities of returning to his native Lercara Friddi near Palermo. He received a rapturous welcome from the native-born members of the Mafia. By lavish use of money in high quarters in the Italian capital he obtained permission to establish himself in a sumptuous apartment overlooking the Tiber in Rome. Within months the graph of illicit dope traffic in Italy showed a sharp rise.

"Lucky", however, was unhappy. Although he had been born and had spent his childhood in Sicily he was an out-and-out American. He pined for what he would always regard as his real home—New York's Lower East Side. At the beginning of 1947 a certain Signor Salvatore Lucania, with a perfectly valid and genuine Italian passport showing he had been born at Lercara Friddi and complete with a Cuban visa, landed at Havana Airport. At once he rented a luxurious apartment in the capital of President Batista and put himself in touch with some of the higher officials of the régime with whom his Mafia buddies had had long and lucrative links.

By one of those amazing coincidences with which the story of the Mafia and "Dope International" is punctuated, there took place in Havana a remarkable series of "accidental meetings" with prominent visitors from New York. These encounters were later to provide much fun for the members of various U.S. Congress inquiries. Frank Costello admitted to the Kefauver Commission that he had "just happened to bump into 'Lucky' in the lobby of a Havana hotel and he rode to the airport with me." When asked what they talked about the scowling "Prime Minister of the Underworld" retorted cautiously: "Oh, about his health . . . and what not."

The U.S. Federal Bureau of Narcotics had its spies in Cuba. It did not take them long to report Luciano's presence. Moreover, they soon knew what he was actually doing just 100 miles from Miami.

The corrupt pre-Castro government was reluctant to remove him. Ordinary diplomatic representations were without result. At last the Americans decided to cut off supplies of all narcotic drugs to Cuba—on the ground that if "Lucky" was in Havana there was no need for the import of legal supplies of heroin and morphia. The Cuban Government capitulated, no doubt at great financial loss to some of its leading members. Luciano was expelled. Back he went to Lercara Friddi. By this time his contacts in Italian high places were such that within a week or two he was back in his luxurious Rome apartment in company with a beautiful Italian ballet dancer named Igea Lissoni. This girl, the daughter of a good-class Italian family, had failed to make the grade as a prima ballerina in La Scala, Milan. She had thereafter become the star of a well-known but somewhat disreputable cabaret in Naples of which Luciano was part owner. There she met "Lucky".

This was something new for Luciano, for Igea was no "dumb broad" but an elegant, cultured and very charming girl. She seemed to satisfy that other strange side of Luciano's character which seemed to pine for the better things of life. He remained devoted to her until she died some years later. Those who knew her said she was very attached to Luciano.

The stream of visitors who had "accidentally" met Luciano in Havana was diverted to Rome. Among the first was his old "buddy" Meyer Lansky, who subsequently told an American Senate Commission that he found himself in Italy "purely by accident". He explained to the not-very-amused Senators that the travel agency which had booked him his holiday had put him on the wrong ship. Once he unexpectedly got to Naples "Lucky" had just called him on the phone, explaining that he had seen about Lansky's arrival "in the papers". Their main conversation in Rome, said Lansky, was about how Luciano was being "crucified". Luciano was referring to the activities in Italy of agents of the American Federal Bureau of Narcotics. As soon as Luciano had been expelled from Cuba agents of the F.B.N. from Washington "tailed" him almost everywhere he went in his native land.

Meyer Lansky was not Luciano's only visitor. Some time later there appeared Frank Scalise, another of the New York Mafia "dons". In the years that followed Luciano entertained his own successor in New York, the sinister "King of the Rackets", Vito Genovese, who had succeeded the ageing Frank Costello as chief of the American National Crime Syndicate. Genovese on these trips was visiting Europe to inspect his safe deposits, in Zürich, Monte Carlo and elsewhere, which are alleged to have contained a fortune approaching £20,000,000.

By the middle of 1948 the American narcotics agents in Italy were sure that Luciano was the master-mind in southern Europe of the rapidly reviving illicit dope traffic. A year later they knew he was the chief European executive of "Dope International". They could trace his links with the top operators in the Middle East, with his own Italian Mafia and its cousins in crime, the French Corsican gangsters, and across the Atlantic to the North American Syndicate in the United States, Canada and Mexico.

In 1949 an American agent succeeded in linking Luciano with a consignment of illicit cocaine picked up at Rome Airport. The Italians, some of whose senior officials almost certainly were drawing a substantial income from Luciano, were reluctant to do anything. However, the United States was giving Italy generous financial aid under the Marshall Plan and so pressure was put on through diplomatic channels. One day an American agent accompanied by two Italian detectives raided Luciano's magnificent apartment at 46 Via Lima. They were almost speechless. In his wardrobe they found seventy beautifully-cut suits, four hundred pure silk neckties, and dozens of shirts and pairs of shoes—all hand made.

When interrogated Luciano denied everything. He was an experienced operator. So was his American opponent. The interrogation continued for a fortnight. Taciturn, sarcastic and most unco-operative, Luciano's only reaction was that he was being persecuted. The Italians were inclined to agree. What had he ever done they asked the Americans? He had been picked up for dope peddling when he was "a baby" (at sixteen). By his sentence for white slavery the Italians were outraged. Running a chain of brothels was a perfectly legitimate business. It was satisfying a natural demand.

The Italian police authorities were becoming increasingly restive about the continued interrogation of Luciano. He was freed. But after a long-drawn-out haggle the Italians bowed to American pressure and "Lucky" was ordered to quit the Eternal City. The Americans wanted him sent to Lercara Friddi where an eye could be kept on him. Backstairs negotiation produced a compromise. He was permitted to settle in noisy, corrupt Naples where nobody would care what he did. He was permitted to establish himself with Igea Lissoni in yet another sumptuous apartment—this time overlooking the Bay of Naples. Luciano was ordered to observe a 10 p.m. curfew and to report to the police once in every twenty-four hours. Later these conditions were somewhat relaxed.

While Luciano was still in Rome British and American detectives of the Allied Military Government in Trieste had uncovered an important dope ring in the still-occupied harbour city on the Yugoslav border. Inquiries showed that the Trieste peddlars, who were well-known citizens, were linked with a pharmaceutical firm in Modena, which also was involved in illegal operations.

From there the trail led to Milan, where directors of two important chemical firms were found to be involved in what became an international scandal. After long investigations the Americans established that Professor Carlo Migliardi, the technical director of the big Schiapparelli chemical firm, had misappropriated 2,500 lb. (more than a ton) of legitimately-manufactured narcotics and passed them to the Luciano-controlled Mafia dope traffickers. His profit was £500,000—at a cost in death and human suffering on both sides of the Atlantic which will never be accurately known. Members of the conspiracy were observed meeting both "Little Joe" Peachy and Luciano personally in Milan luxury hotels. The Italian Government, it was discovered, had *legally authorised* a production of ten times Italy's legitimate need of heroin, and *most of it had gone to Luciano's organization.*

Under pressure, the Italian Government prosecuted Professor Migliardi, who was linked to the ruling Christian Democrat Party. He was sentenced to eleven years' imprisonment.

The Italian diversion of legally-manufactured narcotics to the Luciano gang created an international furore. At a meeting of the United Nations Narcotics Commission in New York, Italy was denounced from many sides. The Italians accepted an American recommendation that the manufacture of all heroin be stopped. They promised to stamp out the illicit drug traffic in Italy. But when it came to Luciano the Italians declined to do anything. The Americans, they alleged, were persecuting a solid Italian citizen. The evidence against him was inconclusive. And Charley "Lucky" continued to go to the races, which had become his main diversion. He had always played the horses in New York. Settled down in quiet, respectable retirement in Naples, he was a regular visitor to the tracks. He followed a steady routine. Getting up late, his first call was to the barber. Then he proceeded to the well-known California Bar, of which he was generally thought to be the owner. He gave a luncheon party every day. His guests always included important Italians —and sometimes a stray officer from the American Fleet H.Q. at Naples.

After a short siesta Luciano went to the races, where he was a lavish gambler. He could never quite forget his past. On one occasion, as a diversion, he decided to "fix" a race. The Italian jockeys were bribed. But organization is not a Neapolitan strong point. The staff work was bad. The wrong horse won. "Lucky" was very sore. He sent his bodyguard to recover his cash from the jockeys with threats of what would happen if they failed to pay up. To an American friend Signor Luciano's final comment was "These god-damned lousy dishonest Wops".

Despite his almost regal existence in the land of his birth Charley "Lucky" Luciano pined for his real home, the streets of New York's East Side, which he was never to see again. He became ultra-cautious and discreet. It is doubtful whether in the last ten years of his life he ever had any personal contact with the dope traffickers moving across the Middle East and Europe whom he controlled. Dossiers in the possession of the international counter-narcotics authorities show that his contacts with the illicit narcotics cartel was entirely through intermediaries. If "Don Salvatore" paused for a chat with a friend at the race track or bought a drink for a visitor to the California Bar in Naples who could say that the incident was linked with the international narcotics traffic?

The American secret agents in Italy kept close to his heels right up to his death. In his later years he certainly had important visitors from the United States. They included old friends, lawyers, criminal associates and ordinary seamen from American ships. These people brought him large sums in cash from the Mafia Grand Council in New York in payment for various consignments of narcotics. He is also believed to have had large sums hidden in the anonymous numbered accounts of some of the smaller Swiss private banks.

Luciano employed an expensive public relations organization to secure a sympathetic press in his native Italy. What none of his P.R.O.s was ever able to explain was where he got the income to maintain his lavish way of life. Apart from a number of insignificant and not particularly profitable "front" enterprises he had "no visible means of support".

Some time before he died one of the American agents who tailed him stated :

"We have no doubt that 'Lucky' is the master-mind of the whole narcotics operation in Europe. But he is much too smart to ever make contact with anyone handling dope. We know that he gets a big cut from the Mafia traffickers in the United States and in recent years he has been the 'President of the Corporation' in Europe at least. We have strong evidence to show that Luciano merely issues policy directives and gives approval for major operations without in any way being involved in the day-to-day operations of the illicit narcotics traffic."

The problem was to convince successive Italian governments to do anything about Luciano. No matter how conclusive the evidence of his participation in the international dope traffic seemed, it was never enough to satisfy the curiously-complacent Italian legal authorities.

In the early weeks of 1962 official Italian resistance at last began to weaken. The dossier presented by the Americans and the international counter-narcotics authorities was overwhelming. There is strong evidence to suggest that had Charley "Lucky" Luciano survived a month or two more he would have been arrested and sent to prison for the rest of his natural life.

Chapter 13

SENATOR McCARTHY

JOSEPH RAYMOND MCCARTHY never killed anyone nor did he indulge in torture, at least of the physical variety. He was neither a monster nor, in the ordinary sense of the term, a sadist. He was just a loud-voiced, vulgar, flamboyant, boozy Irish-American who for five years mesmerized a considerable portion of the population of the United States and fathered an evil which even today brings shudders to all liberal-minded Americans.

He was certainly the most *intellectually* wicked man produced by the Anglo-Saxon nations for a very long time; and potentially he was one of the most dangerous men of the century. Although in life he may have seemed bigger than in retrospect, his great liberal and radical contemporaries in the United States compared him, with justice, to the embryonic Adolf Hitler. That view of Joe McCarthy and the cult called McCarthyism which he inspired was shared by liberal opinion the world over.

McCarthy died a disgruntled, discouraged, drink-sodden non-entity. But for the inherent strength and virtue of American freedom and democracy Joseph McCarthy might have lived to equal the greatest dictators of the century.

McCarthy was certainly the greatest liar of the century—far outstripping that other father of lies, Dr. Paul Josef Goebbels. For whereas the Nazi Propaganda Minister believed at least a considerable part of what he and his party stood for, McCarthy believed neither in what he said nor in what he did. He was the apotheosis of cynicism, insincerity and unscrupulousness rolled into one—and yet personally he was quite a pleasant fellow so long as the TV cameras were not in operation. Yet by a fearsome combination of complete amorality and a superb gift for public relations he succeeded in terrorizing American public life.

245

He was without programme and had neither political organization nor a party of his own; his interest in the public weal was of the flimsiest. Yet in the five years during which he shot like a rocket across the American political firmament he atrophied a large part of the government of the United States. Overseas, in many parts of the world his name came to be synonymous with all that was believed to be bad in American foreign policy and disagreeable in the American way of life.

For years he held two American presidents in thrall. He neutralized the later years of Truman and demoralized the earlier years of Eisenhower's presidency. He kicked around cabinet ministers as though they were marionettes and terrorized the American Senate, of which he was almost certainly the most disgraceful member since its inception.

With the aid of a private inquisition headed by two adolescent nitwits named Cohn and Schine he wrecked American diplomacy, panicked great sections of the American civil service, treated great institutions, such as the American Army, with contumacy and purged American radio and television, the theatre and Hollywood of many of its most advanced thinkers.

McCarthy believed in nothing except the Roman Catholic creed of his forefathers. On his own admission he only "discovered Communism" a couple of months before he began his grand crusade against Communists in high places in the United States. However, having found the gimmick, he exploited to the ultimate the average American's instinctive fear of Bolshevism as Hitler had exploited traditional Teutonic anti-Semitism. He created in the United States something which, given a different twist of fate, might have become as vile and terrifying as German National Socialism.

For his own wanton ends—if he had any ends at all— McCarthy blamed all the troubles of America, real and imaginary, on his enemies—the intelligentsia, the liberals and radicals, or anyone who refused to fall for his pernicious political blarney. To root out his enemies he perverted the machinery of Congress itself until a Senate sub-committee in McCarthy's hands became the instrument for the most vicious of witch-hunts.

To keep that sub-committee well supplied with victims he gathered round himself what may well have been the most

sinister political development of the century in the United States
—the so-called "Loyal American Underground". To whip up
his persecution campaigns he drew secret information from an
anti-Communist "maquis" comprising both a cabal in high
government circles and an underground spy network spread
across the lower echelons of the American public service.

Across the length and breadth of the United States stood
millions of his large and dedicated following ranging from hair-
brained cranks and moronic millionaires to some of the most
sophisticated political minds in America. But Joe McCarthy
fooled the millionaires just like everyone else, for much of the
money they showered on him for the "battle against the Reds"
went into his own pocket—to be gambled on the tracks or in
purchasing soya bean options.

Joe McCarthy was born on 14 November, 1909, in the small
Wisconsin town of Grand Chute. He was the fifth child of an
Irish-German family of nine. His parents were poor and pious.
Shortly before his birth they had managed to scrape together
enough from the poor living they earned as small farmers to
exchange their log cabin for a rather better home.

Little Joe, barrel-chested and short-armed with heavy lips and
protruding eyebrows, was the ugly duckling of the family. For
that reason he was his mother's favourite. She mothered him
much more than the rest of her brood. He went to a local
grammar school and, at the age of fourteen, left to take up
chicken farming. He was very successful. Within a year or two
he had 10,000 chicks, newly-built poultry houses and a lorry
to drive the chicks to Chicago. At nineteen disaster overtook
him; the chickens were wiped out by an epidemic. He abandoned
poultry farming and moved to the small town of Manawa, twenty
miles from his home. There he became manager of a grocery
chain store. He was a bright young man and some of his friends
urged him to resume his studies. On the eve of his twentieth
birthday he went back to high school. As a result of tutoring
by the headmaster he managed to complete the normal four
years' course in twelve months. He was just over twenty-one
when he entered Marquette University at Milwaukee as an
engineering student. After two years he changed over to the law
faculty, since he had decided there were more opportunities for

his talents in the legal profession. While studying he had kept himself by a variety of jobs. He was a dishwasher in a hotel, a nightwatchman and a petrol station attendant in turn. He was also something of a boxer and became the University boxing coach.

Soon after graduation he set himself up as a lawyer in the small town of Waupaca, without any notable success. It was generally believed that he augmented his rare professional fees with his winnings at poker.

After a time he took a job with another lawyer at fifty dollars a week. His employer was a member of the Republican Party. In the tradition of American small-town legal firms McCarthy became a Democrat to get business from "both sides of the street". His gifts as an advocate were never striking. But his native instincts were quick to appreciate that the law offered a rapid approach to politics, where the rewards were infinitely greater than those accruing to a small-town lawyer.

Soon McCarthy was chairman of the Young Democrats Club for one of the Wisconsin counties. As such he ran for the post of District Attorney—and lost, much to everyone's surprise. But he had put up a good show and his employer made him a junior partner. For the next three years Joe McCarthy slogged away as a Middle West small-town attorney. American legal and judicial appointments are bedevilled by politics. At regular intervals the local circuit judges must stand for re-election. McCarthy was thirty when the election for the local judgeship came round. He decided to run for the appointment—but this time as a Republican because the present incumbent was himself a Democrat.

His political conversion was remarkable—but the election campaign proved to be sensational. The real McCarthy of after years began to appear. He campaigned on the slogan "justice is truth in action". To prove his point he lied, and lied, and lied again. The judge in office was sixty-six. McCarthy decided he was too old. "The job of circuit judge is too exacting for a man of his age." But what was the judge's age? With his inborn genius for confusing the facts McCarthy began to play what he would later call "the numbers game". First he announced his opponent was seventy-three. Then he improved that and made the present incumbent of the post eighty-nine. To show that he held no prejudice he decided to knock two years off his own age. On election day he was on the eve of his thirty-first birthday. He was determined to be the youngest judge in the history of Wisconsin. So he made himself twenty-nine.

Even a pathological but otherwise normally inhibited liar would never have attempted to put over such manifest fiction—both his own age and that of his opponent were matters of public record. That worried McCarthy no more than equally well established truths in the days of his power. For McCarthy, like the late Dr. Goebbels, believed that provided he repeated a lie, no matter how outrageous, often enough ordinary people would eventually begin to believe it was true.

He was right. His lying paid off. He won the judgeship. His outraged opponents tried to have the result overturned on the ground of corrupt practices. But Joe's luck held—as it did so often. He became a judge—although scarcely an ornament of the American legal profession—for the next four years. One of his biographers has succinctly summed up this period: "His comportment as a judge revealed that emancipation from convention which characterized his behaviour as a United States Senator."

He was scarcely on the bench before there was a scandal. He granted the State Department of Agriculture an injunction against a dairy company to force compliance with a marketing regulation. Three days later later he suspended his own injunction for reasons he never put on record. In view of what is known of his later career the arguments were no doubt substantial. When the case eventually came to trial he dismissed the department's case on specious grounds. An appeal was made to the State supreme court where it was found the record was incomplete. McCarthy had instructed the court reporter to remove from the records part of the statement he made in dismissing the case! As a judge he did achieve one distinction: he tried more cases than any other in a similar period. From his predecessor McCarthy had inherited a long calendar of untried cases. According to his own claim in six weeks—by sitting often till midnight—he cleared off 250 outstanding cases. He soon became famous for his "five minute divorces"—the hearings of which sometimes started while he was walking down the corridors to his court. Within two years Judge McCarthy was the judicial scandal of the Middle West. At this point the *Milwaukee Journal* commented:

"Judge McCarthy, whose burning ambition for political advancement is accompanied by an astonishing disregard for things ethical and traditional, is doing serious injury to the judiciary of this state."

The United States by this time was in the war—and Joe decided that it might be the better part of valour to join the Marines. At the beginning of June, 1942, he wrote to the U.S. Marines asking for a commission. To local reporters, who as always were his constant associates although not necessarily his greatest friends, he announced that he was "eager to enlist as a buck private—I am more interested in a gun than a commission." McCarthy got his commission if not his gun. To the fury of his judicial colleagues however he declined to resign his judgeship. And before he departed for a Marine base in Virginia he was photographed on the bench trying his last case—in Marine uniform.

Joe McCarthy was a Marine Officer from mid-1942 until the end of 1944. Most of the time he was an Intelligence officer to a scout bombing squadron in the South Pacific. His job was to interview pilots on their return from bombing missions. He was a perfectly normal "run of the mill" officer. He had no sooner left the Service however than he invented a military record which would have done credit to the best fiction writers of the time. McCarthy claimed a number of war wounds. His only known injury was a broken leg which he got when he fell down a companionway in a seaplane tender during an Equator-crossing party far removed from the scene of operations. For his broken leg however he collected an American service disability medal. In subsequent election literature McCarthy also claimed to have been a gunnery officer known throughout the length and breadth of General Douglas MacArthur's Command as "Tail Gunner Joe". He never was a gunner. It is known, however, that he made one or two trips as a passenger in the rear gunner's turret when he may have fired an odd shot. He also claimed that he held the record for the greatest number of rounds of ammunition fired in a single day—4,700. They were fired against coconut trees on Pacific islands held by the Americans!

As years passed and he moved from one election to another he again started the "numbers game" about the missions he had flown. In 1944 he said he had flown 14 missions; four years later it had increased to 18; by 1951 it was 30. At that stage he applied for the Distinguished Flying Cross granted for 25 missions or more. By that time the Pentagon went in fear and trembling of Senator McCarthy—and he was awarded the D.F.C., even although the Washington *Evening Star* stated, "his Marine service record shows no record of his having qualified for an air gunner's wings or being credited with combat missions."

In the quiet of an Intelligence officer's hut in the South-west Pacific Joe's political ambitions had blossomed. He decided to contest the election for the Republican nomination held by Senator Alexander Wiley. There were two serious obstacles. As a serving officer he was forbidden to speak on politics. As a judge he was equally barred from such a course. He took what was to be the classic McCarthy method in such cases. He ignored both. Applying for a month's leave he returned to Wisconsin to fight Senator Wiley. He lost and returned to the South-west Pacific where soon afterwards he asked for a further three months' leave in order to campaign for his re-election as a circuit judge.

The U.S. Marine Corps by this time was a little weary of Joe McCarthy and his ways. So, with the Pacific war at its height, he resigned his commission. A few months later he was re-elected to his judgeship for another three years.

In the following twelve months the flair for personal publicity of the "Tail Gunner Judge" attracted the approving notice of the Republican Party managers in Wisconsin. He did not need any persuasion to let his name be put forward by the hard core reactionary wing of the Republican Party against the sitting member, Senator Robert La Follette Jnr., son of one of the greatest Senators in the history of the United States.

Senator La Follette Jnr. was an intellectual progressive of great distinction. He was no match for the unparalleled campaign of infamy and scandal which McCarthy directed at him. Most of it was lies—but then so was McCarthy's slogan "Joe

McCarthy was a TAIL GUNNER . . . AMERICA Needs
FIGHTING MEN . . . to SAVE AMERICA".

Once again it did not matter. McCarthy triumphed over his
liberal opponent, who committed suicide some years later, by
a narrow majority.

His Democrat opponent in the Congressional mid-term elections that autumn was a lightweight. And, probably to his own
surprise, Joe McCarthy became a member of one of the most
august legislative bodies in the world as junior Senator for the
State of Wisconsin.

His first act on arriving in Washington was characteristic. He
called a press conference. The reporters had never heard of him
and were highly amused when he offered them a radical—and
completely absurd—solution to the problem of ending a coal
strike which at the moment was a national issue. They just
guffawed but McCarthy was unperturbed. He knew how to use
the press. As they left him he shouted after them, "When you
want me don't hesitate to call me—night or day." He sent a
present of Wisconsin cheese to the Washington National Press
Club. That set the pattern for his first three years in Washington.

There was no suggestion during these years that Senator
McCarthy was anything more than the usual publicity-hungry
politician of the most mediocre attainments. Yet he had not
been in the American capital for more than a few weeks before
he had made contact with the seamier side of American political
life. Washington is crammed with lobbyists of every description
and McCarthy almost automatically gravitated towards those
who had little interest in power and were concerned only to line
their own pockets. His closest associate was a well-known soft
drinks lobbyist. In almost no time Joe McCarthy, as the acknowledged spokesman in the Senate of an internationally-renowned
soft drinks corporation, had gained the nickname of the "Soft
Drinks Kid".

He had equally profitable links with the big building corporations which were violently opposed to a measure to promote
low-cost public housing programmes. McCarthy and the other
congressmen in the pay of the building corporation succeeded
in securing the establishment of a Joint Housing Committee.
He was not the chairman but soon the junior senator from

Wisconsin began to dominate the sittings. Cries of "Scandal" and "Outrage" which within a few years would spread terror across Washington were heard coming from the committee room. But no one was much interested in the committee—or in the somewhat hysterical junior senator from Wisconsin. The committee only became notorious later when it was discovered that one of the building corporations had paid Senator McCarthy ten thousand dollars for writing a short article and that the president of the same corporation had met Senator McCarthy's gambling debts totalling thousands of dollars.

McCarthy in these first years in the Senate seemed of no particular importance—and he himself had probably no aspirations towards the role he would come to play in American national life within a few years.

Some shrewd observers of the Washington scene, however, had begun to note the peculiar gifts of Senator Joseph McCarthy. One distinguished American reporter had been quick to discover that the new Senator was a master of what was called "the multiple untruth" . . . a technique almost undistinguishable from the Nazi Big Lie. The McCarthy technique consisted of stringing together a long series of loosely-linked mis-statements or plain lies. McCarthy, with an Alice in Wonderland-like genius, however, could so confuse the real issue that although individual mis-statements might be denied he was able to convey the impression that the rest of his tissue of lies was the absolute truth.

From his earliest days in Wisconsin political life McCarthy had been a master bamboozler. From his earliest days in the Senate he exploited his unparalleled ability to create confusion to cover the farrago of fantasy and fiction which was the very texture of almost every public speech he ever made. Not all the Senators were fooled. After a typical McCarthy performance one of his senior colleagues said: "The Senator is confusing the Senate of the United States by a heterogeneous mass of figures which will not stand the test of accuracy." McCarthy was playing the "numbers game" with the Senate.

Even the most experienced professional interrogators, however, were no match for the wiles of McCarthy. From the bulging briefcase which was to become an inevitable part of the

McCarthy image he would produce document after document. Each document produced, ostensibly to prove his case, was more irrelevant than its predecessor. Interspersed with interjections of "Now y'see what I mean" were repeated offers of "have another Scotch". Eventually even the most expert questioner decided that either McCarthy was mad or that he himself was completely stupid. He departed tending to believe that McCarthy could not be all that daft. For Joe McCarthy was the greatest political "con man" of the twentieth century.

By the first days of 1950 Joe McCarthy was worried. He had to face re-election in 1952. And in the years since he had been elected there had been a marked swing to the Democrats, as evidenced by President Truman's sensational victory in 1948. More important, serious details of his malpractices in Washington had got back to Wisconsin. The Democrat newspapers, which had never forgotten that he was a renegade, had begun to dig up the stories of his scandalous activities on the judicial bench. The attention of the tax authorities had been drawn to the fact that he had evaded paying tax on big stock exchange gains made during the war.

In the first week of January, 1950, at dinner in the Colony Restaurant in Washington he confided to three companions— one of whom was a Roman Catholic priest and professor at Georgetown University—that he had need of a dramatic campaign issue for 1952. Various suggestions were made and rejected. Then the Catholic professor suggested Communism— its power in the world and its capacity for subversion.

Up to that time McCarthy had shown no interest in Communism. In elections he had accused his opponents of being a "pink and the mouth-piece of the Reds". That was nothing more than the common political cant of the day, but McCarthy seized on the suggestion and, according to those who were present, began to vulgarize it.

"That's it," he exclaimed, "the Government is full of Communists—we can hammer away at that."

His companions warned him strongly of the dangers of an irresponsible approach. He assured them that nothing was farther from his thoughts. Within three months all three, including the Catholic professor, were forced publicly to repudiate him. Joe

McCarthy had found the gimmick for which he had been looking.

Soon after the dinner party McCarthy asked the Republic campaign organizers to arrange for him to speak on the dangers of Communism in the government and to make arrangements for him to speak in the near future. The bookings made for him were scarcely top line. He was told that he would address a Republican women's club at Wheeling, West Virginia, on 9 February, and thereafter similar gatherings at Salt Lake City and Reno. There is no evidence that McCarthy in the intervening period made anything more than the most cursory efforts to investigate how many Communists were employed in various U.S. government departments. With nothing but a few scribbled notes he proceeded to Wheeling.

What Joe McCarthy actually told the West Virginian Republican ladies became in the following few months one of the most controversial subjects in the United States. According to a local reporter who was at the meeting he said:

> "While I cannot take time to name all the men in the State Department who have been named as members of the Communist Party, I have here in my hand a list of 205 that were known to the Secretary of State as members of the Communist Party—*and who nevertheless are still working and shaping policy in the State Department."*

At this he flourished a sheet of paper at the ladies who, with that American passion for documentary proof rose to the bait— and presumed that what they had seen *must be* evidence in support of McCarthy's allegations.

In the hullabaloo which followed it transpired that what McCarthy did flourish was a copy of a letter written four years earlier by a former Secretary of State, Mr. James F. Byrnes. This stated that as a result of screening it had been decided not to re-employ 284 members of the State Department, of whom 79 had already left the service. Apparently McCarthy's 205 consisted of the 284 minus 79. That had been in 1946. He was speaking in 1950.

The speech was reported in the local press and a brief paragraph was circulated by an American news agency. The State Department was not slow in learning of the allegation and wired to McCarthy for the names of his 205 Communists.

For the only time in his campaign against the Communists, McCarthy panicked. He obviously feared action for libel. He was clearly quite unprepared for the major sensation which he had provoked. Presumably he had believed that he could put over anything to the West Virginian Republican ladies and that he could use local press cuttings at a later date to prove to the people of Wisconsin that he was a leading Communist-hunter. Faced with something he had never even contemplated he at first put up a smoke screen. Then the sheer amoral audacity of the man came into play. When he stopped at Denver en route to Salt Lake City he said he had been misquoted. At the Mormon headquarters he regained his nerve and started on the "numbers game". He announced that he actually had the names of fifty-seven card-carrying members of the Communist Party in the State Department. In an interview with a local radio reporter he invited the Secretary of State to call him at his hotel and learn the names of his Communist assistants. When Mr. Acheson failed to oblige McCarthy then announced that if "Harry Truman" would call him he would reveal all. The President was equally unimpressed. But McCarthy was not to be put off. Realizing that he was now becoming a controversial figure he again repeated his allegation about the fifty-seven Communists when he reached Reno. By this time the State Department was becoming at least irritated and sent him another telegram which remained unanswered.

McCarthy returned to Washington to find the capital in an uproar. He was at once faced with a demand—which he said he was anxious to satisfy—that he should explain himself to the Senate. On the afternoon of 20 February, McCarthy, complete with bulging briefcase, took his place in the Senate. Thereafter ensued what has been described as "one of the maddest spectacles in the history of representative government".

Challenged at the outset to explain the relationship between his 205 Communists and the subsequent 57 he denied that he had ever mentioned the former. Then he dramatically assured the Senate that he had penetrated "Truman's" curtain of secrecy. With all the glibness of which McCarthy was the master, he announced to the astounded Senators that he would now reveal full details of *81* Communists in the State Department.

Around him in wild disarray were piles of what appeared to be official documents. From these he proceeded to read. Hour after hour becoming more and more hoarse and more and more red in the face McCarthy read out the contents of the files, which the Senators were quick to appreciate were as strange to him as they were to them. He had clearly never seen them until he started reading. From late afternoon until far into the evening the Mad Hatter performance continued. The climax was reached when, stumbling and stuttering through one file, he was forced to admit that this individual *did not* appear to be a Communist at all. Despite that he went on.

One Senator made thirty-four attempts to bring McCarthy to order and make him submit his wild allegations to proof. Others did the same. Skilfully deploying all the tricks of Senatorial procedure, McCarthy brushed aside all interruptions. Challenged again and again about the discrepancies in his figures he burst out petulantly: "Stop playing this silly numbers game." When the bewildered, weary and word-besotted Senators adjourned at midnight, the view of all who had watched was summed up by his party leader, Senator Robert A. Taft: "He must be daft."

All Washington agreed with Senator Taft. Even the extreme right-wing anti-Communist group led by the later vice-president Richard Nixon was furious. They were convinced that McCarthy's clowning was seriously injuring their case. Whatever Washington thought the reaction to McCarthy's Senate speech across the breadth of the United States was diametrically opposite. The American press, radio and TV must bear a great share of the responsibility for what happened.

Owing to the professional traditions of American journalism, which insist that fact and comment, which might have put McCarthy in perspective, must not be intermixed—most Americans heard only straightforward excerpts from his speech. Taken together these snippets aroused the strong suspicion that there were, indeed, a considerable number of Communists in the State Department. The reporters who had watched his lunatic performance in the Senate had reported only the more lucid passages—the bedlam qualities of a McCarthy speech seldom reached the American public. The excerpts, although just as big lies as his nonsense, seemed to many people to make sense, particularly after the Alger Hiss trial and the discovery of Soviet spies in the United States. So McCarthy's technique of the "multiple untruth" began to pay off in a bigger and bigger way.

McCarthy suddenly became a national figure. Despite the merriment and the scoffing in Washington it became obvious in no time at all that the junior Senator from Wisconsin had the ear of the people. McCarthy reacted instinctively. Once again his outrageous mendacity had been justified. He had neither a policy nor a plan of campaign. He continued to improvise as he had done ever since he entered political life in Wisconsin.

The audience gained by McCarthy's Senate demagoguery rapidly developed into a following. Within a few weeks that following had become a McCarthy-led-and-inspired anti-Communist national crusade backed by millions of hysterical and ill-informed sympathizers all over the United States. With support came money for "the fight against subversion"—much of which found its way into McCarthy's pocket.

The Senate was not prepared to let McCarthy's contumacious marathon go by default. Two days after the speech it unanimously instructed its influential Foreign Relations Committee to make a full investigation into whether the State Department employed traitors. The inquiry was handed over to a subcommittee headed by the rich and powerful Senator Tydings and thereafter came to be known, erroneously, as the Tydings Committee. It scarcely broke new ground. It was merely following in the footsteps of no fewer than four similar inquiries carried out by the lower House of Representatives. Soon it transpired that what McCarthy had read to the Senate was the report of one of these earlier inquiries.

McCarthy was far too gifted a demagogue not to appreciate the potentialities of the Tydings Committee, which had really been appointed to put a brake on him. He was the first witness. After shuffling around still more documents from his famous briefcase he announced that he would *reveal all* about the eighty-one Communists in the State Department. For the next day and a half thereafter he devoted himself to the case of a New York woman solicitor who had never been employed by a U.S. Federal Department, who was chiefly known as a devoted do-gooder— and had never been a Communist.

From early in March until well after the start of the Korean War in the middle of 1950 the Tydings Committee solemnly took evidence which in the end amounted to 1,500 printed pages. Time after time McCarthy exploited the sittings of the committee to repeat that travesty of reason and logic with which he had shocked the Senate in February. Every few minutes he would throw out random charges against anyone who came to mind. When he was asked to produce proof McCarthy pulled out his trump card. The evidence, he blandly asserted, was "in the files of the State Department". In desperation Senator Tydings obtained the permission of President Truman to see the mysterious files. When the President's decision was announced McCarthy at once stigmatized it as "a phoney offer of phoney files". When the documents were brought before the committee McCarthy alleged, despite the evidence of the F.B.I. to the contrary, that they had been "raped and rifled".

Eventually the committee had had enough of McCarthy. It demanded that he produce proof. He promised to do so the following Monday morning. On that Monday he appeared briefly to say that he had another urgent engagement—a Senate housing debate. When the chairman pointed out that the debate had been postponed McCarthy, never at a loss for an answer, informed the committee that he must leave at once "because important constituents from Wisconsin had just arrived".

In July the committee issued a report. McCarthy had a good idea of what was coming. Before it appeared he announced it would be "a disgrace to the Senate". When it was issued the report stated that Senator McCarthy had "imposed a fraud and a hoax on the Senate".

McCarthy seemed finished. For a few weeks while the Korean War stole the headlines he lay low. But he was not inactive. He utilized the time organizing an infamous campaign which succeeded in driving the enormously rich patrician Senator Tydings out of the Senate along with two other prominent Senators who had led opposition to McCarthy's outrageous conduct.

By the beginning of 1951 McCarthy, with some primitive demagogic instinct for "public relations", was back in the headlines. He knew the whole technique of news and how to exploit it to his own advantage. He knew what would make a headline and what would not. He knew all the deadlines, all the edition times and when the radio and TV stations gave news. He would always pose for a picture—and always the right one, as with a brush sweeping (Communists) down the stairs of the Congress building. He had even mastered the high-level P.R.O. technique of blanketing criticism by providing the reporters with a newer and more sensational story which would inevitably get the headline in the later editions. He even invented a morning press conference to announce—an afternoon press conference. Inevitably the evening papers came out with a banner line, "New McCarthy Revelations expected". When they did *not* materialize the singularly naïve American provincial morning papers announced "Delay in New McCarthy Case—Mystery Witness Sought".

By mid-1951 Joe McCarthy was getting weary of making attacks on the small fry. He was being pushed off the front pages by the recall of General Douglas MacArthur from Korea. He decided to fight a general—with a general. Looking around for a promising victim he suddenly recalled that the then U.S. Secretary of Defence General George Catlett Marshall, as U.S. Army Chief of Staff, had been at the unfortunate Yalta Conference in 1945 when Stalin had fooled the dying President Roosevelt.

General Marshall, who repeatedly had been recalled from retirement to high office, was the most honoured man in the United States and the President had called him "the greatest living American".

McCarthy decided, to his own satisfaction, that on the record of Yalta and its aftermath General Marshall was a "traitor". He took steps to bring this view to the attention of his millions of supporters. On the afternoon of 14 June, 1951, when business was near an end, McCarthy ambled into the Senate. His briefcase bulged with documents which he claimed would be useful to the Armed Forces Committee.

To a dozen or so astounded colleagues McCarthy then lashed out at the American Secretary of Defence. "Unless we understand the record of Marshall," he said, "it will be impossible to foretell the next move in the great conspiracy. I very much dislike this unpleasant task . . . but it must be done."

Thereafter he launched into a long and not unscholarly review of Marshall's military career, punctuated by characteristic McCarthy charges of Communism. He continued until around five-thirty when, after some consultation with other senators, he announced that he did not wish to prevent "his colleagues seeing the ball game this evening". At that point he stopped and left the forty thousand undelivered words of his attack on Marshall to be inserted in the Congressional records.

In simple terms, McCarthy did not deliver most of the most scandalous speech of his life. Nor did he write it. Its distinguished language was so unfamiliar to him that he stuttered and stammered over unaccustomed words. The speech, most probably, was the product of some of his clerical friends at Georgetown University, where there was a school of history with a somewhat Teutonic twist. This group held the view that Roosevelt's foreign policy had been catastrophic since 1933 when America recognized the Soviet Union right through the Soviet-American war-time co-operation up to Potsdam in 1945.

McCarthy, however, was not finished with the man who had been the chief architect of America's military victory. Said he:

> "He (Marshall) is a man steeped in falsehood . . . who has recourse to the lie whenever it suits his convenience . . . part of a conspiracy so immense and an infamy so black as to dwarf any previous venture in the history of man . . . one in whose activities can be seen a pattern, always and invariably serving the world policy of the Kremlin."

All intelligent Americans knew that McCarthy was talking scandalous nonsense. On the less intelligent the impact of the attacks on Marshall proved the outstanding success of the McCarthy "Multiple Untruth". The McCarthy campaign virtually finished General Marshall's long and distinguished career. He remained in office for a few months more but then retired— virtually barred for ever by defamation almost unparalleled in any civilized country.

After the Marshall affair the Truman administration, for its remaining months in office, was virtually paralysed by the McCarthy campaign. For by 1952 Joe McCarthy, although still only the junior Senator from Wisconsin and without any official post, had become what has been described as "an engine of denunciation".

As the 1952 Presidential election began to loom on the political horizon the Republican Party, to its eternal discredit, climbed on the McCarthy bandwagon. He was the peculiar joy of the party managers. Even the austere Senator Taft, himself a potential Republican candidate, went as far as to state that "the pro-Communist policies of the State Department have fully justified Joe McCarthy in his demand for investigation".

It was not the State Department only which required investigation. Senator McCarthy, too, was under inquiry. Although after the 1950 elections many of the Senators had been scared stiff of McCarthy some at least were not prepared to permit the outrage to the Senate to continue. Towards the end of 1951 Senator William Benton, who had taken over the leadership of the anti-McCarthy faction, placed before the Senate a motion demanding his expulsion. A committee was set up and for many months it tried to persuade the junior Senator from Wisconsin to subject himself to the type of cross-examination which he so abused when he came to examine others. McCarthy was much too crafty to appear before any Senate committee to explain his personal affairs. For by this time he had a bank account of over 152,000 dollars while his assistant had around 100,000 dollars in his account.

He kept in touch with the committee by letter. Finally he wrote to the chairman, "I have not, and do not even intend to read or much less answer Benton's smear attacks."

Most of the members of the committee were panic stricken that the man they regarded as the anti-Christ of the Senate might turn upon them. They drew the line at issuing a subpoena which would have forced him to appear. Instead, this pusillanimous lot issued one of the most amazing official reports in the history of the U.S. Senate. This did condemn McCarthy out of hand but proceeded to ask questions: "Where had he managed to get so much money—and why was he using his family and his staff to cover up details of financial transactions clearly carried out for ulterior motives?" The committee never got an answer. McCarthy had plunged into the campaign for the 1952 elections—to the deep embarrassment of the Republican Presidential candidate Dwight D. Eisenhower.

From the outset Eisenhower regarded McCarthy as a guttersnipe and a cad. He intended to go to Wisconsin and say a few warm words about his old chief and patron, General Marshall. The Republican leaders in Wisconsin heard about this plan and pleaded with Eisenhower to omit all references to Marshall, which he did. They were certain of McCarthy's fury. Unpredictable as ever, McCarthy, when he heard of the affair, announced that "he couldn't care less". He toured his home state with Eisenhower and won re-election to the Senate fairly easily. But all too many Republicans in Wisconsin knew the facts about Joe McCarthy and it was significant that he polled ten per cent less than the Republican total for Eisenhower as president.

Before the election he had proclaimed that the twenty years of Democrat rule had been "twenty years of treason". With the election of Eisenhower he announced that subversion would come to an end. For in 1953 the mere thought of McCarthy sent shivers through the White House. By the spring of 1954, however, the administration had begun to take courage and McCarthy then announced that there had been "twenty-one years of treason".

For much of 1953 there is no dispute that McCarthy shared control of many parts of the government with the President. Within three months he had disposed of three successive heads of the International Information Administration. Eisenhower appointed John Foster Dulles as Secretary of State. McCarthy appointed Scott McLeod as State Department Security Officer. It was doubtful who exercised more authority, because while Dulles made the speeches McLeod appointed the ambassadors. In the face of strong McCarthy opposition the Republicans agreed to the President's request over the appointment of Charles E. Bohlen as U.S. Ambassador in Moscow. But Senator Taft only agreed on condition that there should be *no more appointments offensive to McCarthy*.

McCarthy also set himself up as an agency for foreign relations. On 28 March he announced that as chairman of a Senate sub-committee he had negotiated an agreement with Greek shipping interests. He also announced that he was negotiating another agreement with shipping interests in London.

For most of 1953 McCarthy completely dominated the weak-kneed Secretary of the Army, Robert A. Steven—no American

THE WORLD'S WICKEDEST MEN

Army officer who crossed McCarthy had much future. On the other hand he looked after his friends in the Armed Services.

In the 83rd Congress which assembled in Washington early in 1953 McCarthy was rewarded with the appointment of Chairman of the Senate Committee on Government Operations. The party leader in the Senate, Senator Taft, believed this was a particularly sly move. He believed that McCarthy had been side-tracked into watching dull details of government administration. Like others, Taft underestimated McCarthy. He had been quick to remember that in the previous Congress a sub-committee of the body of which he now became chairman, the permanent sub-committee on investigations, had raked out a great deal of muck about the Truman administration. Given a tough, aggressive chairman the sub-committee could investigate almost anything. McCarthy appointed just such a chairman—himself. Before anyone had realized what had happened he was back on his favourite hobby horse—the sub-committee which soon completely swamped its parent was investigating Communism in the government.

To assist him in his official investigations—for McCarthy, for the first time in his political career, now had official authority—he selected two assistants who would soon be immortalized by the British press as "Cohn and Schine". They would play the major rôle in McCarthy's downfall.

Roy M. Cohn, whom McCarthy made Chief Counsel to the sub-committee, was a bright young Jewish lawyer from New York in his late twenties. Son of a New York judge, he had been something of a scholastic prodigy and after being called to the bar had found a job in the Attorney General's office in New York. There he had prosecuted the Mafia dope peddlars and smugglers while he had also some share in the prosecution against the Rosenbergs, the notorious Soviet spies. He was almost certainly more of a genuine anti-Communist than McCarthy but his performance as McCarthy's chief investigator was heavily loaded with self interest.

His crony, David Schine, was the twenty-six year old playboy son of a well-known American hotel-owning family. He had dabbled in both Hollywood and Tin Pan Alley and was the author of a number of lugubrious ditties notable chiefly for their lack of grammar. The chief justification for his appointment as "Chief Consultant" to McCarthy's committee was a six-page brochure, written for the family hotels, called a "Definition of Communism". It contained more factual errors than would have been thought possible in such small compass.

Cohn and Schine really ran the McCarthy investigation committee for most of 1953. Joe was always available to give his by then famous performance of the ranting, threatening anti-Communist determined to drag out and expose the traitors to America. But he was lazy. He was more than willing to accept the facts which were given to him by Messrs. Cohn and Schine and the considerable staff they employed.

A staff was necessary, for by this time McCarthy had all too many "secret agents" in all sections of the government. The "Loyal American Opposition" which had originally been based in the Voice of America now extended to the Pentagon, the State Department, and even to the F.B.I., which provided McCarthy with all too much confidential—not to say secret—information.

The first investigation of the Cohn and Schine partnership was aimed at the Voice of America, where it was well supplied with informants. The investigation was never completed. It just quietly faded out when McCarthy at the end of March decided that its potentialities for creating uproar had come to an end.

A week later, on Sunday, 4 April, 1953, Messrs. Cohn and Schine set out for Paris on one of the most sensational journeys of recent years. In ten days they went through the U.S. diplomatic missions in western Europe like a dose of salts. Spending a few hours in each city and making contact with the most disreputable informants they "rooted out subversion" and spread consternation from Paris to Bonn, Munich, Frankfurt, Berlin, Vienna, Belgrade, Athens, Rome and London. News of the sensational purge could not be concealed. The two brash, but eventually furious, adolescents were followed round Europe by gleeful British and European newspapermen chanting inevitably, "Positively Mr. Cohn, Absolutely Mr. Schine".

The basis of the purge—if it had any other beyond the Cohn and Schine fantasies—seemed to be any vague association with books by radical or liberal authors which might be found in the

THE WORLD'S WICKEDEST MEN

libraries and reading rooms of the excellent U.S. Information Service in the main cities of western Europe. There were numerous victims—liberal, intelligent, hard-working American diplomats, most of whom had been doing a big job advocating American interests for years. The most notable was a senior information officer in Berlin who said what everyone else felt by describing Cohn and Schine to newspapermen as "junketeering gumshoes". Many American diplomats, ashamed and outraged at what had happened, resigned. Hundreds more were on the point of doing so.

Cohn and Schine struck a blow at American diplomacy from which it did not recover during the Eisenhower administration. For many years afterwards the disgraceful journey of Cohn and Schine was standard ammunition for every anti-American group in Europe.

The "junketeering gumshoes" had been back in Washington for only two months when someone in the Pentagon decided to break up the partnership. Schine was called up for the army. His call-up was the signal for the McCarthy-Army feud which continued for another nine months under the gaze of not fewer than twenty million fascinated American television viewers. In the words of one biographer of McCarthy:

> "The entire country found nothing more absorbing than an investigation centring on Schine's efforts to serve his country in other ways and on the efforts of others—notably McCarthy, Cohn and the Secretary of the Army, Robert Stevens—to accommodate him."

The details of the feud were never important. What liberal, intelligent Americans and their foreign friends and sympathizers will never forget is the picture of McCarthy, beetle-browed, threatening, almost foaming at the mouth, as he appeared on the television screens screaming, insulting and browbeating witnesses. It seemed like some supernatural throwback to the dark ages and the Star Chamber.

It made no difference to McCarthy who the witness was. He continued to storm, rave and shout threats. His most notable victim was General Ralph Zwicker, companion in arms of Eisenhower and one of the heroes of the Ardennes Battle of the Bulge. To Zwicker McCarthy shouted:

"You are a disgrace to the uniform. You are shielding Communist conspirators. You are not fit to be an officer. You're ignorant. You're going to be put on public display next Tuesday."

The basis for all this was an argument about the promotion of an army dentist.

It was scarcely surprising that the Secretary of the Army, Robert Stevens, refused to let the General appear. "I cannot submit loyal officers of our armed forces to such unwarranted treatment."

The Minister ordered the General *not* to appear. But McCarthy had a quiet word with Stevens. Members of the Eisenhower cabinet were in terror of the Senator from Wisconsin. The Minister's order was rescinded. The General was *ordered* to appear. From McCarthy he got another hysterical lambasting. Then McCarthy adjourned the sitting to go to the lavatory. As soon as he was out of range of the cameras he chatted genially with everyone. That hysterical outpouring was just an act.

By the early summer of 1954 the abasement of the American Army by McCarthy and his adolescent minions had become not only a national but an international scandal. The President himself was a soldier and McCarthy's attacks, if permitted to continue, must inevitably affect the prestige of the American forces serving overseas. In addition, vast numbers of decent, ordinary Americans were becoming terrified by the thought that this absurd clowning demagogue might reach the White House. Nowhere were these views more strongly held than among the more responsible members of the United States Senate. On 30 July, 1954, therefore, the veteran Senator Ralph Flanders introduced a resolution of censure based on McCarthy's contempt of the Senate, his contempt for truth "and his habitual contempt for people".

Shortly before this, when Flanders had compared McCarthy with Hitler, McCarthy had called the old man "senile".

Three days later the Senate, by a big majority, appointed a committee to consider the charges and report on:

"Whether the conduct of the Senator from Wisconsin, Mr. McCarthy, is unbecoming to a member of the U.S. Senate, is contrary to Senatorial traditions and tends to bring the Senate into disrepute."

267

The Vice-President, Mr. Nixon, after consulting with Senate leaders, appointed a carefully-selected committee of Senators. The chairman was the gaunt patriarch Arthur Watkins, a Mormon elder from Utah. Senator Watkins proved to be the living embodiment of both the greatest traditions of the Senate and of American democracy. From the start he made it clear to McCarthy that there would be none of his usual performances. He declared one prepared statement by McCarthy to be "neither material nor relevant to the issue". As a charitable gesture he let McCarthy read it. The committee leaned over backwards to be fair. In the end, however, it urged the Senate to express its disapproval of McCarthy on two counts:

1. His contempt of the committee inquiring into his personal affairs in 1951-52.
2. His abuse of General Zwicker in 1954.

The debate on the report had to be postponed because McCarthy was in hospital. The report was modified in some respects but on 2 December, 1954, the Senate approved the report by 76 votes to 22. In the words of Vice-President Nixon it had "condemned but not censured" McCarthy. He was still a member of the Senate—but he was finished. He never seemed to recover from that vote. He was no longer a threat to anyone or a major political force in the United States. The Eisenhower administration, which for so long had gone in living terror of McCarthy, was quick to disown him. Within a few weeks he seemed to suffer a collapse.

In the two and a half years left to him he spent much time in hospital being treated for ill-defined complaints. He drank more and more. Occasionally, he appeared on the floor of the Senate to make a speech on one of his old topics. No one listened and the reporters walked out. He became interested in money and made substantial paper gains on Wall Street. Then he went to hospital, lost control of his investments and had to face heavy cash losses.

McCarthy had a happy domestic life and he and his wife adopted a baby girl. Although Joe became a devoted father the zest had gone out of life. He had lost heart. On 28 April, 1957, he was admitted to the Naval Hospital at Bethseda, Maryland.

The doctors said he was "very ill". On 2 May, just after six o'clock in the evening, he died—just in time for the seven o'clock news, as one of his old reporter acquaintances said, not un-affectionately.

The real cause of his death was uncertain. Some time previously he had suffered from jaundice. To sufferers from that disease large quantities of alcohol can be poison. In one sense Joe McCarthy probably drank himself to death.

His death provided the obituary writers with a problem. All agreed he was a "controversial figure". Few wished to be really unkind and tell the truth. Perhaps the truest assessment of Joe McCarthy came from a woman who, although she detested the role he played in American life, liked him personally:

"The poor bastard," she said ". . . he was a stinker."

INDEX